The Fable as Literature

The invention of a fable is to me the most enviable exertion of human genius: it is the discovering of a truth to which there is no clue, and which, when once found out, can never be forgotten.

William Hazlitt

H. J. BLACKHAM

The Fable as Literature

THE ATHLONE PRESS
London and Dover, New Hampshire

First published in 1985 by
The Athlone Press Ltd
44 Bedford Row, London WC1R 4LY
and 51 Washington Street, Dover, NH 03820

Copyright © 1985 H.J. Blackham

British Library Cataloguing in Publication Data

Blackham, H.J.
The fable as literature.
1. Fables——History and criticism
I. Title
809'.915   PN980

ISBN 0–485–11278–7

Library of Congress Cataloging in Publication Data

Blackham, H. J. (Harold John), 1903–
The fable as literature.

Bibliography: p.
Includes index.
1. Fables—History and criticism.   I. Title.
PN980.B56   1985   809'.915   84–21674
ISBN 0–485–11278–7

Typeset by Inforum Ltd, Portsmouth
Printed in Great Britain at the
University Press, Cambridge

To the memory of my tutor
A.M.D. Hughes

Contents

Preface

A fable is a story invented to tell the truth, not a true story. A common definition used to be: a short story in which the action is natural and the agents imaginary. It could as well be the other way round. Enough to say at the outset that the fable is a metaphorical statement of its own kind, worth discriminating from its near literary kindred for its special uses.

This study undertakes to follow historically the development of the fable in the European literary tradition, with an examination of some of the principal examples, from Phaedrus and Lucian to Thurber and Kafka. The last two chapters offer an analysis of the form and its uses. For there has been this gap in the critical literature.

Acknowledgements

Edwin Muir's poem 'The Combat' is reprinted in Chapter VI by permission of Faber and Faber Ltd from *The Collected Poems of Edwin Muir*; and by permission of the Oxford University Press in New York for rights in America.

The lines in the same chapter from W.H. Auden's poem 'The Truest Poetry is the Most Feigning' are also reprinted by permission of Faber and Faber Ltd, taken from *Collected Poems* by W.H. Auden edited by Edward Mendelson. Random House, Inc. has given copyright permission for the United States and Canada.

I gratefully acknowledge main dependence on the scholarship of Professor B.E. Perry for *Aesopica* and on L.J. Hervieux for *Les fabulistes Latins d'Auguste à la fin du Moyen Age*. These are extensive areas of complications and obscurity. I am indebted to John Flinn for order in *Le Roman de Renart* and its many sequels.

Introduction

A reviewer who refers to a book as 'fable', casually or more intentionally, probably has in mind an eighteenth-century *'conte philosophique'*, described by Voltaire as a work which says more than it seems to say; he might indeed be thinking of *Candide*. Any non-literary person asked about fable would most likely think of Aesop. The two are not as far apart as they seem. *Aesop's Fables*, in one compilation or another, have an honourable lineage in literature and in education; they are fables, not nursery tales. In the early days of Greek and Latin fiction, when different forms were being tried out, comic fiction took the kind of liberties made familiar in Aesop and popular on the stage. Improbable but amusing stories were invented to provide, in a striking way, something to be thought about. It can be said that the embryo of the fable of which Aesop was one parent was fully formed in classical culture by the end of the second century AD, to be developed down the centuries in different cultural contexts by different applications and uses, to become a vehicle of literary expression with special resources.

If 'fable' is to be studied as a literary genre, the prevalent rather loose notion of it needs to be refined. Clearly, in this sense it is not merely a word for any fiction, nor a word specifically for the plot of an epic or a play, senses in which it has been used and may be used. Nor is it merely or mainly a story with animals for characters, nor a story with a moral. This last comes nearer, suggested by the dictionary word 'apologue', defined as 'a moral fable'. There are many stories with a moral, stories invented to bring home a moral, which are not fables at all. Improving stories for the young to show how those who do wrong come to a bad end will not be fables. They are too simplistic to require a fable to arrest and engage the mind. A fable gets past the garrison of resident assumptions, the mind's defences, to bring home its point or raise its questions: it is a tactical manoeuvre to prompt new thinking, Voltaire's story that says more than it seems to say – not a didactic story.

To start with, fable is narrative fiction in the past tense. A very early definition of the Aesopic fable was, 'a fictitious story picturing a truth'.[1] The 'picturing' implies a metaphorical representation of the 'truth'; so that a fable is basically a metaphor. Something in the mind

is brought into the mind's eye by an image of its likeness. Thought
and speech are steeped in metaphor. This was summed up long ago in
the Epicurean dictum: Nature is its own standard; one thing throws
light on another. Fable runs its metaphorical traffic on narrative rails:
'The mountain was in labour, and brought forth a mouse'. Brief,
incongruous, effective: a miniature story representing graphically a
familiar truth. There are three elements, idea, image, expression. The
idea is in the image, the image is its metaphorical expression; the
metaphor is in the narrative, which is its formal expression.

Since a fable as a fictitious story is an imagined action, and is a
metaphor, the action is used to portray something else which it
resembles in some way, and this something else is in the mind, a
'truth'. A truth can be formulated as a general statement; that is what
it is. If it is related as a fable, there should be some sufficient reason.
This may simply be to make it graphic and memorable, for ready
application: sour grapes, a leonine bargain, the lion's share, a wolf in
sheep's clothing, an ass in a lion's skin. These metaphorical expressions are made available to apply to a variety of instances with the
generality of a 'truth'. The particular story is put to general use as a
truth, although not possibly true. A more ambitious fable will not
merely express a truth graphically and memorably, but mainly will
generate and store new meaning in the conception it represents,
whereas a general statement relies mainly on established meanings.
What *Animal Farm* says could be formulated, and may have to be for
any evaluation of its 'truth'. But summary statements cannot resume
all the meaning generated and stored in the images and events of the
narrative. This may be true, with greater consequence, of *Brave New
World*.

The metaphorical expressions which familiar fables have made
current – a dog-in-the-manger attitude – make familiar also the
nature and use of metaphor which they exemplify. No word or
phrase is normally a metaphor in itself, since 'metaphor' implies
transference of words from use in their proper contexts to use in an
alien context. The word or phrase is borrowed for its descriptive
power in the new application. In 'a stream of abuse', 'stream' is
chosen as most appropriate to the occasion of use. Otherwise, it
might have been, 'he fired abuse'. 'Abuse' is in general a verbal
utterance, and can be a 'stream' or a 'volley' only in particular
instances. A metaphor is chosen, and exists only in particular use. It
may be a stereotype, 'a crushing bore', or specially chosen and fresh.

The most successful become stale, and fail. We say, excusably, 'blood was literally streaming from the wound', and less excusably, 'killing time is literally killing life', or, 'things began literally to fall apart'. To say 'literally' of a metaphor is of course absurd, as though to say: 'This is no metaphor' – when it is solely as metaphor that the word serves. The addition of 'literally' betrays inarticulate anxiety. Thought and expression are primitively and permanently metaphoric in their fabric. The implied comparison – 'a running sore', 'running with sweat' – does not in practice entail double reference: there is a compound reference which is grasped directly. In narrative form, the fable is an extended metaphor. There is a compound reference to the image presented and the conception represented.

This compound reference is read off, as it were, directly. The fox and the crow with a piece of cheese is wholly and solely about profit and loss in flattery, and does not otherwise refer to a transaction between a fox and a crow. The brevity and simplicity, and impossibility, of an Aesopic fable make this evident, so that it has become habitual to say what the fable is about in a title or moral. Thus a collection in Penguin Classics, selected and translated by S.A. Handford, gives a title to each which indicates an application, and a moral which explains it. However, this is only an editor's privilege; it is exemplary, not restrictive. A history of editions of the fables would show that. There is no definitive 'moral'. The metaphor is open; the comparison invites exploratory reflection.[2] One can see in the primitive Aesopic fable a potentiality for development as a mental artefact, which detains the thought that conceived it in the further reflection it prompts. Stripped and focused as it must always be, fable is then, like any work of art, dense enough to abide repeated examination, and to abound in stimulus. It is this development, with the achievements that have marked it, which the present study sets out to describe.

(ii)

Before saying more about that prospect, distinctions must be made between fable and other forms of allusive fiction with which it is liable to be confused, particularly parable and allegory. The books of the Bible are in general rich in imagery, and are studded with similitudes and allusive forms, allegories, dreams, visions, parables, and the like. Among them all, one is recognized as a fable. The trees at some time looked for a king among themselves, and asked first the olive, then the fig, then the vine. All refused because they had their own proper business to look after. Last, the bramble gave ironical consent upon an absurd condition that entailed a fearful penalty. This was Jotham's invention to bring home the realities of a situation to the perpetrators of it (Judges 9:8–15). In so far as it is a fable, it is so because it can stand on its own with a more general application – and there are Aesopic fables which it does resemble.

It used to be said that the only parable in the Old Testament was the story which Nathan told David (2 Samuel 12:1–7) to bring home to him his guilt in taking Bath-sheba: 'Thou art the man.' It is invented by Nathan for his purpose, and used and done with, which is what marks the parable; it is ancillary, brought in to explain or illustrate a particular point, dependent; not remaining as an independent statement in narrative form for general application, as a fable does – as in Kafka's *Metamorphosis*, in which a member of the family wakes up as a loathsome insect, with which all parties have to come to terms and live. A not uncommon occurrence is endowed with new meaning by these peculiar circumstances. This is fable using its daring metaphoric power in a transformation act of general significance, which the homely parable does not attempt. It might be objected that Jotham's story was invented for the occasion and done with as much as Nathan's. That might be fair comment, for Jotham's story is not as self-contained as a fable should be. But it is in the mode of a fable, and it does scrape into the collections (Perry, p. 475).

For, though the point of separation holds between parable and fable, dependence and independence, the borderline may be blurred. 'The Good Samaritan' is invented for an occasion, to answer the question, Who is my neighbour? Logically, however, it is a fable, in that the particular story is invented to represent a general pattern of behaviour, with the widest application. It is a conception, neighbour love, defined in a special narrative. Given some understanding of the relations between Samaritans and Jews in that cultural situation, it has an independence that takes it out of the main universe of discourse, about the kingdom of heaven, in which the other parables of Jesus have their occasion. The plainness of the story makes it uncharacteristic of fable. Surely, it is no more than a simple illustration of neighbour love, which is something anybody would immediately recognize and understand. So is the dog carrying a bone over a stream an illustration of greed, which is something everybody understands. In their originality, both broke new ground in ways familiarity now obscures. The difference between parable and fable is not between a story that might be real and one that could not be, as is sometimes supposed. The distinction is between independence and generality in the one case, dependence confined to the particular in the other. The parable of the Prodigal Son could not reasonably be said to be a fable, although indeed it can stand on its own as a story, and it does represent a general and familiar pattern of behaviour. As told by Jesus, it does belong intimately to the universe of discourse about the kingdom of heaven, and the point of its telling is in that. Its universality otherwise is trivial, merely the universality of what does happen more or less frequently, without any feature to make it significant. The same story is a different matter told in the *Gulistan* (below, p. 95) or by Thurber, 'The bat who got the hell out'. Fable generates conceptual meanings, does not merely furnish an illustration in a particular instance.

An allegory in narrative form may seem close to fable. Again, the principal difference is that the allusion in allegory is to something particular, and in fable to something general. Rather, although both may embody general conceptions in particular forms, with roles in a particular action, fable will do this to focus attention on an illuminated patch exposed to thought, whereas allegory tends to explore labyrinthine manifestations with delight in the description. Allegory constructs a series of specific correspondences in two systems, so that one translates into the other, either way. Bunyan's *The Pilgrim's Progress* represents the stages and vicissitudes of the Christian life, translating spiritual experiences into physical adventures, to give them imaginatively concrete reality. Personification has been largely used in allegories to give some abstraction, say Famine or Greed, a human appearance and a name, and a role in the action. Personification differs from an Aesopic image in a way that epitomizes the distinction. Personification describes an abstraction as a person who manifests in appearance and behaviour the name it bears, so that such agents may be used as characters in the argument of a plot, or paraded as figures in a pageant. The image of an Aesopic fable is a single action, in which the elements of meaning derived from the agents are integrated. In allegory, there is elaborate detail in detailed elaboration of the theme, heavily dependent of description of visual imagery. In fable, depiction jumps from particulars to the enactment. The ant and the grasshopper are not brought together because of what they are in nature. Popular beliefs are drawn on to construct an image of the carelessness of carefree enjoyment of life in humiliating confrontation with the righteousness of prudent foresight. Typically, allegory may represent human life as a voyage, in a sequence of images that recognizably correspond to features of life as lived. This is alien to the way of generalizing in fable, which would represent human life as lived by resuming it under a single aspect in an action imagined to bring home some part of human fate or folly.

(iii)

The images created by fables of the Aesopic type are deceptively homely: they have a quasi-mathematical abstractness and applicability. G.K. Chesterton likened the animals, in a Preface to a collection of Aesop's *Fables*, to an alphabet of humanity of which a language is made to write down and hand down the first philosophic certainties, and for this the figures had to be like abstractions in algebra or like the pieces in chess. This is roughly right, although the language of images is concrete and particular and picturesque. The virtue is that they can be and are used with the universality of abstractions. The essential theme of *Animal Farm* is anticipated in 'The Wolves and the Dogs'. The longer complex fables go beyond the simple images of the Aesopic fable, but simplify the abstractions they represent in a kind of model, as modern scientists build models of their invisible conceptual entities, based on measurements. Such models can be examined and questioned to give thought a firmer hold on experience. It is this power of fable not merely to represent but mainly to inform a conception that is its genius, beyond the scope of allegory. Anyone can write an allegory of sorts, or find an illustration. The invention of a fable is akin to that of the poet, as Plato recognized (*Phaedo*, 60–61) – in connection with Aesop. Hazlitt had that insight, and it justified his enthusiasm: 'The invention of a fable is to me the most enviable exertion of human genius: it is the discovering a truth to which there is no clue, and which, when once found, can never be forgotten. I would rather have been the author of *Aesop's Fables*, than of *Euclid's Elements*!' ('On Wit and Humour'). This could hardly be said of parables or allegories. There is a recognized distinction, examined in more detail in Chapter V.

Formal definition is likely to be less than helpful if it has to say in general terms not only what fable is but also what fables do. The first part is straightforward, in that fable is not straightforward narrative but a device, and can be called a narrative device. What it does with that device varies with the fable, as does the device itself. This includes ways to move things around, bring together, take apart, switch contexts, shift perspectives, unsettle, reorganize; in short, imagination manipulates the environment, to take hold of things as they are taken to be in order to show the way they are. The play of fiction drops any pretence to play real life as it appears, in order to show seriousness that does not appear; and thus sharpen perception, or broaden understanding, or quicken passion. In each case the action represented forms a conceptual artefact fabricated for a special use. A formal definition might be: a narrative device, to provoke and aid concrete thinking, focused on some general matter of concern. That hardly hints at the incongruities or the ironic comparison or the baited bafflement or any of the temerities by means of which so many fables achieve their effects. Varieties of the fable idiom are analysed in the last two chapters, after they have been exemplified in the first four. Meanwhile, there are some identifying general characteristics to be noticed here related to ways in which fable does its work.

(*iv*)

(1) Professor Perry has listed the following types of story as materials used in early fables:[3] a fairy-tale (*Märchen*), an aetiological nature-myth, an animal story, a series of amusing actions, a novella, a myth about the gods, a debate between two rivals, an account of the circumstances in which some aphoristic or witty remark was made. The point he is making is that the narrative material is indifferent; it neither makes nor excludes a fable. What makes a fable is the peculiar purpose and implied comparison that govern and shape the material. The type of story is not a criterion. The use made of it is. As fable developed and longer narratives were used, those in current vogue were often adopted and adapted, as voyages, travellers' tales, Eastern folk-tales or fantasies, and, latest, science fiction. These examples are of narratives which rather easily take human behaviour out of its normal contexts.

(2) The Aesopic fable established itself as a convention, and was its own excuse, however radically adapted. Longer fables had to make their own way in finding readers on their own terms. There were difficulties. The narrative is organized for the purposes of the fable. In this sense and for this reason, it is not written for the reader, as the bulk of fiction is. The story may have to be read before it can be 'read', in order to recognize what it is that is said more than seems to be said. It has been said, 'each poem contains its own poetics'.

Similarly, every fable has to justify itself in the telling. Cultural conditions may even forbid the attempt, when the conventional rules are too strict, or the climate of thought too uncongenial. But there are nigh-universal responses that help. This kind of serious fiction in which the writer must prevail, and prevail with the reader, has been regularly baited with the comic and the satirical. A reader's confidence, or interest, may be generated by tone of voice, encouraging, alluring, ironic, rapid. An author may banter and tease the reader with tricks, ploys, bluffs, a light buffet or two about the ears with the fool's bladder, to alert attention to the lurking intent. Above all, the reader is not tried too long. The story is simple enough and short enough to be memorable as well as telling. And since its main ostensible content is the plot, an action, it can often be translated without loss. People are not in the round, like Mr Pickwick or Mrs Poyser. It is not likely to matter what happened at the meeting in the wood, nor what passed between certain persons at yesterday's picnic. There is not the visual field of broad daylight. A spotlight is focused on an object, or a floodlight isolates a chosen area.

(3) Fable is a special form of literary composition, in the sense that it is occasioned, there is a reason for it. There must be cultural conditions not merely to make it possible, but mainly to make it expedient. Generally, these may be political or philosophical. Politically, opinions, a message may be cast in the form of a fable to baffle or deceive the official mind with meanings that cannot be literally construed as evidence, but get through plainly to those for whom they are intended. This is to use fable merely as a practical device; but it is legitimate, and when it is live its wit and bite are sharpened by incomparable excitement. Interaction between the two levels of meaning, literal and implied, is a different mechanism when the intention is philosophical, for the act of communication is at a different level, understanding or awareness, rather than praxis. Fable then has its proper generality and permanence.

(4) As a genre fable has a boundary, but every fable has its own neighbours, and its own affinities. One may be close to an allegory, another to a folk-tale, a third to what may be taken for an ordinary story. The boundary may sometimes be ill defined, but unless it is recognizably thereabouts at some point of distinction, there is no point in looking. What the neighbours are, however, is often relevant to what the fable is and does.

(5) Last, not least, the medium is the message. The message is not

delivered – certainly not in the 'morals' tagged to the Aesopic fables: it is embodied. It is in this sense that fable is a conceptual artefact, which remains to be used. Interplay continues between the thought provoked and the representation that provokes and aids it.

(*v*)

Enough has been said in a preliminary way about what fable is and does and how it differs from similar narrative forms. The first three chapters of this study trace the development from obscure beginnings into maturity by the end of the eighteenth century. A conspectus of this history may help to establish the theme.

The sources of fable are found in the 'wisdom literature' characteristic of early civilization. Short pithy sayings and poetry spring spontaneously from the native soil, for later cultivation. The nucleus of the Book of Proverbs in the Old Testament was probably in oral currency at the time of the monarchy; and the later Wisdom literature of the Hebrews seems to have been in some sort of communication with Greek thought. The maxims with which this kind of literature is studded were useful in the instruction of children by their parents. The last chapter of Proverbs explicitly repeats what King Lemuel was taught by his mother. In the Apocrypha, these books go beyond moral instruction into the intellectual provinces of knowledge: 'To know the constitution of the world, and the operation of the elements . . . the diversity of plants and the virtues of roots' (Wisdom of Solomon: 7). The Indian fables were used to teach 'political science'. Fables abounded in the wisdom literature of India, but there were none in the Hebrew. However, in the old Mesopotamian literature, dating back to the eighteenth century BC and earlier, collections have been made of one-sentence fables of the Aesopic type, a clear anticipation. The developed Aesopic fable was useful material in the schools of rhetoric both as a linguistic discipline, in paraphrase, expansion, compression, and for apposite citation in the development of an argument. Rhetoric, the art of discourse, of persuasion and of thinking, was the main discipline in higher education throughout the classical period to the fall of Rome. It involved humanistic studies, as Cicero called them, including history, poetry and moral philosophy. The Aesopic fable was too useful to be forgotten in this context, if used sometimes half-apologetically. *Aesop's Fables* remained a school book in English grammar schools until the eighteenth century. When the fables were put into Latin verse of some accomplishment by Phaedrus and into Greek verse by Babrius, both in the first century AD, they found a lowly but secure place in polite literature, a status to be put beyond challenge by La Fontaine some sixteen hundred years later.

The philosophic background of fable in wisdom literature, and the loose connection of the developed Aesopic fable with the rhetorical discipline which had philosophic roots with the Sophist Isocrates (in opposition to Plato), had implied recognition when Lucian, the most famous rhetorician of his day throughout the Roman world in the second century AD, had it in mind to mate Socratic dialogue with the Aristophanic imaginative licence of the Old Comedy to produce a new kind of fiction that would use jest to put before the reader something to think about. With his *True History* he is said to have initiated a new genre of which *Gulliver's Travels* is a much later, and indebted, example.

The staple material of the Aesopic fable was destined to survive, and was found in the Latin inheritance of the European Middle Ages. The development achieved in classical culture was also destined to be re-enacted or paralleled, spontaneously. Marie de France and others put the fables into vernacular verse of some merit. They were available for use in homilies. In the great *Roman de Renart*, Aesopic material was worked up into a parody of courtly poetry that was so successful and continued so long that it left a lasting mark and a striking precedent, if it did not initiate a new genre, like Lucian. Although fable showed this manifest liveliness, it was not at home in a culture dominated by the Church, in which meaning was allegorical and predetermined. It had little independence; as parody or satire, it was parasitic. The Renaissance recovered Lucian, with lively appreciation on the part of such as More and Erasmus – particularly Erasmus, who imitated him in his Colloquies, and who incidentally produced a sustained independent and deadly Aesopic fable in one of the many revisions of his *Adages*. But it was in the eighteenth century, the Age of Reason, that fable achieved classical maturity, with books of accomplished modern fables in verse or prose (Gay, Lessing), with La Fontaine's sophisticated *comédie humaine* of these antique puppets, and with the new *conte philosophique*, whether of Lucian extraction – like *Gulliver's Travels* – or of Indian extraction, descending through the Persian versions that had become popular and had been in European circulation since the Middle Ages, a story type adopted and adapted by Voltaire or by Samuel Johnson in

Rasselas. At this time, fable came of age and displayed the resources available to its purpose, uniquely serious in fiction.

However, the device was not to be used during the next century in England, save (almost accidentally) by the maverick Samuel Butler in *Erewhon* (1872), a notable exception. Some reasons for this void or avoidance are offered, which may be probable but must be speculative. What is certain is that this was the period in which the novel established its dominion and became the dominant literary form; and one that opened ample scope to serious purpose. Since then, with most artistic forms, it has had its share of subversive movements; the anti-novel may be the most serious form of fiction. Experimental freedom has left the fable as a device where it was at the end of the eighteenth century with the *conte philosophique*, outmoded because unnecessary. So it has been said. All the same, the protean fiction of the present time is rich in reputations made by productions that have the distinctive odour and inner logic of that philosophic fiction, whatever the class name they may get today. And Aesop survives in modern varieties that seem to conform more to Mendel's principles of transmission than to the legendary theory of Pythagoras.

An example of the modern return to fable is Michel Tournier's translation of a story which is not a fable, Defoe's *Robinson Crusoe*, into one that is – *Vendredi*, 1967 (*Friday or The Other Island*, tr. Norman Denny, 1969). Defoe's story is his imaginative construction of what might have happened in such a case as that of Alexander Selkirk left alone on a desert island. He builds up day-to-day detail, so that Sir Walter Scott could say, 'Robinson Crusoe is more real to us today than any real seaman who was ever wrecked'; and he added that the story had set every 'elf' acting it out for himself. No elf would set himself up on The Other Island, although Tournier's Robinson starts off in the same way as Defoe's Crusoe, and adapts himself to the same plight and prospect, in a designed parallel. Defoe's Crusoe had endured hardships and captivity before the twenty-four years he spent in solitary confinement as an island prisoner, and the four that followed with Friday. Throughout the time he worked and worried, regulated and filled his days, thanked God for his mercies or felt an abandoned wretch, was a king content and proud to rule his realm or a fretting or despairing castaway. In short, he not merely survived, he persisted the same restless, dissatisfied, half-reflective, middle-class, eighteenth-century Yorkshireman, Robinson Crusoe. Not so

Michel Tournier's Robinson, alike in particulars of background and situation. For the modern author knows that human personality does not survive prolonged solitude; that as a castaway infant does not become human, a castaway adult in time loses human attributes. Therefore, the Journal of Crusoe which recorded the vicissitudes of mind, body, and estate becomes the Journal of Robinson that monitors the phases of his transformation, as it becomes apparent to him.

At the outset, Robinson gives up, overcome by the shock of his plight. He is, as it were, demoralized and dehumanized in anticipation, drops on all fours and wallows in the mud with and like the wild pigs. Then he pulls himself together, recognizing that salvation from this madness depends on his constructing a model of the society he had known, in which to continue his life; that to survive as human, he has to conquer nature, to assert himself, to organize, to make and abide by rules – to behave as human. The island itself becomes for him a substitute for humankind, the piece of earth in which he can be anchored to Earth, the home of his kind; and he calls it Speranza. Thereafter, he institutes with due pomp the productive tasks and routines and rules and offices and observances which he has brought with him in remembrance, regardless of their uselessness. He maintains this self-imposed nonsense punctiliously, knowing that he needs the discipline – at the same time, exposing the fatuity of much of it anywhere by stripping away its context of custom and consent. Gradually, he establishes a relationship with Speranza which he makes personal and special, and in which he incorporates his own intimate past as son and as husband. He is aware of growing disenchantment with his elaborately maintained way of life, a routine regulated by a water-clock.

A new chapter is opened towards the end with the appearance of Friday, as in the parent story, and in similar circumstances. Robinson is now Governor, Commander-in-Chief and Spiritual Pastor, with a subject and dependant of inferior race, whose service he is entitled to and for whom he is responsible. Friday is so utterly docile and obedient that the puppet prompts reflection upon the play-acting. Robinson begins to study Friday, to discern the difference from himself, innate and cultural, and to sense a deliverance from himself in which Friday would be his guide. What he recognizes in Friday is not merely a mocking disregard for all his thought for the morrow, his tasks and rules and organization and its fruits; not merely the negative aspect of Friday's attitude, but mainly an altogether different principle of order, like that of the lilies of the field. Friday lives in and for the moment, but remains fully capable of the sustained striving and spontaneous virtuosity required to achieve what he sets his heart on and puts his mind to. By a train of incidents, Robinson's homestead is completely destroyed in an explosion of the kegs of gunpowder he had recovered from the wreck and stored. This turns his mind from the past to the future; he will throw in his lot with Friday, and learn from him. The new relationship is consummated in a thrilling experience, the inventive outcome of a dangerous venture of Friday in trying to subdue an exceptionally splendid he-goat. All seems set for an indefinite idyllic life together, when a sail is sighted and a vessel puts in to try to obtain water, the first visit to the island in the twenty-eight years Robinson has been there. The ship is English, and Robinson has dinner with the captain. This encounter, with the crew, the mate, the captain, observing their behaviour, hearing their talk, brings back concretely the greed, arrogance, violence which prevail in the civilized world, disillusioning him face to face as he had been disillusioned gradually in abstraction by his play-acting based on garbled recollections of the society he had left and lost. He decides that he cannot leave, that he and Friday must return, and they do. In the night, Friday slips away to join the ship. Robinson is alone again, a generation older. Too disheartened, he prepares to die; and in setting about it discovers the cook's boy, about twelve years old, so grossly mistreated on board that he has taken the chance to escape – Robinson's second refugee. This time, there is no bondage to the past nor the present nor the future.

The story exposes to thought aspects of the social and personal nature of human being, ways of being human that are conditioned by social consent, and ways that are not; a human being's relations with the environment, natural and cultural, with the past, with another human being, with the present, with himself, with the future, with what happens when time has a stop. The range of reflection is both abstracted from normal circumstances and grounded in concreteness, and the story shows how a particular action can be invented to focus and facilitate thinking at a general level.

Finally, a negative example. The BBC has twice broadcast a televised version by Derek Mahon of a novel by Jennifer Johnston, *How Many Miles to Babylon?* One press comment said: 'It is also a play of ideas, exploring the connection between class and militarism with subtlety and intelligence'. A just comment which perhaps suggests a theme for a fable type of fiction. The story is not a fable, and does not suggest anything of the kind. It is wholly human in texture, about formed characters and their multiple relationships. The action is determined and sustained by the strength of a friendship that begins and ends in unusual circumstances. It falls victim to the militarism that fails to break it; and it is a friendship that breaks class barriers, between Alex Moore, son and heir of an Irish landowner, and Jerry, a village boy. They enlist together at the beginning of the First World War. Major Glendinning, their Commanding Officer in France, is a dedicated professional soldier, despairing of the fighting material in his hands but determined to 'make a man' of the subaltern Alex Moore. In the Major, one gets a glimpse down the centuries of the ideas and ideals of a class celebrated by Froissart and formed by the feudal system – root of the connection between class and militarism.

In a fable focused on this connection between class and militarism, there would not be the 'human content' of this story. The particular action would have to be constructed by agents and agencies that transcended the age-long link which survived until the war to end war, by showing its link with technology in a longer perspective. The invention of the stirrup was adapted to war by the use of trained mounted armoured knights (cp. tanks), levied on the landed class bound by the oath of fealty. This order was gradually modified, but not superseded until transformed by a technological mutation of unimaginable scope and consequence. Human subordination to the war-machine, which is militarism, or rather the subordination of all humane considerations as an implied imperative of the machine itself – whether of the ideals of the corps of chivalry or of the discipline of manned mutual atomic destruction – needs to be represented in fiction as the takeover it is, if it is to be seen as of general consequence rather than as a particular stupidity as it touches local concerns.

An example to illustrate the level of abstraction at which a major fable makes its representation particular and concrete.

1   The Fable in Literature

Early popular narrative

(i)

Most animal stories are not fables. Richard Adams's *Watership Down*, one of the most widely read (not only by children), is certainly not a modern fable, as *Animal Farm* certainly is. Margaret Blount, in her comprehensive and perceptive study of animal stories of all kinds (*Animal Land*, 1974), devotes the first and shortest part to 'Animal Fables'. In her Postscript, in the light of her synoptic view of the changing ways in which animals have been used or presented in fiction, she concludes that they now 'seem better than we are'; their societies, or those invented for them, are exemplars of a higher morality. *Watership Down* is seen as one of these examples, in truth a modern fable, not merely a story for children, with nostalgic overtones for grown-ups. This is more than hard to take seriously. On the general point, that animals 'seem much better than we are', fables have been ready to say this, with great emphasis, in all periods. The animals of a fable, however, are neither heroes nor villains. That is not the kind of story in which they play their roles.

Katharine Briggs, in *A Dictionary of British Folk-tales* (1970), has a short section, 'Fables and Exempla', thirty in all. She distinguishes four kinds: (a) the true Aesopic fable, e.g. 'The Yaller-legged Cock'rill'; (b) a mock origin myth, with implicit moral, e.g. 'The Wood Pigeon's Nest'; (c) exemplary tales with a supernatural element, e.g. 'The Greedy Peasant Woman'; (d) a simple moral tale, e.g. 'The Choice of a Servant'. She adds that even tales with no explicit moral generally embody a social comment.

About a third of her items in this section are versions of Aesopic or Indian fables, or can be paralleled in them. Two are of special interest. 'The Grateful Beasts' is a version of the Bidpai story of the traveller who finds a goldsmith fallen into a pit along with a tiger, an ape, and a snake. The animals rescued warn him against helping the man out because nothing in all creation is more dangerous. In the sequel, the animals prove their gratitude and the goldsmith deals treacherously with his benefactor. In the other story, 'The King of the Beasts', representatives of all the species are in mortal combat to determine by survival which is fit to provide the king. The lion, exhausted and cruelly hurt, is the survivor, but he notices a donkey who has kept out of the fight cowering with his head in a corner. The lion drags himself over to despatch this other survivor, and is himself finished off by a desperate blow from the heels of the donkey. Hardly a variant of 'The Old Lion' (*Phaedrus* I, 21), it is a match.

'The Yaller-legged Cock'rill' is an example of the fable in oral currency, since it was taken down in Lindsey (West Suffolk) folk-speech as told by a local who recalled what his grandfather had said about a swaggering young coxcomb. This must be an unstable mixture of remembrance and improvisation, like folk- or fairy-tales, which emerge in literature only if and when retold by a Perrault or a Tolstoy, unless in a version recorded by a collector and published.

(Katharine Briggs cites in her Preface a letter from Lady Alington to Margaret Roper in which she describes how she was fobbed off with fables by the new Lord Chancellor, who boasted that his only learning was in Aesop, when she went to intercede with him for Sir Thomas More—cp. R.W. Chambers, 1936, p. 308. More himself remarked that he had often heard Wolsey tell the first fable and that the second could not be by Aesop because it was Christian, and neither applied to his case. The reference by Katharine Briggs is to show how common fables were in everyday speech at that time. Henry VIII gave Anne Boleyn a copy of Aesop, now in the Bodleian Library.)

(ii)

Editors of collections of early popular narrative do recognize the fable as a special class. Moriz Winternitz, writing of the Indian *Jataka Commentary* as a 'very old and highly important collection not only of folk-tales, but also of literary productions of the most varied kinds', distinguished seven: (1) fables; (2) Märchen (fairy-tales, many of them tales of animals); (3) anecdotes and comic tales; (4) tales of adventure and romance; (5) moral tales; (6) moral maxims; (7) legends (Hastings's *Encyclopedia of Religion and Ethics*, vol. vii, pp. 491–4). This is a division representative of many early literatures, and in most cases there is a proportionately small membership of the fable class. The classification does represent real distinctions, but there are fusions of these elementary types, evident in many fables.

W.G. Lambert, in his *Babylonian Wisdom Literature* (1960), gives six fragments of the type of fable which became traditional in Akkadian literature, quite distinct from the Aesopic fable which may have been current orally. The Babylonian literary fable is a stylized

verbal contest between creatures, substances, or other personifications ('The Tamarisk and the Palm', 'The Ox and the Horse'). A
mythological introduction leads to a meeting of the contestants, who
dispute superiority, mainly in terms of their usefulness to man; a
judgement scene settles the affair. Another group in Lambert's
collection, 'Popular Sayings', includes short animal or insect fables
told mainly for amusement.

> A mosquito, as it settled on an elephant,
> Said, 'Brother, did I press your side? I will make off.'
> The elephant replied to the mosquito, at the watering place.
> 'I do not care whether you get on – what is it to have you? –
> Nor do I care whether you get off.'

This droplet finds its way via *Babrius* (No. 84) into the European
stream.

The discovery of manuscripts at the beginning of this century in a
hidden library at Tunhuang in North West China was a find of
Chinese popular literature, stories and ballads. Arthur Waley (1960)
describes the discovery and the manuscripts in an Afterword to his
translation of a selection. They are popular, he says, in the sense of
composed by people of the scribe or village schoolmaster class (as
were the fables composed or edited by monks in medieval Europe),
not as recorded after age-long oral transmission: 'Many of the
characteristics of this literature are similar to those of the folk literature of peasant Europe and of folk-tales in many parts of Asia, such as
the repetition of stock passages, and asides in which the story is
related to the origin of place-names, or of rites and customs.'

There is only one fable in his collection, 'The Swallow and the
Sparrow'. In a Note, he gives the date of composition as not long
after AD 721, and remarks that it does not seem to go back to any
legend about swallows and sparrows, but that fables about birds have
always been a favourite Chinese way of letting off steam about
unpopular government measures: 'Not long ago a Peking daily
printed on its front page a fable about a bird-catcher who gained the
confidence of birds "by speaking to them in their own language". He
was then easily able to catch them and pop them into cages. That the
fable referred to the Hundred Flowers episode is obvious.'[1]

After the squat, the plot speeds to a conclusion, using the ingredients of puppet comedy: abuse, knockabout violence, frequent

proverbial sayings, take-off of characteristic behaviour in officials, rogues, wronged persons, wives caught in the trap of their husbands' less successful exploits, partisan onlookers and busybodies. Justice is not done in a case of recognized injury, the squat, in case 'the files will become unwieldy'. Reconciliation of the litigants ensues because rough injustice endured by both blossoms into good humour and bears fruit in self-help. This satirical piece stands alone in the selection; the other twenty-five are mainly 'marvel-stories' – legends, ballads, Buddhist pieces, stories of the afterworld, some with political undertones. None of these resembles the fable.

The distinctive function of the fable is observed also in less developed literatures. In the Yoruba (Nigeria) folk-tale tradition, for example, the folk-tale (*àló*) is distinct from the story (itàn), and is explicitly fictional and supernatural in characters, plot, and scene. Told in the evening to groups of children, it includes songs with choruses in which they join. However, it may also be treated allegorically as adult instruction, and regarded as a parable or fable (*òwe*).

There are a few fables in Grimms' collection. Some are variants of Aesopic fables: 'The Wolf and the Seven Young Kids', 'The Fox and the Cat', 'The Hare and the Hedgehog'. Others have a fable content: 'The Cat and the Mouse Set up House', 'The Wolf and the Man', 'The Wolf and the Fox', 'The Mouse, the Bird, and the Sausage', 'The Fisherman and his Wife'. These are assimilated in manner to the Märchen, but do the work of a fable, as others which seem to have a kinship with fables do not, or not quite: 'Mrs Fox's Wedding', 'The Fox and the Geese', 'The Fox and the Horse', 'The Dog and the Sparrow'. There are aetiological stories of a kind often included in collections of fables, although not properly fables: 'The Hedge King', 'The Flounder', 'The Bittern and the Hoopoe'.

This glance at early popular narrative sees something of its diversity, and that the differences are recognized. Fable is identified among them, and numbers among the fewest in representation. Nigerian practice shows particularly that it is the use of the material that is to the purpose, rather than the material itself. The Babylonian stylized literary fable is not a fable in this sense, but the form was later adapted to the purpose of fable – by John Lydgate, for example.

Sources: Aesop

(i)

Aesop is a legend whose original seems to have been a colourful personality of Samos in the early sixth century BC, a freed slave who made a telling use of fables as he went about. Whatever the obscure origins of this way of speaking, Aesop is associated with an innovation, for the metaphorical or implicit statement was alien to the thought and language in Homer, as the frankly fictitious was to the assumed historical character of myths. (Lucian, some seven centuries later, was trying to sort out confusions in the truth claims of narrative.) Although popular in origin, like proverbs, the Aesopic fable proved apt for cultivation in the urban climate of the city-states. Later, Aesop was idealized as spokesman of the wisdom of the common man. Erasmus recalls that 'Aulus Gellius does not hesitate to put those absurd fables of Aesop before the famous doctrines of the Stoics, stern and fallen from heaven as they are'.

From early on, Aesop and his fables enjoyed this comic mixture of apology and esteem. When he is made to appear in the fables themselves, as by Phaedrus, it is naturally as a sage old man of great prestige, who intervenes to open people's eyes, or who administers a sharp rebuke or a smart retort, or who gives good advice. His appearance in fiction of a later time is rather different. In Lucian's *True History*, Aesop is found in the Island of the Blest in the fellowship of the heroes as their jester, a superior menial, a professional. He is present in Plutarch's famous conversation piece 'Dinner of the Seven Wise Men', a dinner party given by Periander (ruler of Corinth, 625 BC), a patron of literature and philosophy.

'Aesop too, as it happened, having been sent by Croesus only a short time before on a mission both to Periander and to the god at Delphi, was present at the dinner, seated in a low chair next to Solon, who occupied the place just above.' The former slave is quite at his ease in this exalted but unpretentious company, offering leads in the talk; and after he has been shut up for distracting the conversation from the matter in mind, he comes back in his own defence later when they are all caught in a similar deviation. 'Aesop told the following story: "A wolf seeing some shepherds in a shelter eating a sheep, said, What an uproar you would make if I were doing that".' At the end, when each is capping the other with tall stories about the

marvellous sympathy of dolphins with the human race, and the many
rescues they have effected: ' "Well! well!", said Aesop, "you all
make fun of my jackdaws and crows if they talk with one another,
and yet dolphins indulge in such pranks as this".' As befits legendary
sages, they sum up by discussing the famous Greek apophthegms:
'Know yourself', 'Avoid extremes', 'Give a pledge, and mischief
ensues'; and someone remarks that for a long time those present have
been praising the stories which Aesop has composed touching each of
these principles; to which Aesop rejoins that he gets the credit only
when he is being made fun of – otherwise, on serious occasions,
Homer is their inventor.

Aesop's presence in the company reflects the popularity of the
fable in intellectual circles in classical times, and the quizzical apolo-
getic attitude of the serious to the apologue, as something witty and
apposite, but uncomfortably close to old wives' tales or nursery
nonsense. This ambivalence is explicit in literary terms where Seneca
remarks that no Latin author has attempted to turn Aesop's fables
into literature, as though the Roman genius and the Greek invention
were worthy of each other, at the same time as he speaks of the fables
with some disparagement by comparison with serious literature
(*Consolatio ad Polybium*, ch. viii). This mixture of respect and
apology persists down the centuries.

Professor Perry has woven four sizable pieces of the fabric of
Aesopic legend from scattered threads: fifty-two sayings attributed
to Aesop on various authorities; references to Aesop or the fables
from one hundred and five sources, including passages in *Babrius* and
Phaedrus; a collection of proverbs (179) attributed to Aesop,
brought together from four sources; above all, the first critical
edition of the texts of the 'Life of Aesop' (two Greek, one partial
Latin) which originated in Egypt early in the first century AD and
was subsequently many times edited and added to until the end of the
eleventh century, when a Byzantine version became the source of the
only modern reproduction, published by A. Westermann in 1845 but
based on an imperfect text. Although not authentic lineaments of a
real original, these features of the legend reflect the position held by
Aesop and the fables in the ancient world, and show traces of a
pervasive influence within the classical literary tradition.[2] With no
reliable evidence the figure of Aesop is remote and dim, but an
impression remains of an independent superior intelligence – not the
questing intelligence of a systematic thinker, rather that of a close

observer of his fellows, with a sharp mother wit and a metaphorical imagination – as authentic a product of the independent Greek genius as Euclid or Diogenes.

(ii)

The foundation stock of Aesopic fables eventually transmitted to Europe was a collection in Greek prose made by Demetrius of Phalerum, a principal and distinguished Athenian statesman and orator of his time (*c.*350–280 BC), 'intended to serve as a repertory of literary raw materials for the use of writers and speakers' (Perry, 1965, lxxxv). Diogenes Laertius lists among the many works of Demetrius also a collection of Anecdotes. His collection of Aesop's fables, which is not extant, seems to have been *Aesop* for the classical world, the stock source for the schools and the rhetoricians and writers, and in due course for Babrius and Phaedrus, who gave *Aesop* literary form and currency. 'The oldest and largest extant collection of prose fables ascribed to Aesop, known as the Augustana . . . contains some 231 fables from the ancient collection and can be traced to an archetype of the fourth or fifth century. The original compilation was probably made in the second century, if not in the latter part of the first, but it was unknown to Phaedrus and uninfluenced by Babrius except for a few fables which may be later accretions' (Perry, xvi).[3] This is the raw material for the literary versions of later authors. In all these prose collections the fables are attributed to Aesop, and the version bears no genuine name. With Babrius, Phaedrus and Avianus, and later with Marie de France and others, the poetic versions are literary compositions for which their authors claim recognition.

Thus *Aesop's Fables* is not a canonical text. There is a corpus of some 725 Greek and Latin fables in the Aesopic tradition, of which critical texts have been provided by Professor Perry in *Aesopica*. This corpus includes many items which are not true Aesopic fables as defined by Theon, 'a fictitious story picturing a truth'. Phaedrus says explicitly in the Prologue to Book IV: 'fables which I call Aesopic rather than Aesop's, since he brought out only a few, and I compose a larger number using the old form but treating new themes'; and his use of the old form is rather free. On the use of the term 'Aesopic', Perry says:

the range of what may rightly be called Aesopic, both by tradition

and by kind, is so vast and so repetitious as not to be worth
including, even if it were possible, within the compass of a single,
necessarily monstrous and chaotic volume. A fable invented by an
eighteenth-century writer, or by one today, may be just as truly
'Aesopic' in all essential respects as any of those which were made
up or adapted from popular lore in antiquity after the time of
Aesop, which is to say any of the fables extant in ancient collections with the dubious exception of less than a score. If Aesop
really used or invented those few particular fables, then they are,
ipso facto, in a special sense, more 'Aesopic' than the products of
later or more modern times, but otherwise not necessarily so.

Any modern translator of Aesop's fables may select from several
modern critical editions, principally: B.E. Perry, 1952; E. Chambry,
1925–6; and A. Hausrath, 1956–9. The many *Aesops* which exist in
English selections since Caxton's in 1483, a few of them famous like
the one he used, are evidence of popularity and esteem. S.A. Handford's Penguin selection of 1954 has had eleven reprints.

(iii)

Aesop's fables seem generally to be thought of as cautionary tales
illustrating foolish or bad conduct, and teaching prudence in an
amusing way that is memorable and appeals to children and the child
in everyone. Phaedrus suggests as much in his Prologue to Book II:
'That which is Aesopic in kind is confined to instructive examples;
nor is anything else aimed at in fables than that the mistakes of
mortals may be corrected, and that one may sharpen his wits by a
close application to them.' Stored in handbooks, a fable had no
immediate context; it was furnished with a promythium, a statement
of its application, for the convenience of indexing, so that a writer or
speaker could find what he wanted to make his point; and/or an
epimythium, an explanation or repetition of the 'truth' intended.
This collecting and editing did not leave a fable to speak its own
language direct to the reader, which was its whole vocation.
    More than half the 207 fables selected and translated by Handford
in the Penguin edition are descriptive, less than one quarter are
simply prescriptive, and the remainder are both, but predominantly
at a simple level, given general force. They say, in effect, this is how
things are: how dependence on others is certainly unsafe; how a
cunning ruse sometimes comes off, more often is seen through; how

what is won by cunning has to be kept by force; how a kindness or service is sometimes repaid, sometimes provokes insult or injury; how foolish it is to deal fairly or kindly with a rogue; how self-preservation is the strongest motive, violating natural ties, forcing the last ounce of exertion, compelling the strongest to swallow humiliation; how a deadly hatred may be unappeasable and fatal; how goods are enjoyed at a price – sufficiency with servitude, freedom with privation, peace of mind with poverty, security with expense; how it is idle to expect respect for rightful claims unless one has the power to enforce them; how dealings with absolute power demand the utmost wariness; how boasting, conceit, vanity, greed, jealousy, infatuation, pretensions, and acting out of place are not only ridiculous but also self-defeating; how many ways there are in which impulsive, thoughtless behaviour lands one in disaster or in trouble; how stupid and futile it is to ignore or flout nature or established usages, or to repine at one's lot; how the whirligig of time brings in its revenges, and the irony of events reverses fortunes; how there is no way of making oneself immune to misfortune, and even the most circumspect foresight may be mocked; how the biter gets bit; how the most dreaded and deadly meet their match; how we rationalize our failures and represent losses as gains; how the race is not always to the swift nor the battle to the strong.

To generalize the promythia or epimythia in this way is to show, at least, that the Aesopic fable is not for the nursery. Locke thought Aesop almost the only book he knew fit for children, one which would join childhood to manhood. Philostratus said: 'Homer, Hesiod, Archilochus cared for fables, but Aesop treated all sides of human life in his fables, and made his animals speak for the sake of thought, that through them children may learn the business of life.' Quintilian called the fables 'the natural successors of the fairy stories of the nursery', as Locke said, joining childhood to manhood. If they teach morality, it is not the morality of the Sunday school; rather, an open-eyed Baconian morality.

Anyone botanically informed knows what he sees in a recognized specimen; and then sees what he knows. To know what one sees and see what one knows is reciprocally informing in this way. A fable embodies the general in an invented particular which, when it is recognized, informs the general notion with more perceptive recognitions. One knows what one sees in the action of the dog that snatches at the reflection of his bone in the stream, say 'greed'; and in seeing and studying what one recognizes in this instance, one sees greed bound up with covetousness, and both with a self-defeating attitude: what one sees informs what one knows, so that what one will see in other instances is better informed.

There are several versions of the hunted fox who is concealed and then betrayed by a woodcutter (Handford, 4). The story shows literally the actions of one who wants to stand well with all parties as they come along, as a child says what he thinks will please someone he likes, even if it contradicts what he has just said to another he wants to please. When the woodcutter gets nowhere with the huntsmen, he still wants the gratitude of the fox – or a gratuity in real life. If the fable is taken as merely 'actions speak louder than words', which is what the caption says, or as an example of hypocrisy, which is what the moral says, that is to see the woodcutter's behaviour as the fox does. To make fable sense, the image will inform the perception by which it is recognized. If the image recognized here is of habitual ingratiation, for gain or merely to please, perception sees that this is necessarily bound up with undependability and is a main source of it.

'The Stork and the Fox' (77) is said, or made, to represent an ill turn repaid in kind. The image might be recognized as inconsiderate behaviour of a less deliberate sort, a bland assumption that the ways and customs of others are, or ought to be, the same as one's own, without regard to differences of class or culture or religion. In some versions, the Stork arrives from abroad. It could be a fable on race relations: this is an English school for English children, loving of course to extend hospitality to little foreigners who are here. In Odo of Cheriton's version the bees invite the beetles and offer them honey, and on a return visit are offered ordure, which is intended to represent what the doctors of the Church have to offer and what men of the world prefer. The action of the fable is so nicely conceived in concrete terms, and so neatly simplifies the fixity of cultural patterns, that it seems a pity to waste it on a mere prank.

As a botanist knows what he sees, the reader of a fable has to know what he sees in the image presented and to see it in a new light. The part of the reader in recognition and response is more personal than the botanist's can be, and he learns more from his examination of the specimen. In this the reading of fables, even Aesopic fables, anticipates modern insights into fiction and its possibilities. That is, when the reading has been freed from the tyranny of tradition, the arbitrary rule of promythium and epimythium, in which editors usurped the role of readers.

The animals in fables are not beasts of the field, of course, but neither are they stereotypes of moral attributes, fixed symbols. The serpent is evil incarnate, thrown out of heaven by Zeus as such, yet resorts to Zeus on another occasion with a plea for help, and is given advice. The ass is 'that blot on creation', but not always stupid nor contemptible, even representative of innocence. The fox may be outfoxed. The lion is afraid or humiliated. The kinship of wolves and dogs, and their relations with shepherds and sheep provide a nexus for several themes. Nature or symbolism or legend or myth is material to be adopted and adapted if apt for the image of an action which is the core of the fable. Improvisation, adaptability of the material to the purpose, gives fable its inventive scope. Plasticity made the fable excellent material for linguistic exercise in schools. Quintilian recommends paraphrasing fables in simple and restrained language, going on to freer paraphrasing that remains faithful to the meaning whilst making abridgements or embellishments (*Instit.* I ix 2, 6). Those who had learned to do this well were said to be ready to learn anything. Fables were the junior or preparatory humanities in classical education.

Fables were at home in any place where people congregate – in the assembly, the law courts, the council chamber, the market place, the club, at the dinner table; and were readily brought into discourse to make or reinforce a point. In the compilations they were stored for use, not for reading, and served their purpose only in use, applied on occasion. Yet in due course their popularity destined them for reading, and they appeared in literature.

(iv)

Fable as literature in classical times meant poetry. Callimachus, in the third century BC, had taken fables as themes for poems: a contest between the olive and the laurel, rudely interrupted by a bramble bush, a familiar folk-tale motif (Iambus IV); or Iambus II, which refers to a time when all animals shared speech with mankind, another familiar piece of folklore. Much earlier, in the seventh century, Archilochus had introduced the 'Iambic', a word used for his poetry of a certain kind employing ridicule, invective, and improvisation, with borrowings from folk-speech and fables, for a personal purpose, satirical attack. *The Battle of Frogs and Mice* (c.480

BC) has small literary merit, but as a burlesque of the epic is an early example of fable as parody – the war is occasioned by the drowning of a mouse by a frog (cp. Perry, 384). Of course, Horace made free use of fables in his Satires and Epistles, with a dozen allusions and the famous retelling with relish at length of 'The Country Mouse and the City Mouse', to savour both his taste for convivial good fare and his ever-faithful preference for rural simplicity and peace of mind above the baited attractions of the city.

Phaedrus was the first to have produced 'a series of fables in verse meant to be read consecutively, each for its own interest and literary value, without a context or a specific application' (Perry, p. xi). This literary innovation by an upstart was ignored by Roman critics and writers, to the extent that this has been used as an argument that the fables attributed to him were never written in classical times. Why should these devices from the rhetorician's workshop have seemed to have the makings of an attraction for its own sake in the literary market? Why did Phaedrus choose Aesop as the subject for his poetical composition?

Hervieux suggested that the main motive was to fight against growing moral degradation after Augustus and Tiberius. For this purpose he chose the genre which allowed the moralist greatest immunity; and he refers to the Prologue to Book III. Certainly, someone with a place in the imperial household who wanted to display 'the ways of men and women' would have to be wary of the hostility of such as Sejanus. In the Prologue, Phaedrus explains the origin of the genre by saying that a slave dared not speak outright, and in order to say what he wanted to say he projected his feelings into fables that eluded censure as jesting fiction. Where 'the former slave' Aesop had made a footpath, he (another former slave) had built a highway. There probably was this motive for an attack on the morals of the time, with the appropriate example of Aesop; and Phaedrus, if ignorant of Greek history, was steeped in Greek literature. However serious he may have been as a moralist, he was most serious in his literary ambitions; and to exercise his talent and prove his power late in the achievement of Latin poetry, he needed a fresh subject. No neglected stone that might respond to polishing looked more promising than the fable, perhaps. It was the most elementary combination of the two traditional functions of poetry, entertainment and instruction:

Poets would profit or delight mankind,
And with the pleasing have th'instructive joined.
Short be the precept, which with ease is gained
By docile minds, and faithfully retained.
    (*Ars Poetica*)

Horace himself, in the Satires and Epistles, had made his central theme the self-defeating consequences of irrational behaviour, and its prevalence.

The innovation of Phaedrus was to take the fables as composite subject matter for poetic composition, which was quite different from their conventional use. As Perry remarks (p. xci), the precise analogy is in Ovid's treatment of the myths, which likewise had been stored in handbooks for reference, apart from the supreme literary use of some of them in Greek tragedy. Ovid's *Metamorphoses* retells the myths in a sequence of poems linked only by a metamorphosis in the story, Phaedrus retells the fables in a sequence of poems linked only by their being included as fables. The one link is as strong or weak as the other, but the literary achievement is not comparable. Ovid has been perhaps the most readable and read of all classical poets, Phaedrus the least. What Phaedrus attempted was fully justified by what La Fontaine did. It is he alone who would be worthy of comparison with Ovid, if they could be compared. Their styles and temperaments are as alike as a Dutch water-garden and the cascades of Tivoli. And myth and fable are different universes of discourse. Yet the tenth book of *Metamorphoses*, the best to Dryden's taste, is at least in form a moral testament, as a plea for reverence for life in conformity with the Pythagorean principle of the unity of all life. At least the Indian fable writers shared this view.

Phaedrus and Babrius show remarkable diversity in telling the same fables. In Babrius's of the dog carrying his meat across a stream, the larger reflection of the meat excites greed; with Phaedrus, it is seeing another dog with something that prompts the impulse to take it from him. Babrius takes eight lines to Phaedrus's four to tell 'The Fox and the Grapes', but he paints the heavy clusters of ripe grapes ready for the vintage, which takes all colour of excuse from the invented consolation. In 'The Fox and the Crow', Babrius puts into the mouth of the Fox a final word which raises the irony of the flattery to a crowning insult: 'You have indeed a voice; you have everything, except brains'. Babrius, in general, shows greater poetic skill and livelier imagination, but Phaedrus also has the pith and point which Horace says make the charm of such tales. The speech of the dying lion, whose last sufferings from his subjects have culminated in his being dashed in the face by the heels of an ass, is a consummate expression of the loftiness of the proud on the floor of humiliation:

> Fortis indigne tuli
> mihi insultare; te, Naturae dedecus,
> quod ferre in morte cogor, bis videor mori. (I, 21)

(I have borne the undeserved insults of the brave; but since in death I have to endure you, a blot on Nature, I seem to die a second death.) Could anything like this be found in the raw fables stockpiled in collections for the use of rhetoricians? La Fontaine cannot do better than echo it.

All the same, fables standing independently in sequence for their own sake have to earn their place, and do tend to have their narrative value exploited for entertainment regardless of the 'pictured truth', which may be trivialized or ignored. Elevated as poetry, they are degraded as fables. Sometimes, however, integration of 'statement' and expression is achieved, and the result is superb, unsurpassable. Art strives for, and is justified by, a perfection rarely attained. This first presentation of Aesop's fables as a book of poems justified itself as an innovation which gave this kind of fable a new use, and therefore an altered character; and it was justified by refining together the narrative and the gnomic elements with a gift of poetic expression which could make fewer words please more and say more, the elegance and extreme brevity which La Fontaine found so praiseworthy in Phaedrus.

The collection as a whole is marred by the inclusion of too many inferior pieces which are not fables at all, anecdotes of a kind that appear in the columns of daily papers, as Hervieux remarks (vol. i, p. 31), and other irrelevant material. The personal modelling of the collection as a commentary on life, which his innovation made possible, is not impressive; but he did make the innovation, which another used to better purpose. It is astonishing that Hervieux should have thought that Phaedrus was perhaps superior to La Fontaine as a philosopher on the strength of Aesop's advice to a farmer to give wives to his shepherds (III, 3) and a dubious personal piece, 'The Butterfly and the Wasp' (Appendix, 31).

That Aesop's fables scraped into classical literature in form as well as by repute is due to Phaedrus, who was confident of his worth and of his poetic achievement, although this had little or no acknowledgement in his time. Afterwards he suffered total eclipse as a poet, since the earliest publication was not until 1596. Meanwhile, he survived unacknowledged in prose paraphrases.

Indian

(*i*)

Perry makes the claim that in the entire Greek tradition 'there is not a single fable that can be said to come either directly or indirectly from an Indian source; but many fables or fable-motifs which make their first appearance in Greek or Near-Eastern literature are found later in the *Panchatantra* and other Indian story-books, including the Buddhist *Jatakas*' (p. xix). On the other hand, he says, 'Nine or ten fables in Babrius, two of them (138 and 143) not found in other Greek or Latin texts, seem to have been derived, directly or indirectly, from the Assyrian *Achiqar*' (p. lx), which had been translated into Greek, reputedly by Democritus. He strongly suggests that the moral habit of mind of the Western Asiatic neighbours of the Greeks – shaped by the Sumerian-Babylonian-Assyrian literary tradition, many centuries before the Greeks had begun to write anything or to think philosophically – must have been a profound influence.[4]

Indian classical literature is charged with fables – the *Panchatantra* notably, and even the great national epic, the *Mahabharata*. The *Hitopadesa* has a frame story which gives rise to four main fables in the course of which there are thirty-eight dependent fables which spring up with the expected frequency of arias in opera. Many of the Buddhist Jataka stories are fables or bring in fables. But the book which has spread the fame and influence of Indian fables far and wide since the middle of the eighth century AD is the *Fables of Bidpai* (or Pilpay), otherwise known as *The Book of Kalila and Dimna,* the title of the main fable in the collection. This book was said by an English translator in the late nineteenth century to have had probably more readers than any other except the Bible, a remark which could apply only to Christendom; but the book was as popular throughout Islam.

The original of this book is lost. It was a translation from Sanskrit into Pehlevi, the literary language of Persia, made for Khosru Nushirvan, King of Persia (AD 531–79) by a learned physician, Barzoye. The story of the Persian mission which obtained the copy for this translation is partly legendary and it is uncertain whether Barzoye made his own selection of fables from the rich Indian mine or directly translated a book already put together, but there is no doubt that the Persian translation did represent the content and the presentation of Indian fables at that time, better than the Sanskrit texts do today after generations of editorial study and elaboration. This Persian translation disappeared in the destruction of the Persian Empire by the Arabs in the seventh century, but the fame of the book was then such that later Caliphs had a search made for it, and when it was recovered in the eighth century a Persian convert to Islam, Abdullah ibn Almokaffa, was asked to translate it into Arabic. From that translation derive all the numerous versions that have made the book widespread: translations into Syriac, Greek, Persian (again), Hebrew, Old Spanish, Italian, Old Slavonic, Latin, Turkish, French, German, Danish, Dutch and English. Not all these translations were made direct from the Arabic version of *c.*750, but indirectly, through dependent translations, they all derive from Almokaffa's text. Particularly, the Latin translation was made from the Hebrew by a converted Jew, John of Capua (*c.*1270), and this version was the main source in Europe, and for translations into the vernaculars.[5]

This book translated from Sanskrit was thus domesticated in Zoroastrian, Islamic, Christian and Hebrew religious cultures; and the various versions have interpolations and adaptations suited to the purpose of the translator in his own cultural context. Hervieux, after showing that a Latin version by Raymond de Béziers in 1313 – allegedly translated from an Old Spanish version of 1251 – was largely cribbed from John of Capua, goes on to show that a second manuscript of this version, double its length, must have been the work of a monk who interpolated citations in verse and prose from Christian sources, quite incongruously, to turn it into a work of Christian propaganda. This is an extreme case.

The book was not a sacred text, and in general Indian fables were detachable from the canonical maxims which justified their original use (as Aesopic fables are from promythium and epimythium); so that *The Fables of Bidpai* could be generally regarded as a compendium of ancient wisdom, offensive to none and a valued vade-

mecum for all in the conduct of life, especially when translated not
only into the language but also into the cultural inheritance of the ✓
people for whom it was prepared. Here in good form, and with the
sanction of antiquity, was the combination of entertainment and ✗
instruction which made fable so acceptable.

(*ii*)

The most unified of the Indian collections is the *Hitopadesa* (Hale-
Wortham, 1906), in which there are versions of many of the fables in
Bidpai, particularly the principal one in both, 'The Lion and the Ox'
(or 'Kalilah and Dimnah'). In the frame story a king called Sudarsana,
himself a virtuous ruler, is distressed by the ignorance and frivolity of
his four sons, and he calls together his wise men in the hope that one
of them will undertake to instruct the young men in 'Political and
Social Science'. The task is taken on by a pandit named Vishnusarman, who engages to make the princes thoroughly conversant with
the subject in six months. They sit out on the terrace in front of the
palace, and Vishnusarman says, 'To entertain your highnesses, I will
tell you the story of "The Crow and the Tortoise", along with
others'. (The stories, it is explained earlier, are 'drawn from the
Panchatantra and other books'.) There follow these main fables: on
the destruction of friendship and mutual trust by a third party ('The
Lion and the Ox'); on the making of friendships and alliances ('The
Ring-Dove' in *Bidpai*); and, at the request of the princes, one on
making war (with similarities to 'The Owls and the Crows'), and one
on making peace. At the end, the princes say: 'Sir, you, through your
goodness and learning, have taught us all the round of our kingly
duties: we have learned our lesson, and are satisfied. Vishnusarman
concludes with his blessing.

'The Lion and the Ox' is the most dramatic story. The mischief is
done by a jackal (one of a pair, Kalilah and Dimnah) who poisons the
mind of the Lion against the Ox, his faithful minister, making him
believe that the Ox is conspiring to dethrone him and usurp his place;
the Ox is put to death. The fable of the Ring-Dove is a story of
friendship and prudent alliance across the barrier of species, with
trustworthy partners. 'The Owls and the Crows' represents a natural
enmity. The narrative is overcharged with dependent fables that
impede its course, but the complete reversal of fortunes brought
about by the character and conduct of the Crow who volunteers to go
into the enemy's camp, and the good nature of the King of the Owls

who disastrously refuses to listen to the ruthless advice of his ablest counsellor, make a compelling story.[6]

(iii)

In the Bidpai collection, 'The Lion and the Jackal' is a more remarkable story. This ascetic fruit-eating jackal, who has been ostracized by his own species, is importuned by the Lion to serve as his chief minister. The Jackal is without ambition, and the invitation is incompatible with his chosen life-plan. However, he is overruled and takes up office. His stewardship is exemplary, all that his royal master had counted on. Inevitably, even-handed administration inaccessible to corrupt approaches disobliges all those spirits that count on and live by 'working' the system, and they conspire to disgrace the Jackal and bring about his removal. Their plot works only because the Lion is too lightly suspicious, and he is saved from folly only by the intervention of his mother, who sees how things are. When the Lion wants to make reparation and to restore the Jackal to office the Jackal has something to say, reminding the King of his own reluctance in the first place; of the vulnerability and thanklessness of the job itself, exposed to the envy of all; of the weakness of the King in succumbing to chance appearances without test. The King was not worthy of trust, and he himself had been discredited in the eyes of many; nothing was as before. However, the King again prevails and persuades him to return to his stewardship, after a public vindication.

The frame story which links the dozen main fables in *Bidpai* is simply a request from a king of India to hear from the philosopher and chief of the wise men, Bidpai or Pilpay, similitudes representing situations which he specifies, e.g. 'Show me the similitude of two men, companions or friends, between whom a false or astute cunning individual has produced dissensions, so that they have turned from mutual love and harmony to hatred and enmity.' The frame story of the *Hitopadesa* is not altogether dissimilar. In general, education of the well-born is the underlying motive. The main fables told in this setting have many short fables inserted as the story goes along, ostensibly to illustrate what is being told; but often that is an excuse for the diversion. The characters, dialogue, and action of the main fables are thoroughly realistic, except that all the parts are played by animals whose behaviour is entirely human. This does not turn the story into fantasy, nor satire. The tone is uniformly serious, the narrative deft and vigorous, often showing remarkable subtlety in characterization. The convention has the effect of distancing the story from history and from contemporary life, and from other forms of fiction. The story is offered as a similitude, 'a fictitious story picturing a truth', in a completely different cultural context from that of the Aesopic fable.

(iv)

This formula does not apply to the other main Indian source, the *Jataka Tales* (Francis and Thomas, 1916). These are Buddhist birth-stories, of which some date back to the fourth century BC, and the originals drawn from folk-lore must have been much earlier. The early ones were adopted and adapted for the purposes of Buddhist teaching, as the Aesopic fables were sporadically by the Christian Church in the Middle Ages; but they were formally recast to serve the purpose. There are more than five hundred stories, each told about Buddha in some incarnation. The story is a story of the past occasioned by some incident in a story of the present. Thus any ancient story could be made to serve, so long as the Bodhisattva could be made to appear. Verses are recited in each one, like a chorus, and these lines are the canonical words which carry the message for which the story is told.

Clearly, stories suited to this purpose are unlikely to be akin to the Aesopic fable and most of them are quite alien, oriental tales with such ingredients as royal persons and palace scenes, inter-regal conflicts, intrigues and conspiracies, hermits and the ascetic life, brutal betrayals and callous murders, arbitrary cruel punishment, forgiveness of injuries, royal alms-giving and royal justice, sensual gratification, pomp, luxury, display, magic. However, some of the shorter tales are in the form of beast fables not unlike Aesop's, and there are a few, some dozen, which are recognizably the same, however it came about. Buddha, the Great Being, exists in these stories as a cock or a wolf or a tree spirit or a bird or a monkey, even a jackal or an outcast, as he comes to life also as a royal heir or a priest or a minister – never a woman. This makes beast fables appropriate material for the Jataka, and the tales have a numerous animal population.

Some of those which resemble Aesop and seem variants of the same fable are quite different in meaning – for example, 'The Ass in the Lion's Skin' (Sihacamma-Jataka, 189). Aesop's silly Ass capers about giving himself airs in his giant's robe, till his pretensions are cut short by exposure. The Ass in the Jataka story is a hapless victim who has neither luck nor mercy. He carries the goods of a pedlar who on his rounds of the villages turns him into barley or rice-fields to forage for himself, throwing a lion-skin over him to protect him from being driven off. When villagers collect in force with drums and sticks to mob him he brays in fright, and is beaten to death. A similar version, with different meaning, comes into *Hitopadesa* (p. 120). 'The Jackal and the Crow' (Jambukhadaka-Jataka, 294) is another with a difference. The Crow sitting in a tree eating fruit, flattered by the Jackal, willingly shares the plentiful fruit and flatters in return to show his gratification. This mutual indulgence goes on till they are both scared away by the Bodhisattva, who happens to be the tree spirit. There are significant differences in several other pairs which are obviously the same story. One or two are equivalent: 'The Woodpecker and the Lion' (Javasakuna-Jataka, 308) is practically the same as 'The Wolf and the Heron' (*Babrius*, 94) and 'The Wolf and the Crane' (*Phaedrus* I, 8).

Whether or not because of the Buddhist belief in the equivalence of all life, the animals in the Jataka tales have their own inside stories and are not mere agents in the image of an action. In 'The Discontented Ox' (Munika-Jataka, 30), the discontented young one and the older one who puts him wise are real brothers, whereas in Babrius (37) the old bull and the young steer merely speak their parts. Because of the inside story to match the bare relation to an action, the Jataka fable is sometimes like an embroidered linen cloth compared with a piece of hessian. For example, there is this kind of difference between the fable of a fox who squeezes into a hollow tree to eat a goatherd's dinner and is too swollen afterwards to get out (*Babrius*, 86) and 'The Greedy Jackal Caught' (Sigala-Jataka, 148), in which a jackal finds himself in a similar predicament. The Jackal has tackled the carcass of an old elephant, and found that the only part he can get his teeth into is the rump. He eats his way in through this soft part and gorges himself, falling asleep inside the beast. Finding both food and shelter, he stays. The carcass dries and shrinks rapidly in the scorching sun; he is unable to get out by the way he got in, and no outside light can be seen. In a frenzy, and in vain, he hurls himself at the sides, 'bobbed up and down inside like a ball of rice in a boiling saucepan'. Torrential rain then soaks the carcass and relaxes the tissues; light is to be seen. The Jackal retreats into the elephant's head to be able to throw himself with maximum impetus at the exit, head-first. He gets out, stripped of all his hair, 'smooth as a palm-stem'. The situation in the two fables is similar, the panic is the same; the terror of the one is Poe or Kafka, of the other not even mentioned, because not relevant.

This skill and delight in circumstantial story-telling does not necessarily dissipate the focus on a typical action of which the story is a 'similitude': the successful practice of deception upon an unwary ruler; the advantage of mutual aid to those without power and exposed to perils; the folly of trusting an enemy, however plausible; the disastrous tendency of hasty action; the folly of thoughtless trust, and actions which extinguish the possibility of trust; the vulnerability of the powerful, and their liability to folly. The animal as human actor does not simply avoid the distraction of engaging human sympathy. Instead, in the longer narratives, it is an added piquancy and an additional resource. The Ox Sanjivaka, in 'The Lion and the Ox', has the simplicity and patience associated with an ox as well as the incorruptibility of a trustworthy minister. The fruit-eating jackal is even more set apart from his fellows, even more his own man, than a mere ascetic.

(v)

The ethos of the Indian fables is of a world that turns on the poles of city and forest, court and hermitage, worldliness in its most luxurious and voluptuous forms, and world renunciation and spiritual enlightenment. The background of the Aesopic fable is less evident and relevant. In the Indian collections the minor fables are like parables (called *parabolae* in the Latin translation) which are invented to illustrate a point, though mainly of course drawn from a stock of elaborated anecdotes. They are discursive, often with named characters, and provide an instance in circumstantial daily life terms of the behaviour being examined.

The fable is akin to the wisdom literature dominant in India at the time, and joins it with narrative that, like music, is intentionally pleasing. Thus was established a convention reinforced by taste and practice, as in opera, whether or not in the particular instance the fable is needed or useful: convention encroaches on function. The ready and regular incidence of minor fables in the main narrative was likened above to arias in opera. The main fable itself may be likened to opera as a convention which imposes itself on the material. In the Greek context the fable is a rhetorical device used incidentally in writing or speaking, regularly in linguistic training; until, late,

Phaedrus and Babrius make fables the subject of poetic compositions. The convention which made the genre was not supported by an
elaborate convention that sustained its use.

Fables for the instruction of young members of royal families of
the Far East and the far past are an unlikely product for export.
However, *The Arabian Nights' Entertainments* became universal
among readers young and old. The translatable narrative interest of
the Bidpai collection made it the highly popular book it became in so
many lands, not merely as narrative, like the *Nights*. When the
Indian king asks Bidpai, the philosopher, to show him the 'similitude' of two friends alienated by the cunning of a third party, he
wants to see concretely something he knows abstractly, to examine
it. Why a 'similitude' instead of a straightforward story with this
plot? The 'similitude' does not simulate a history; it devises a concrete representation that is simplified, accented, and memorable of a
general form of behaviour. The longer narrative cannot have the
gnomic point and condensed image of the Aesopic fable but shows
that an interesting story with realistic action can be devised simply
and obviously to 'picture a truth', perhaps an unpalatable truth. In
the *Bidpai* version of 'The Lion and the Ox', after the jackal has
accomplished his design with the death of the Ox, his skilful arguments overcome the scruples and regrets of the Lion and restore his
peace of mind. (In the *Hitopadesa* version the story ends there.) This
unpunished triumph of rascality was not acceptable to the translators, and a sequel appears in either the Persian or the Arabic version
(probably the work of Almokaffa) which brings the jackal to trial and
execution. From a literary point of view, the dramatic and rhetorical
power of the jackal's defence is abundant justification. But it is an
unwarranted tampering with the 'truth', the philosophy. In other
places, the story may overreach its purpose. 'The Greedy Jackal
Caught' depicts the plight and pluck of an unlucky young animal.
This is not *Bidpai* of course, but a 'parable' in the *Jataka* series.

(It is worth a remark that women are poorly regarded and extravagantly censured in the context of Indian fables:

Neither shame – nor sense of propriety – nor decency – nor
timidity – none of these things is the reason for a woman's fidelity.
The sole reason is the absence of a suitor (*Hitopadesa* L, 125).
No one comes amiss to women: they are always wandering about,
like cows in a forest, looking for fresh pasturage (IV, 7).

Women eat twice as much as men: they are four times as cunning: six times as vicious: eight times as much given to falling in love (IV, 8).

These are maxims in *Hitopadesa*. In the actual fables, women may be superior. In two, the Lion is saved from folly by the decisive intervention of his mother.)

'Kalilah and Dimnah', 'The Lion and the Jackal', and such Indian stories have the concrete abstraction which is the literary signature of fable narrative, and they are admirable stories. Their popularity, world-wide and centuries long, made the Indian similitude comparable with the Aesopic model in influence.

A Prometheus in words: Lucian

The Aesopic fable remains a fertile tradition in Western literature, but the larger and later fable (whatever the oriental influence) owes some of its scope and character to Lucian of Samosata, a Syrian writing in classical Greek in the second century AD, whose literary influence since the Renaissance in Europe has been acknowledged by his distinguished admirers, from More and Erasmus to Fielding. Trained as a rhetorician, he acquired some wealth and fame by his public lectures as he travelled about the Roman world and then turned to the development of a line of his own, a comic fiction that blended Aristophanic fantasy with the dialectic of Socratic dialogue. This coupling risked producing a monster, as he well recognized, and it is questionable whether what he did achieve was this kind of hybrid, but the virtuosity of a rhetorician was in his eclectic skill and Lucian, drawing on his congenial sources, succeeded in dazzling the literary world in his own day and since. His philosophic interests, his Aristophanic bent, and his experimental approach to fiction combined to break new ground. In recent years, scholars of the period have tried to cut him down to size (testimony to influence). In particular, his originality is discredited, or reinterpreted. Indeed, so many different opinions of the man and his work have been expressed in the reassessment, including the extravagant and bizarre, that he has become a controversial figure in classical circles about whom an outsider should be wary of saying anything.

The literary movement by which he was formed and within which he worked was the so-called Second Sophistic, which had an ascendancy from the time of the Flavian emperors to the end of the second century AD. The orators and the teachers of rhetoric who made the movement played a part comparable with that of the humanists of the Renaissance. Indeed, it was a renaissance of Hellenism, the Hellenism of Isocrates and the first sophists, and was under the patronage of philhellenic emperors like Hadrian and the Antonines, who founded chairs in philosophy and rhetoric, gave high priority to education, surrounded themselves with Greeks, and themselves thought and wrote in Greek. Like the humanists, the sophists of this period were used in public employment, and their profession was the principal road to wealth, fame and influence. The models were the classics, but the new 'Greeks' were citizens of the cosmopolitan Roman Empire, particularly Asians, who brought in an infusion of talent and enthusiasm. Formed by the discipline of the schools of rhetoric, bound by the conventions of the movement, but with the incitement and scope of large educated audiences in the great cities of the empire, Lucian followed his successful career as a public lecturer, ending with a public office. He bequeathed a literary legacy that has been the delight of generations of admirers, translators, and imitators who have included such eminent and serious jesters as Erasmus, More, Jonson, Rabelais, Dryden, Swift, Voltaire and Fielding.

One major reassessment of Lucian is based on an elaborately detailed study of literary mimesis as the essential feature of the Second Sophistic, since the sophists of this period, like the humanists of the Renaissance, took possession of their literary patrimony by schooling themselves on models, with scrupulous respect for the authority of the classics. J. Bompaire (*Lucian Écrivain*, 1958) has studied Lucian's practice with leechlike tenacity in a large volume dense with references, using statistical counts as well as analysis of composition and style to show that Lucian's pages are pastiche or parody or a mosaic of references and allusions, drawn from his reading or from the many different compilations available for the purpose. His was a bookish performance to delight a bookish audience with their recognition of the echoes and his own clever use of them, with the kind of relish a star performer gives a modern television audience in a verbal or musical parlour game. First-hand observation, references to the real world, any non-literary reference or purpose was excluded by the rules of the game, a solecism that would require explanation or apology – like the slip of the tongue in greeting for which Lucian did compose an apology. '. . . le monde lucienesque est à la base constitué par des clichés empruntés aux traités de rhétorique ou à la tradition comique, mimique, élégiaque' (. . . Lucian's world is founded on stereotypes borrowed from the treatises on rhetoric or from the tradition of stage comedy and of elegy) (p. 235): the literary emasculation carried out by Bompaire is an intended appreciation of the actual performance by the criteria of the time. A Canadian scholar, Barry Baldwin, in a volume as thin as the other is thick (*Studies in Lucian*, 1973), has rejected the dogma of mimesis as vacuous, and tried to show that Lucian is at least aiming at real contemporary targets all the time: literary sects, historians, religious beliefs, superstitions, social injustices; above all his own enemies, motivated chiefly by personal malice, sectarian in-fighting, and self-advertisement.

(ii)

Whatever the truth may have been about his character and conduct, whatever the truth is about his methods of literary fabrication, there is no dispute about the reputation and influence of Lucian's literary art. (Probing the composition of 'Homer' does not affect the epic quality of the *Iliad* and the *Odyssey*.) Interest here is in those features of it which may be said to have affected development of the fable. There are some six out of some sixty-six of Lucian's undisputed extant works which could have had this kind of influence, but they are among those for which Lucian has chiefly been read and relished since the Renaissance. These are: *The True History, Charon, The Cock, Menippus, Icaromenippus, The Fisherman.*[7] There are also features of some of the others which illustrate relevant points about Lucian's methods or purpose – an extra-literary purpose and a literary purpose of his own, despite 'mimesis'.

The True History is the most famous of his pieces, and the most imitated. Belying the title, and taking leave from poetic licence, Lucian blasts off in an explosion of fantasy after a declaration which parodies the usual preliminary verbal assurance given by historians: 'Be it understood, then, that I am writing about things which I have neither seen nor had to do with nor learned from others – which, in fact, do not exist at all and, in the nature of things, cannot exist. Therefore my readers should on no account believe in them.' The description of a voyage into space, with all the happenings that befall, parodies various sources like a medley of wild tunes that echo one after another snatches familiar or recognizable to his listeners, but carries the narrative on with the gusto of a large and liberating jest, which the author has professed it to be, fortified with 'a little food for thought that the Muses would not altogether spurn'. The 'truth' here is the claim of fiction not to be burdened with any pretension to truth, whether the truth of what happened or of what might happen, history or verisimilitude. Such truth as fiction may have is truth to thought, not truth to life.

In an essay, 'How to write history' (vol. vi), Lucian insists on scrupulous faithfulness to scholarly standards, and marks the distinction from fiction:

> . . . history has aims and rules different from poetry and poems. In the case of the latter, liberty is absolute and there is one law – the will of the poet . . . even if he wants to harness winged horses to a chariot, even if he sets others to run over water or the tops of flowers, nobody gets annoyed.

Of course, fiction never does enjoy absolute liberty; there is always a covenant, as there are rules of practice, even when the time comes for deliberate rule-breaking. Lucian seems to have felt that the example of the classics, particularly the *Odyssey*; the semi-sacred myths of gods and goddesses; the popular passion for marvellous tales, as well as the introduction of legends and incredible stories into their works by some historians, notably Herodotus, had confused the credible, the incredible, and pure invention. The incredible, by its context or its auspices, passed as true because people wanted to believe in marvels. The time had come for fiction to disclaim all pretension to truth, and claim its freedom simply to entertain.

In a short piece addressed 'To one who said "You're a Prometheus in words" ', Lucian accepts that he works in clay, that he makes figurines, dolls, fragile as pots, lifeless, and exhibits them like puppets for the sake of empty enjoyment and play; and he deprecates praise for originality in daring to try to combine the old Dionysian comedy with the seriousness of philosophic dialogue, since this was to mate incompatibles and risk producing a freak. The emptiness of fiction, for enjoyment, can hardly contain even a little food for thought. Lucian shows that he was well aware of the risk in what he was trying to do, that he had involved himself in a contradiction it was his skill to resolve, in a successful fable. *The True History* is the charter of his fiction and his freedom, which starts with a declaration of intent. Thus it would cleanse fiction of false pretensions, as in general his fiction would cleanse his world of false beliefs and expectations.

(iii)

In *Charon*, the grim ferryman takes a day off and prevails upon Hermes to show him the life men live in the world before they come to him and are rowed across. From a height attained by piling Pelion upon Ossa (enacting a metaphor) on top of Olympus, they are able to see far and wide; and by reciting more verses from Homer, Hermes enables Charon to see as well as if he were close at hand. The detailed spectacle of human behaviour (drawn from historical and literary scenes) makes Charon laugh; but cumulatively he is worked up to amazement: human life is like a stream of bubbles of various sizes and duration, but all bursting; or, as Hermes reminds him from Homer, like leaves – a favourite quotation of Pyrrho. Charon is actually moved to want to intervene, to shout down to them and help them to see their lives in perspective, and live more sanely. He is restrained by Hermes, who says that ignorance stops their ears. What Charon wants to do, anyhow, is done by the enlightened few.

Lucian takes another traditional theme, the longing for riches, in *The Cock*. A poor cobbler is awakened from enjoyment of the gratifications of wealth in a dream by the crowing of his cock. His scolds and curses are answered by the Cock, who says he thought he was giving him an early start with his day's work, and goes on to rebuke his master's astonishment at hearing a cock speak as sheer illiteracy; in any case, he is a reincarnation of Pythagoras. In the course of their long and vivacious conversation, the cobbler learns from the experiences of the Cock in various incarnations about the perils and miseries which the envied great and powerful have to endure; but in the end he has to confess that for all that he is not yet able to unlearn the desire to become rich which he has had since boyhood. The Cock undertakes to cure him by taking him to see with his own eyes how the rich neighbours he envies are really living. One is the man at whose banquet he had enjoyed a rare treat the night before, which had excited his dream. Another is a cobbler like himself who had inherited a fortune. They enter the houses of these neighbours and the cobbler sees for himself what they are up to, and the entanglements they are involved in which spoil their lives.[8]

Menippus, a Cynic philosopher of about the third century BC, a legendary jester and satirist about whom little is reliably known and whose writings do not survive, makes a characteristic persona for Lucian in several dialogues. In the one called *Menippus* the theme is a philosophic quest, the ethical 'choice of life' of Johnson's *Rasselas*. Menippus says that as a boy he had taken the gods as examples but, finding their behaviour in the myths condemned by the laws, he had resorted with his question to the philosophers, whose verbal responses – and example – confused him further. In despair, he had decided to seek out the prophet and sage Tiresias in Hades, to find out from him what the best life is, the life that a man of sense would choose. Conducted by a Chaldean magician, he gains admission to Hades and eventually, under pressure, Tiresias tells him: 'Make it always your sole object to put the present to good use and to hasten on your way, laughing a great deal and taking nothing seriously.' However, he had already formed his own conclusions, informed by what he had seen among the shades about the hazards of Fortune in the affairs of men and the abrupt and equal end of all dramas, grand or petty.

In *Icaromenippus*, Menippus ascends to Heaven, having made himself wings, borrowed from a large eagle and a strong vulture, following a clue from Aesop (Perry, 3) and Aristophanes (*Wasps*, 1446 f.), to take his questions to Zeus, this time questions of physics and metaphysics, on which he had failed to get satisfactory answers from the philosophers.[9]

The Fisherman is Lucian's justification of his attacks on the figure of contemporary philosophers, which had provoked protest; particularly his *Philosophies for Sale*, in which the schools and sects had been auctioned off with scant respect. The author, as Frankness, is mobbed in the streets of Athens by famous dead philosophers back in the world. Urged on by Socrates, they are yelling for the most cruel and humiliating death for one who has brought them into disrepute. However, he makes himself heard, and demands a trial. This takes place, with Philosophy and his persecutors as jurors and prosecutors. Plato is chosen as spokesman for the philosophers, and bidden to put together the points that had given him success against the sophists. But Plato reminds them that Frankness is a professional speaker who will need expert handling and suggests Diogenes, telling him to speak for all of them. Diogenes then argues that Frankness has played to the gallery to gain the applause of the common sort who delight in jesters and buffoons, especially when what is most highly respected is pulled down for their benefit, as when Aristophanes made fun of Socrates. Worse, Frankness has bribed their serving-man and Menippus their one-time colleague to take part in his farces. Exemplary punishment is called for.

In his defence, Frankness says that when he turned from rhetoric to philosophy, thinking to pass from chicanery to peaceful pursuit of all that is best, he was shocked to find charlatans masquerading as philosophers like the ass in the lion's skin (the first known reference to the fable in Greek literature), getting philosophy blamed for their disreputable behaviour. Therefore he had made it his mission to expose them, in order to confine to them the ridicule and contempt their conduct was bringing upon philosophy and true philosophers. The prosecution is entirely won over by this speech, and Frankness is acquitted by unanimous vote. He is then set up as accuser of the false philosophers, summoned from the city below to come before them all. They do not answer to the summons of Philosophy through Syllogism, but come like swarming bees when Frankness announces a distribution of gifts. Representatives of the sects squabble for the first share of the distribution, or for special gifts. When Philosophy threatens to discover who really do live by the rules of philosophy, and punish the rest, the throng melts away, leaving the few who do not fear the test. Philosophy asks Truth to devise means for telling the self-servers from the true enquirers, but Truth suggests that Frankness be commissioned to make the purge, and brand impostors on the forehead with the image of a fox or an ape. Frankness undertakes to bring some of them back forthwith. Borrowing a rod, hook and line (a fisherman's votive offering), and baiting the hook with a fig and with gold, taking his seat on the crest of the wall, he makes a cast from the Acropolis into the lower city. The scene then turns into a fishing sport with Investigation and Frankness as commentators, guessing the species and describing the specimens that swim up to the hook; until Philosophy sends the philosophers back to their abode, and Investigation and Frankness to carry out their mission of branding or crowning.

(*iv*)

All six pieces are poetic fiction, images of things which 'do not exist at all, and, in the nature of things, cannot exist', applied directly or by implication to what exists in common knowledge or can be recognized as possible – the behaviour of philosophers, for example, in different contexts: and of their satirist. Even when a dialogue is not as a whole effectively a metaphor, a sustained metaphor is often used to pull the argument together or to pick out the theme. Mycillus, the cobbler, says, 'Do you not see how you have already taught me to make comparisons, friend cock?'

Lucian's ease with images and unease with abstract ideas (in spite of his philosophical preoccupations) are best illustrated by *Hermotimus*, his longest dialogue, in which the Socratic model is least parodied and most used as the effective method it is for exposure and exposition. Hermotimus is an adherent of the Stoic sect and devotes his life to the study of their doctrines, for the attainment of the promised goal. His friend Lycinus (Lucian) argues that all the schools have an equal claim as long as it remains uncertain which is true. He keeps probing Hermotimus with matter-of-fact questions and proposes practical tests, all in the language of comparisons and examples, until Hermotimus is led into confusion and made to consider disturbing points he has never thought of. When he complains that Lycinus has reduced his treasure to ashes and shown his life to have been wasted, Lycinus replies: 'You will not be nearly so hurt if you remember that you are not the only one left outside the hoped-for blessings. No, all those who study philosophy are, as it were, wrangling over the shadow of an ass' (Perry, 460).

Lucian's targets are all in the same neighbourhood: men's self- and mutual deception in entertaining improbable or contradictory beliefs and unattainable ends, all the deluded aims and pursuits which distract men from the business and pleasures of ordinary daily living, including super-human blessedness, and commonly desired attainable things that let one in for what he had not bargained for, and could not want. He uses dialogue in *Hermotimus* in a soberly Socratic manner. But when he blends it with the twists and shocks of comedy and fantasy, it is to the same purpose. Mycillus is left in the mind to reconsider his lot and his dream of bettering it.

In *The Ship*, three friends on a day out indulge themselves in confessing what they would like to have if they could have their wishes. A fourth friend in the party amuses himself with making rational comment on their choices, based on pointing out what the real consequences would be if they had their way. *Hermotimus*, *The Ship* and *The Cock* are three different forms of Lucian's fiction. They all try to induce a sleeper to wake up, but they are not interchangeable forms. Hermotimus has to be tackled on philosophical grounds by reasoning. The three friends are in exuberant holiday mood; the wishes they elaborate are marvellous tales, fairy-stories; fiction of this kind can be enjoyed as a holiday spree, but the rationalist friend is there to remind them that the spectacular lights in which the city blazes with excitement at night are out when the sun gets up and the day's work begins. Cock-crow awakens the cobbler from dreams to the reality of day-labour, but from the dreams of avarice a meta-phorical awakening is called for. The situation between the experi-enced bird and his shrewd, blunt, stimulated master is relaxed and playful, classically comic. These three forms are examples of Lucian's experiments in comic fiction, diverse when thematically the same, experiments of an artist who adopted, adapted, and innovated.

Bompaire, apropos the second part of *The Fisherman*, writes of 'cette imagination zoologique, à la façon des *Guêpes* et des *Oiseaux*' (this zoological imagination, in the manner of the *Wasps* and the *Birds*) (p. 693); and elsewhere he refers to the untutored fantasy of the *Birds*, beyond formulas (p. 328); in another place, he expresses the view that Lucian is fully himself and at ease only 'à l'ombre de l'aède ou de l'auteur des *Oiseaux* ou de l'Hérodote des quatres premiers livres' (in the shadow of the minstrel or of the author of the *Birds* or of the Herodotus of the first four books) (p. 705) and remarks that Lucian was 'un amateur de la littérature ésopique' (he had a taste for the Aesopic literature) (p. 460), as he was of the Old Comedy and the Cynic literature. In *Downward Journey*, Lucian even brings a Bed and a Lamp into the cast to facilitate the dénoue-ment. On the fetters of mimesis, Bompaire's thesis which would undermine the fabulist, let Barry Baldwin have the last word. The two final sentences of his book reconcile the literary conventions of Lucian's time with the literary freedom of a writer and the moral freedom of a man of any time. 'Virtually all that he wrote is relevant to, and was inspired by, his age. Topicality and universalism are quite compatible, the former is based on the latter.'

Graham Anderson, in *Studies in Lucian's Comic Fiction* (1977), argues that Lucian is the author of the extant version of *Onos* (*The Ass*) and also of the lost original *Metamorphoses* of which the extant version, doubtfully included among Lucian's works, is a supposed abridgement and from which the *Golden Ass* of Apuleius independ-ently derives. He also takes *de Dea Syria* (*The Syrian Goddess*) as

Lucian's work. He adds these two examples to *The True History*, *Toxaris* and *Philopseudes* to show Lucian's versatility in writing comic fiction, all of them marked by his special skill and method. His conclusion is that this performance, together with his achievement in satiric miniatures, show that he was capable of being 'a creative novelist fully in command of his medium' (p. 119), and the equal of Longus and Petronius. He adds that their interests and methods bring Lucian and Petronius closer together than is usually allowed.

Of *The Ass*, he says that it 'reinterprets Ideal Romance in Aesopic terms, and so forms a hybrid as bizarre as Satiric Dialogue itself' (p. 116), since many of the episodes are related to fables, and the usual adventures of the ideal hero happen to an ass. The result is that 'the novel is brought down to the level of *Aesopica*'. This does not mean that Lucian in *The Ass* composed a fable in the manner and on the scale of a popular romance. On the contrary, the fable is degraded to degrade the novel; each parodies the other. The relevant point that comes out of Anderson's discussion is Lucian's readiness to adopt and adapt to narrative form any material that interests him, and his skill in doing so for different purposes. 'He proves himself the manipulator *par excellence*'; and he is a reminder of the literary conditions of the time: 'how easily the simpler materials of story-telling can pass from one milieu to another'.

(v)

Socratic dialogue, Menippean satire, Aristophanic comedy: these were Lucian's preferred models, because they suited his bent of mind, his way of thinking concretely. His idea of mating Socratic dialogue with Aristophanic comedy, of their compatibility, came from within; it was a projection of his own way of thinking, integral not eclectic. The congenial comic fantasy and irony, tools of satire, were equally useful for exposing a matter to reflection. In this way he permanently enlarged the vocabulary of fable, with a resource not found in the Aesopic gnome or the Indian similitude. As 'a Prometheus in words', Lucian would enlarge and purge the realm of fiction. In this, he gave fable its charter: to devise an amusing fantasy focused on something left behind to be thought about, something 'the Muses would not altogether spurn': that is, something memorable.

2   Renart to Volpone

The Latin inheritance

(*i*)

The principal legacy of Rome to medieval Europe was the idea and ideal of an Imperial and Christian unity, never realized, never wholly abandoned. Classical literature was partially salvaged and preserved by the Church as a precious part of the inheritance. In the educational tradition, Aesop passed into the schools and was Christianized. The wolf who became a monk was a stock theme for centuries, being both the Aesopic wolf in sheep's clothing and the false prophet who comes in sheep's clothing, but inwardly is a ravening wolf (Matthew 7: 15). *Le Roman de Renart*, the self-generating satirical star comedy that went on like 'M.A.S.H'. and filled so large a space for so long in the literature of the Middle Ages, originated as a clerical creation out of the fables.

The Church also had its own literary animals in Bestiaries and in legends of beasts and saints. Helen Waddell translated a selection of the latter from Latin (*Beasts and Saints*, 1934). There are evident respects in which these are unlike fables. The narrative is intended not to be fictitious; evidence is often adduced as reliable testimony to its truth. Unless true, it fails completely, like a miracle that has not happened. What the story provides is not a similitude but an example or illustration of the power and mercy of God and the holiness and blessedness of the saint, and of the docility and seemliness of animals as creatures of God. To be serviceable to their purpose they are stories to be taken literally, not metaphorically. In a later view they are legends, with the characteristics of legend, such as the recurrence of themes: tenderness in not removing a cloak or hands in which a bird happens to have laid her eggs until they are safely hatched; or removal of a thorn from a lion's foot, repaid with gratitude and service. A regular theme is the salvation of crops, human sustenance, from animal predators and spoilers, with penitence of the offenders; another is the service of animals to sustain saints who have renounced the world and separated themselves from their fellows. The saints are protected and served, the creatures are brought into the fellowship of all. Also to be remarked is the delighted realism of natural descriptions. The stories are told to the greater glory of God and the holy renown of the saint, and are not in any sense apologues.

In three respects, there may be a tenuous connection with fables. The fox shows the wiles and habits for which he is notorious – the better to repent and reform. One of the weakest of the fables, 'Androcles and the Lion', has the same motif as the legend of St Jerome and the Abbot Gerasimus. Taken together the tales may be said to produce an image of a truth, the community of creation, including plants, in obedience to the will of God. However, in form and function these are legends, not fables. Decisively, their ethos is alien to the spirit of Aesop.

(ii)

Bestiaries were a more curious production. It is likely that Aesopic fables did provide one of the many sources of *Physiologus* (*c.* fourth century), along with the Bible, works of the Fathers on the six days of Creation, and of others who had borrowed from Pliny and Solinus and Aristotle. It was written in Greek, and translated into languages of the Middle East, and also into Latin. This was the basis of the medieval Bestiary. There was no systematic treatment of the animals, birds and fish about which *Physiologus* collected available information, most of it fabulous; but the purpose was to use the nature and habits of the creatures of the natural (and preternatural) world as images of biblical teaching. Later, the encyclopaedic survey of animals, birds, insects in all their diversity, domestic and wild – with central reference to man – classified and put together by Isidore, Bishop of Seville (560–636), was a main source of additions, and of classification.[1] Isidore's references are mainly to the Bible and to the Latin poets, particularly Lucan. With its attempt at system, the compilation remained lore and legend, with scraps of natural history.

The Bestiary was established in Europe in the twelfth century in an amplified Latin version largely taken from Isidore, and translated into the vernaculars. New material was assimilated or invented as the Bestiary was copied. Some were illustrated, and a Bestiary became a principal picture book for those who could afford it.[2] Fanciful etymology was almost obsessive in this expansion, stimulating conjecture. The Old English Bestiary in the East-Midland dialect before the mid-thirteenth century was a free translation of a *Physiologus* in Latin verse by Bishop Theobaldus (of which a copy was printed in Cologne in 1492, from an original of the twelfth century). The

Bishop, in his *De Naturis Animalium*, says he has selected twelve species as mystical and allegorical (also, they correspond in number to the twelve apostles). They are: lion, eagle, serpent, ant, fox, stag, spider, whale, siren, elephant, turtle-dove, and panther. In the Early English translation, some thirty lines on the nature of the lion or eagle or ant are followed by as many for the *significatio*. The lion represents Christ, whose earthly life, death and resurrection are pictured in the similitude of the lion's (reputed) habits. The eagle's changing his nature from feebleness and malformation to majesty by the healing power of a spring clearly portrays the salvation of man's fallen state by grace. The ant provides the usual example of prudent industry in season that assures survival in a hard time so long as we continue on earth, with enough to spare for good works. The panther comes nearest to the lion as a representative of Christ. The serpent has high marks for exemplary performance, but elephant and whale rank low. The fox represents the devil, and doubles this role with his portrayal of deceitful man.[3]

A Bestiary is not mainly a species of narrative, although it may include anecdote; and the similitudes are not invented to speak for themselves. Mainly, it is an allegorical representation derived from natural history, legend, biblical hermeneutics; dependent on Christian doctrine, in particular the scheme of salvation. Richard Rolle's piece 'The Nature of the Bee' in his *Moralia* (early fifteenth century), later than the heyday of the Bestiary, follows their pattern. In effect, 'the nature of the creature' is a brief text for a brief homily. Preaching circulated and invented animal imagery: 'if it were not for the strength of the Aesopic tradition and the influence of other fabulists in the Middle Ages, it would be reasonable to attribute to Scripture this immense vogue for animal symbolism in the contemporary preaching'.[4] The allegories and references were not systematic nor consistent enough to make a symbolic notation for discernment of signs of the divine and of the demonic among the bewildering forms of natural phenomena in an unredeemed world. Rather, allegory and symbolism in diverse forms manifested a general habit of mind, engendered and sustained by belief that natural and supernatural were the same creation, so that analogy was a built-in feature of the world and a clue to its interpretation. This was as manifest in literature, in some forms of the French *dit*, for example, as in sermons.

Although Bestiaries were so different from fables in structure and function, what is obviously the same material does occur in both. On the nature of the dog:

> if it happens to cross a river carrying some meat or anything of the sort, when it sees its reflection it opens its mouth and, while it hastens to pick up the other bit of meat, it loses the one which it had.

Or the account of Castor the Beaver who bites off and casts his testicles for which he is pursued by the hunters (a fable in Perrotti's Appendix to *Phaedrus*, No. 30; and mentioned by Isidore). Or the lion's fear of a cock (Perry, 82). Or a sick lion that searches for a monkey to eat in order to be cured (*Phaedrus* IV, 14). Or a monkey that gives birth to twins, and by nature esteems one highly and scorns the other (*Babrius*, 35). Only two of these are truly fables, which have been incongruously taken over as natural description. But the overlap indicates no congruence of any kind, merely the absurd confusion of materials characteristic of the Bestiaries during the centuries of their career. They were there along with Aesopic compilations in the manuscript collections, but there was no organic connection between them, and the Bestiaries contributed nothing to the use and development of fable. By the end of the thirteenth century they were already becoming archaic compared with the more direct observation of animals, perhaps stimulated by Michael Scott's translation of Aristotle's *History of Animals* from Arabic into Latin and evident in a work on field sport by Frederick II of Germany, an exceptionally enlightened man of his age.[5]

There is no legacy from the Bestiaries to the occult, as there is none to science nor to theology nor to literature. The accumulated riches all go to the visual arts and are still on display, images in stone and wood and line and colour.

(*iii*)

The many collections of Aesopic fables in prose and verse which were made throughout the Middle Ages all derive from a collection that was early lost, 84 fables in Latin prose dedicated to a certain Rufus. It is known as *Aesopus ad Rufum* and was made possibly early in the ninth century, a fruit of the Carolingian literary renaissance, apparently based on *Phaedrus*. Hervieux, in his usual personal circumstantial account of his adventures in research, describes his finding the famous Wissembourg Manuscript deriving from *Aesopus ad Rufum*, and brings out very well the perils of literary transmission when the work was left in the hands of menial and ignorant copyists and was later corrected by over-ingenious, perhaps lazy, editors, inventing new sense or borrowing from other versions. But this manuscript – paired with the only other direct derivative, the even more famous 'Romulus' – shows in places an identical text derived from a common original.[6] 'Romulus' consists of 84 fables, of which 51 are found in *Phaedrus* or imitated. Thirty-two are not in *Phaedrus* as we have it.

The name 'Romulus' is taken from the dedication by 'Romulus' to his son Tyberinus. This dedication has itself suffered extraordinary transformations as preface to derivative versions. 'Romulus' becomes emperor (presumably, the last and least illustrious on the imperial roll), and is either himself the translator from Greek into Latin, or orders the translation for his son or sons. Or the emperor is Tiberius or Theodosius, who commissions the choice or composition of amusing fables to distract him from the cares of office; and it is the learned Romulus, or even Aesop himself, who receives the charge and translates the fables from Greek to Latin. All these variations in the preposterous signify at least the prestige of the fables, as well as the historical ignorance of the time.

Supplementing the prose paraphrases of *Phaedrus* in 'Romulus' were 42 fables in Latin elegiacs written by Avianus about the end of the fourth century, of which 26 are based on a Latin translation of *Babrius*. Sixty-one manuscripts of Avianus survive, and there were 67 printed Latin editions (1494–1887). There were the usual translations and selections for inclusion in other collections. Alexander Neckam, subsequently Abbot of Cirencester, rewrote the first six of the fables in the same language and metre, presumably as an example for his students at the University of Paris of how to reproduce the poet's thought in the same form, abridged or expanded. He gave three versions of 'The Eagle and the Tortoise': Copiose, Compendiose, Succincte. In the first, there are 32 lines to the 11 of Avianus; in the second, 10; in the third, 4. It is a distinguished literary exercise, greatly excelling the original.

The most famous edition of 'Romulus' was printed in the earliest days of printing. The editor and translator into German was a Dr Henry Steinhöwel, a doctor practising in Ulm. The edition has no date and no pagination, and is illustrated with woodcuts. The contents begin with a Life of Aesop, followd by the fables of Romulus, divided into four books of twenty each. There are three versions given: the Latin prose text, Steinhöwel's translation into German, the Latin text in elegiacs. The fourth book is not given in Latin verse. There follow 17 'Fabulae Extravagantes', also attributed to Aesop. A further 17 attributed to Aesop, newly translated by 'Remicii', are added, taken from a translation of 100 fables of Aesop by Ranutio d'Arezzo, published in 1483. Then comes a group of 27 fables of Avianus, translated by Steinhöwel into German. There is a last group of 23 taken from Pierre Alphonse and Poggio. There were many editions and translations of this work of Steinhöwel, German editions continuing into the nineteenth century. A French translation appeared very soon by Julian Macho, a monk, with a second edition in 1480, and up to fourteen successive editions. This was translated into English by Caxton and printed in 1484. There were more than seventeen reproductions, and a reissue in 1967 (*Caxton's Aesop*, edited with an Introduction and Notes by R.T. Lenaghan). As Mr Lenaghan remarks, this collection, widespread throughout Europe in the sixteenth century and since, was a representative anthology of fables at the end of the Middle Ages, founded on the 'Romulus' paraphrase, supplemented by selections from other collections and sources.

The Latin elegiacs based on the first three books of 'Romulus,' which Steinhöwel reprinted, were popular. Hervieux identifies the author as Galterus Anglicus, Walter the Englishman, who was chaplain to Henry II of England. Henry charged him with the instruction in letters of his intended son-in-law, Guillaume le Jeune, King of the Two Sicilies. This relationship led to Walter's becoming Archbishop of Palermo and Primate of the kingdom. Walter wrote for his pupil *Pro Latinae linguae exercitiis*, and seems to have given him the exercise of turning 'Romulus' into Latin elegiacs, which he then corrected. In this way the bulk of the fables in 'Romulus' were reproduced in Latin verse, and from the end of the twelfth century there were successive editions till the end of the seventeenth century, with five further reprints in the nineteenth century, and with many translations into European languages. The enormous celebrity of these Latin verses takes up nearly two hundred pages of Hervieux (vol i, pp. 472–668), although he himself thinks they are no better than the school exercise they were; and not as good as the work of another distinguished scholar and teacher, Walter's compatriot and contemporary Alexander Neckam, who also turned 'Romulus' into Latin elegiacs that enjoyed a reputation in their day. In correct verses, Neckam gives some nice touches of his own in retelling[42] the old tales in *Novus Aesopus*. In the last of his four lines on the dog with a piece of meat, it is the reflection that is lost: 'umbraque nulla fuit' (and the shadow was no more) (XIII). The poor ass who emulates his master's pet dog is not only beaten off but also deemed insane, and loaded with fetters and subdued by hunger and thirst:

Insanumque putans, vinclis oneravit Asellum.
Per tormenta famis et sitis excrucians. (V)

(And thinking him insane, loaded the Ass with fetters – greatly distressed by the torment of hunger and thirst.)

This is one of the fables cited in the *Gesta Romanorum*, where it is given an absurd allegorical interpretation. The pet dog is Christ's ordained priest; the ass is a lay person of the world who aspires to an office he is not qualified to perform.

Of the many collections, Hervieux concludes: 'toutes ces collections du moyen âge forment une chaîne, dont les anneaux se tiennent si visiblement qu'il est impossible de mettre la main sur l'un d'eux sans toucher aux autres' (all these medieval collections form a chain, of which the links are held together so visibly that it is impossible to put a hand on one without touching the others) (vol. i, p. 667). One other should be mentioned, a Latin collection composed in England at the end of the eleventh century or beginning of the twelfth, and translated into English. It was this English translation of an English Latin collection which Marie de France translated into French verse.[7]

This summary detail of editions was needed to show how precarious was the transmission of Aesopic fables, and indicate some measurement of their reproduction and dissemination. They became the common property of Christianized Europe, valued as a linguistic discipline – as in the ancient world – and also for their moral content, although secondary meanings were as likely as not to be construed allegorically, with a theological sense. What was officially valued had to bear witness to the Church. The Bible itself was allegorically tortured for the purpose. Studies of the sermons of the time show the abundant use of *exempla*: moralized anecdotes, symbolic figures, legends, illustrative material of many kinds, including 'fables', all drawn from a variety of sources. In all this material the fable proper is least used, although occasionally it is used properly and effectively. G.R. Owst goes so far as to call Odo of Cheriton, Nicole Bozon and John Bromyard medieval La Fontaines of the pulpit, and at least picked out those few preachers who understood, valued, and cultivated the Aesopic fables, particularly the first two named (p. 209).[8] It was available as source material, and was used and abused sporadically; it was not stock.

Le Roman de Renart

(i)

Although a masterpiece of medieval French literature with an influence throughout Europe for more than four centuries, *Le Roman de Renart* is not a single work by one author. As J.J. Jusserand described it at the end of the last century, 'It was built up, part after part, during several centuries . . . like a cathedral, each author adding a wing, a tower, a belfry, a steeple . . .' I risked likening the great Indian fables to opera in some aspects, and with the same looseness might liken *Renart* in some respects to jazz; not mainly in its popular appeal, but structurally in its improvisations, its continuations and repeats, its co-operation and virtuosities, even its differences of mood. Before the French performances broke off, the play was taken up by other hands in other lands, returning to the classical structure of a single work with a beginning, middle, and end.

Inspired by the Aesopic fables, and using these fables freely in its making, *Le Roman de Renart* is obviously not itself an Aesopic fable. Described as a 'beast-epic', whether it is itself a kind of fable, or is a parody of heroic poetry, or an allegory, or something else is hardly a profitable question, since in the long run it is all these and not consistently anything. It originated in fable, and it contributed through its popularity and versatility to the literary value and resources of fable. What distinguishes the work is not characteristic of fable – the creation of Renart as a literary figure, a 'character' as familiar as Mr Pickwick in his day, who walked out of the pages that brought him to life into the sun. Emerging as an amusing rogue, entertaining the world with ingenious tricks played upon Isengrim, his compère, and others, and by even more ingenious escapes from the consequences of his audacities, Aesop's fox becomes Renart, the comic hero of beguiling guile, who in later sequels, when his outrages trail death and desolation, achieves an apotheosis as the devil of the Bestiaries, symbol in particular of that aspect of evil with which the Middle Ages were most preoccupied, the hypocrisy which infected the Church, like the double-think feared as a modern manifestation of a righteous order imposed upon the world. The literary acclaim of this creation of French genius is perpetuated in the word 'renard' in French dictionaries, a proper name that has superseded 'goupil', which was the word for the anonymous animal imported from the fields and woods.

The twenty-eight 'Branches' of *Renart* cannot be integrated into one poem. (There really is no 'cathedral'.) Study of the work has to follow an attempt to piece it together chronologically in order to see how it developed, what individual contributions were made by the score of poets who took it up, and the changes in tone and intention that occurred.[9]

How it all began has been a matter of controversy, in the main between those who wanted to find the roots in folk-lore and oral tradition, whether immemorial or contemporary, and those who found it evident that the source is bookish and clerkly, in the Latin collections of fables derived from Greece and Rome that were in the schools and in clerical hands. In particular there was a long satirical Latin poem, *Ysengrimus*, composed about 1149 by a Flemish cleric, Nivard de Gand, in which the dominant theme of *Renart* was already broached – an implacable conflict between Renart and Isengrim, the Fox and the Wolf, who enter on their literary careers with these proper names. Some close parallels between parts of *Renart* and *Ysengrimus* indicate the earlier poem as chief source and inspiration. Contemporary poets (Chrétien de Troyes, Marie de France) and the Arthurian cycle of romances were encouragement not only as objects of parody but also as models of narrative scale and tempo. King Arthur and his knights, Louis VII and his feudal nobility, Noble the Lion and the animal seigneurs of his court, Aesop's lion and the beasts he rules and injures, are variations of one pattern. The court of Noble makes the *mise en scène* of *Renart*, where the action starts or to which it returns; and behind it is the feudal order of Christendom, which provides whatever organizing principle there is in the ramifications of the stories. This is the framework of parody and satire, containing a family of familiar personages of whom first and last is Renart, with Isengrim his foil, his compère and his enemy, and with Noble, his suzerain and his dupe. Although satirical, even outrageous in the burlesque of liturgical rites, the twenty-eight Branches contain nothing subversive, no attack upon the institutions. The *trouvères* belong to the establishment and share the contempt of their class for the people, including the parish clergy who come from and belong to the people. There is nothing bourgeois, still less populist, about *Renart*, however popular, until the appearance later of independent polemical works based upon it. The stories show the class prejudices and assumptions that still show in Froissart, although perhaps some boredom with the ethos and the literature of chivalry. When Renart describes to Noble with relish his degrading treatment of a *vilein* asleep under an elm, he provokes the remark from Noble:

> Je n'ai mis vilain tant chier,
> Autant ameroie a touchier
> A un ort vessel de ma main
> Comme je feroie a vilain.   (XVI, 1183–6)

(I don't count a villein of much worth, I would as soon touch a dirty pot with my hand as I would a villein.)

Although it is very clear that the framework and temper of *Renart* are bookish and feudal and that the source is Aesopic, the content of some of the stories is drawn from folk-tales. Thus Branch III has the story of the fox who lies in the road shamming dead, to be picked up by a carter and thrown on a wagonload of fish. The fox then throws out the fishes, and jumps off. Later, he tricks the wolf into fishing by dropping his tail in the water and holding it there, until it freezes into the pond. The story, with some of the same elaborations, is to be found among Ukrainian folk-tales (*Ukrainian Folk Tales*, selected and translated by Anatole Bilenko; Kiev, 1974).

The twenty-eight Branches of *Renart* were composed between 1174 and about 1250. They were followed by continuations markedly different in tenor and intention, until the end of the fourteenth century. As a pendant some hundred years later, Guillaume Tardif, professor at the Collège de Navarre, translated for Charles VIII the Latin fables of Laurent Valla in what were in effect new versions that recovered the authentic *Renart*. After that, there is scarcely a reference to *Renart* in French literature.

(ii)

The original tales composed in the last quarter of the twelfth century created the dramatis personae and some of the action out of Aesopic material. The lion's court was there (Perry, 285; 585). The lion was acknowledged king of the beasts (*Babrius*, 102, 103, 106; *Phaedrus* IV, 14). The fox was linked with the lion, in out-smarting him or in some kind of partnership (Perry, 394, 258, 416, 585; *Babrius*, 103). The fox was notorious for his ruses, and already there was the rivalry and enmity between fox and wolf, or identity in different versions of a few fables. In short, there was linked material in Aesop's fables, and actual episodes, for adoption and adaptation and further invention, whether in *Ysengrimus* or the *Renart* sequence. With this material, in a setting that reflected the feudal scene – with a courtly literature to be parodied structurally by the device of setting this material in this scene – there were the ingredients to hand for the first comic mix. Aesop's fox, like Napoleon, already knew how to make tools of others, including the royal beast, by manipulating their greed, vanity, fears, as well as by his own rhetorical art of making the worse seem the better case. Some of the fables are woven into the narrative incidentally for their episodic and cumulative effect, adding to the tale of Renart's villainous mischiefs, triumphant or baffled, multiplying Isengrim's misfortunes and grievances. The old apologues which thus reappear in this context disappear like candles in daylight, having no application, general or particular. In this they are unlike the constantly occurring fables in an Indian context, where the fable, however forced, is always a literary ritual introduced to further some matter in the course of the main narrative. Here in *Renart* fables are remade with their sequels to make the fabric of the tale, and unless the tale is itself a fable, there is no fable any more. What does emerge, apart from parody, is at first a playful satire on the behaviour of men and women in the institutions of their time and in domestic scenes: their cupidities, lusts, deceits, revenges, whims, predicaments, frights; their relationships and solidarities, temporary or enduring; above all, their hypocrisies. Thus in the early Branches of *Renart* are developed the public features of a resourceful and subtle fiction, which is too deadly not to be seized and used in personal and partisan causes, in several serious and powerful fables that transcend the original Aesopic material and turn to profit the success achieved in the first phase of *Renart*. If the Aesopic fable disappears as a fable when it appears in the context of *Renart*, in turn when it reappears later as an apologue again the narrative is longer and richer – as most notably in Chaucer's version of the Cock and Fox. Conversely, when *Renart* offers a later fabulist material for his purpose, it is stripped for that purpose of its narrative complications and circumstantial detail – as Odo of Cheriton simplifies the *Renart* story of Renart and Isengrim in the well (IV).

(iii)

The burlesque note is struck at the outset, at the beginning of Branche 2, which is chronologically first:

> Seigneurs, oi avez maint conte
> Que maint conterre vous raconte,
> Comment Paris ravi Elaine,
> Le mal qu'il en ot et la paine;
> De Tristan qui la Chievre fist,
> Qui assez bellement en dist
> Et fabliaus et chancon de geste.
> Romanz de lui et de sa geste
> Maint autre conte par la terre.
> Mais onques n'oistes la guerre,
> Qui tant fu dure de grant fin,
> Entre Renart et Ysengrin,
> Qui moult dura et moult fu dure.

(Lords, you have heard many tales which many story-tellers have told you, How Paris carried off Helen, the ill which he had of it and the punishment; of Tristan who caused *Chevrefeuille* [Marie de France], and who fares so nobly in common report and in *fabliaux* and *chansons de geste*. Of him and of his exploits stories abound. But never have you heard of the war which was so hard and great a conflict, between Renart and Ysengrin, which lasted long and was very bitter.)

There follow the familiar episodes of Renart with Chantecler, with Tibert the cat, and with Tiecelin the crow. He is then close upon his most notorious exploit, the violation of Hersens in the full view of Ysengrim her husband, described circumstantially as a piece of animal behaviour; thematically, a piece of malice that sticks, a wound that becomes a running sore – and a parody of the infidelities of romance.

The matter of the Branches is varied, from Renart's fast ones in the manner of a trickster in a folk tale (III), to parody of a jongleur's indecent *fabliau* (Ib), or to planned episodes of break and enter, with no honour among thieves (XIV, XVI), or to set pieces at Noble's court. The same characters pass from animals in a folk-tale to proper-tied seigneurs and ecclesiastics, of set and deft purpose. Of the regular appearances (and non-appearances) of Renart at court to answer charges occasioned by his outrages, the one that issues in his single combat with Isengrim is the most dramatic, and is a detailed burlesque of feudal protocol.

After everyone with a grievance has laid his complaint against Renart, Isengrim sums up his own:

> En un des plus lons jors d'este
> N'auroie je pas reconte
> Les mals, les anuis que m'as fes. (VI, 769)

(During one of the longest days of summer I should not be able to recount the wrongs and hurts you have done me.)

But it is vengeance rather than justice for which he thirsts, and he challenges Renart to the test of arms. Noble allows the challenge, hostages are taken from both sides and a day is appointed for the meeting. When the court reassembles for this public event, the contestants refuse appeals for reconciliation and neither will modify his position. An oath is administered to each: Renart denies the acts with which he is charged and reaffirms complete innocence; Isengrim maintains that Renart is perjured and he himself is in good faith. In detail, all the procedures are duly completed, the behaviour of the supporters of both parties is described and the fight, with shields and weapons, begins. The combat is long and grievous, accompanied by verbal exchanges between the combatants. At one point Renart taunts his adversary, galling him with the thought that many of the spectators will be amused to see them made to work like this to mollify him for his wife's amour. Isengrim breaks out in a bitter cry, eight lines summed up in:

> Par famme est plus guerre que pais,
> Par famme sont honis maint homme,
> De touz les maus est fame somme. (VI, 1284–6)

(Women bring more war than peace,
Women bring shame to many men,
Women are the sum of all evils.)

Isengrim is partially disabled as the fight goes on, but his superior strength is too much for Renart, whose ruses do not prevail. The end comes with a collapse of Renart's morale when in his extremity, aware of his perjury, conscience takes sides against him. He is beaten to the ground, and left for dead. Isengrim and his party celebrate their triumph. But Renart is not dead, and the outcome of the trial by combat condemns him: he must be hanged. He repents, to save his skin, and by the intervention of his friends and the partiality of Noble he is allowed to seek absolution and to become a monk. Of course this does not last long, and all is as before. In all these earlier Branches Renart is often defeated, humiliated, punished, and here frightened to death, always resilient. This is in contrast with the later Renart in whom resilience has hardened into a tough mastery of this world worthy of the devil.

The issue of the combat is different in the later Dutch version of *Renart*, translated by Caxton. Renart's ruse does prevail, and by victory he wins friends and influences the great. He is taken by Noble as his chief counsellor, despite his treachery of which Noble has had bitter experience. This shows the indispensability of 'renardie' for worldly success, the keynote of the later versions and adaptations. The other main variant in the Dutch version is the careful preparation – mental, moral, and physical – of Renart for the fight by the she-ape his aunt. They are to fight with teeth and claws, and he is shaved and oiled, to be made as slippery to the touch as he has been elusive to his victims and enemies. The difference in the versions illustrates the evolution in the story from Renart as folk-hero in burlesque of the knights of chivalry to Renart as cynical Lord of Misrule outside the licensed revel, infiltrating Christendom with 'renardie' – as it were, from a university rag to the urban gangster.

Branche XVII narrates the death and funeral of Renart. He is taken ill, his relatives are summoned, he dies. There is a state funeral, with an elaborate burlesque of the office. Bernart, the archpriest, delivers a funeral oration in which the deceased is lauded with the usual bland falsehoods, carried to absurdity: he has lived the life of an apostle and martyr:

> Que de lui ne sui en dotance
> Qu'il ne soit en bonne fin pris.
> Onques ne fut Renart repris
> Nul jour a nule vilanie.
> Il a este sanz felonnie
> Et sanz malice et sanz orgueil.
> Onques jour ne virent my oeil
> Prince qui fust de sa vertu.

(I am in no doubt that he has ended a good life.
Never at any time was Renart found in any villainy.
He has been without crime and without malice and without pride.
At no time would be seen a prince of his virtue.)

A prayer for the deceased follows, in which to the absurdity of his superhuman virtues is added the incongruity of reference to his life and work as a fox:

> En maint peril vous estes mis
> En bois, en forest et en plain
> Pur avoir vostre vantre plain,
> Et pour porter a Hermeline
> Vostre fame coc ou geline,
> Chapon ou oe ou cras oison.

(You were put in many perils, in wood, in forest, and in open field, in order to fill your belly, and to bring home to your wife Hermeline a cock or fowl, a capon or goose or plump bird.)

After this bathos comes the interment by Brun. At the conclusion of the archpriest's benediction, Renart pushes up the lid of the coffin and escapes. Noble is furious. The barons, Chantecler in the van, give chase. Renart is caught between a dog which a vilein has loosed on him and the pursuing court. Chantecler is near, and Renart appeals for help. The upshot is that Chantecler is mounted on Renart's back, and tears him with beak and claws. He is left for dead in a ditch, deserted by everyone. His family carry him home, and his friends demonstrate his death to Noble by annexing a fresh open grave.

Although Renart lives to fight another day as usual, this is the end in 1205 of the *Renart* created by Pierre de Saint-Cloud and his successors. The nine numbered Branches that remain differ in spirit and in manner and in themes, and Isengrim is the central figure in several. 'Les semailles, ou le labourage en commun' (XXII) stands apart as an independent fable. The composition of these last Branches goes on till the mid-thirteenth century.

(iv)

In the second half of the century there were three independent satires based on *Renart: Renart le Bestourné* (1261), *Le Couronnement de Renart* (1263–70), *Renart le Nouvel* (1289). The first is a savage attack on the mendicant orders and their influence over Louis IX by the *trouvère* Rutebeuf, who was biased against the orders for personal reasons. The second, by an unknown author, is a political pamphlet in the allegorical form of a fable against the rising bourgeoisie. Renart conspires with Jacobins and Franciscans to overthrow and replace Noble. Money has taken over with the new rich, and can do or undo anything, save raise the dead. The reign of Renart – displacing the old virtues and values represented by Noble – is the rule of money, with the greed, pride, and double-dealing that go with that. The satire reflects the industrial revolution in the Netherlands which left the cities entirely in the hands of patricians enriched by trade.

In *Renart le Nouvel* by Jacquemart Gelée, the allegorical method is used for an attack on the corruption of the Church by the clergy, who have totally submitted to the rule and the arts of Renart. The chaotic poem ends with a tableau in which Renart, crowned, sits on top of Fortune's wheel, flanked by Pride and Guile, with his sons at the foot. He has been assured that the wheel will no longer turn, since he has destroyed Faith, Loyalty, Right, and Humility, and given all power to Pride and Duplicity. This is far removed from the world of *Le Roman de Renart*. At the same time, the allegorizing and moralizing are relieved by superbly comic episodes, involving the degradation of Noble and some of the most outrageous tricks of Renart, which recall the best of the earlier branches and of the *fabliaux*. This was the first of all the Renart tales to be printed in France.

The last and most curious independent work based on *Renart* was *Renart le Contrefait* by the Clerc de Troyes (1319–42). The author states what he and Renart have learned from experience: 'C'est l'art de Renart qui confère la Fortune et la réussite dans le monde; sans lui, tout savoir, toute connaissance des autres arts ne servent à rien. C'est l'art que doivent apprendre rois et comtes, empereurs et papes.' (It is Renart's art which brings Fortune and success in the world; without that, all wisdom, all knowledge of other arts are worth nothing. It is the art which kings and counts, emperors and popes ought to learn) Here, explicitly if ironically, is justification of the drift of so many of the Renart poems, in which, in spite of inexpiable crimes and unforgivable outrages, Renart is perforce restored to royal favour, and is made steward or chief counsellor. This seems to say that he is necessary to worldly wisdom and successful statecraft. Machiavelli said the same, in a treatise, but using the similitude offered by the fables. Of the way in which princes must keep faith, he wrote:

> A prince being thus obliged to know well how to act as a beast must imitate the fox and the lion, for the lion cannot protect himself from snares, and the fox cannot defend himself from wolves. One must therefore be a fox to recognize snares, and a lion to frighten wolves. Those who wish to be only lions do not understand this.
> (*The Prince*, ch. xviii)

To digest such 'reasons of State' has always been painful for moralists, and although in the *Renart* tales it is seen as corruption rather than statecraft, there is in the end recognition that there is no hope of success in managing the affairs of this world without 'renardie'. The solution has to be in transcendental terms, and the author of *Renart le Contrefait* engages in metaphysical discussion to try to resolve the problem of evil. But it is Noble advised by Renart who is the principal target, the absolute and arbitrary power of monarchy. This is the voice of the new bourgeoisie, in revolt against tyranny, and in defence of the oppressed and dispossessed poor. The author is no longer of the establishment, and this *Renart* is 'contrefait'.

(v)

Attempts to integrate the original *Roman de Renart* into a single self-contained and self-explanatory poem were made outside France, first in Alsace by Heinrich der Glichezaere at the end of the twelfth century with *Reinhart Fuchs*, and then in Flanders in the first half of the thirteenth century with *Reinaert de Vos*, by an author unknown. This version was in the next century remodelled with additions drawn from *Renart*; and it is this second version, *Reinaerts Historie*, which has been endlessly reproduced and translated and is the source of the survival of the Renart story today.

Reinaert de Vos was sharply satirical (it classed itself with hagiography, lives of the saints and martyrs), realistic in description, and subtle in portraiture. Noble is no longer the rather stupid, impulsive, and good-humoured feudal lord, with an obvious weakness for Renart the rascal; he is calculating, not easily deceived, and with the utmost distrust of Renart, whom he is anxious to get rid of. Renart is therefore driven to outwit an astute and watchful adversary, which he does by preying on the king's cupidity, at the same time dealing him a last insulting piece of malignancy before making his exit from the story, totally triumphant, leaving Noble and his peers to escape their guilt and slake their fury by seizing an innocent scapegoat. A Latin translation of the poem was one of the first books printed in Utrecht, about 1474.

Some hundred years later appeared the new version, *Reinaerts Historie*, in which the language is modernized and a sequel added. Renart does not quit the scene, but comes back to trial and once more outwits the king and his enemies, ending as the king's chosen counsellor, after his victory in single combat over Isengrim. It is the triumph of his influence: 'In any court where kings or lords assemble, when counsel is wanted, it is Renart who provides it' (verse 1425). That his gospel has thus been received has been made possible by submission of the clergy to his example.[10]

Impressions of *Le Roman de Renart* gained by acquaintance with any of these vernacular versions of a complete poem will not be a fair impression of Branches I–XVII of the original, but the vitality of Renart forces its way through in all the productions inspired by the original. Even the later independent French poems mentioned above, so different in mood, method, and purpose, having hitched their wagons to *Renart* for its drawing power, had to keep the engine in good repair to make that use of it. Utility as much as literary respect served and saved the original; and in some cases contributed new wealth to the inheritance.

In review of these diverse *Renart* productions in verse and prose during some three centuries, there are two main things to be said. The original *Roman* composed of Aesopic materials was too loose and episodic to be itself a fable – as, conversely, other material may be used to make a fable. The original showed, however, that this was serio-comic fiction that could be used for a concentrated purpose; and it was adapted in the later independent French poems, in an allegorical form, for particular polemical attacks. In the final Dutch form the original is restructured to make what is a telling fable, profiting by the cumulative transformation of Renart to use the action as an image of 'renardie', general and permanent, the mark of a fable.

After Renart

Conspicuous among the fabulists influenced by *Le Roman de Renart* is Odo of Cheriton, a learned English cleric who died in the mid-thirteenth century. The 81 fables of his collection (1219–21), adapted mainly from Romulus and *Renart* and many of them composed by himself, are related with graphic clarity and terse vigour; but even more than in style and invention, his distinction is in his purposive organization and use of the fable. His Prologue is based on the similitude of Ruth's gleaning corn under the protection and with the encouragement of Boaz. Odo is concerned with the reapers who serve Boaz, that is, the apostles, disciples, prelates, who are charged with the care of souls. He reminds them that if they fail in what they are required to do for the edification of the laity (Ruth), the judgement on them will be most severe, more severe than on heretics, which is more severe than on Jews and Saracens, which is severe enough. Nourishment of the soul by the word of the gospel is greater service than nourishment of the body; and since verbal illustration is more compelling than the abstract word and stays more firmly in the memory, he will say what he has to say in that form, as fables and as parables.

This is Odo's perspective in the composition and use of fable, and it is moral and political, not literary. But when G.R. Owst calls him and Nicole Bozon 'La Fontaines of the pulpit' (above, p. 40), that is not merely extravagant but mainly a clinical mistake, a confused perception in the case of Odo, who did not use fables in his sermons for the instruction of the laity designedly. For this purpose he used 'parabolae'.[11] Fables he adopted, adapted, or invented for systematic exposure of the behaviour of nobles and prelates. They are independent, not preaching material; and the distinction he made is the more interesting because he made it to serve two different purposes in practice, although for both he had chosen a graphic form of expression. There is a difference between selecting and retelling fables for their common purpose and general application, and adopting, adapting, and inventing a collection as a battery for systematic attack on a specific target, the conduct of prelates and nobles. The target was general, not named individuals nor established institutions, but Odo by adopting this device for his single-minded purpose demonstrated the contemporary relevance and force which the Aesopic fable in itself does not have, and which were to be the justification of major fables in later times.

Odo had to make good the effect of his story by making sure of its application. Sometimes, this will exceed the fable in length by some six times, with citations from the Bible or the Fathers or Seneca. Or five lines on 'The Wolf and the Lamb' are followed by two which simply say that in the same way the rich devour the poor without cause. Best of all, the seven lines which tell of the Wolf with a bone in his throat are crowned by three which say that peasants and the poor when they do service are not able to have any remuneration, for their master says: 'Homo meus es; nonne magnum est, si te non excorio, si te vivere permitto!' (You are my man; is it not of worth if I do not skin you, if I allow you to live!)

The influence of Asian fables, through the Middle East, is notable in Odo's collection (XLV, LXIII; or in Perry's summaries, Nos 609, 619, 630, 634, 635). He became a source for others and his fables were adapted, abridged, translated for other compilations. Particularly to be noticed is an abridgement by John of Sheppey, Bishop of Oxford (1352–60). His collection of fables was annexed by him to the third volume of his collected sermons. This collection of 73 fables, of which 52 are found in Odo, is an independent work. Seven have no counterpart in 'Romulus' either. Two of these are listed by Perry (644–5) as 'Composed by John of Schepey': 'The Buzzard and the Hawk' and 'The Lion and the Unicorn'. However, the first is word for word the same as Odo's Fable IV in the opening lines. The action of John's ends neatly with a citation from Horace; Odo cites an English proverb, and goes on to apply the story to the Church, with an allegorical interpretation. John usually leaves the fable to speak for itself, and groups them under captions by which they are linked, as 'De ingratitudine', 'De peccatis ypocrisis', 'De vana gloria', 'Contra gulosos et delicatos'. He follows Odo occasionally with brief applications to the Church and its ministers, with independent citations. His narrative style is consistently crisp, so that his versions are among the most readable.

Another Englishman, Nicole Bozon (*c.* 1320–50), a minor friar in the north of the country, collected stories of all kinds, some of his own, written in Anglo-Norman and some of them fables; and he used analogies and images in the manner of French *dits*. His imagination was one of the most fecund in this kind, and his sermons are packed with similitudes, metaphors and stories. He does not distinguish the fable as an independent genre. One that is a fable in his collected stories is of special interest. It is the theme of La Fontaine's 'Les animaux malades de la peste', which the eighteenth-century critic Chamfort regarded as the finest of La Fontaine's apologues, and the finest apologue. Odo has versions, recorded by Perry (628, 628a, 628b), who also records the version of a Byzantine rhetorician, taken from an Indian original (452). La Fontaine's story, short as it is, unfolds gradually and with irony to the culmination. Bozon makes his story monstrous from the first, and tells it with the forceful rapidity of a Bible parable (Hervieux, vol. iv, p. 256). The rhetorician's version is a rhetorician's version, overdone and spoiled. Substantially, the story is of an ass in the company of notorious sinners making their confessions. He is compelled to think of some blameless incident with which to charge himself, and incurs the blame and punishment due to the others, who have the power to impose or spare, or the interest to get spared – a sword of sharp service to Odo and others in the endless fight against religious hypocrisy.

English churchmen educated in Paris, like Odo and John of Sheppey, might easily have known *Le Roman de Renart*, but there is little evidence that it was available in circulation in England. John Flinn thinks that in the thirteenth and fourteenth centuries it was bound to have circulated among the Anglo-Norman nobility and the educated, as did the *fabliaux*, which are also scarce. He thinks that English puritanism asserted itself early, and the monks were in a position to exercise censorship as copyists and librarians, so that nothing survives of this literature that cannot be reconciled with didactic or religious use (pp. 681–8). Towards the end of the fifteenth century, there was Caxton's translation from the Dutch.

Aesop as vernacular poetry

(*i*)

Marie de France was the first to produce in a vernacular a book of fables in verse refined in expression and with a personal stamp. Having ended in classical literature with Phaedrus and Lucian, the fable can be said to have reappeared in the late Middle Ages with *Renart* and Marie de France, with no other link than a slender collection of Aesop in prose. Marie de France wrote as well as *Fables*, *Lais*, and an evangelical work, *Espurgatoire S. Patrice*, in the later part of the twelfth century. The *lais*, she said, were composed from what she had heard and what others had recorded, poems of love, adventure, and marvels; the fables were faithfully translated from English; and the *Espurgatoire*, legend of the Purgatory of St Patrick, was translated from Latin to make it more widely available. She seems to have been head of the Abbey of Shaftesbury in 1181, and to have died about 1216. She had high connections and claims to have translated the fables at the behest of a distinguished nobleman, who may have been the Earl of Pembroke, Regent from 1216 to 1219. She mistakenly attributes to King Alfred the English version of the fables which she translated. No manuscript of the English translation does survive, but two of the manuscripts of Marie's work attribute this English translation to a King Henry, who must have been Henry II, 'Beau-Clerc'.

In her Prologue, Marie says it is the duty of the learned to commemorate and pass on ancient wisdom so that those who have a mind to improve themselves may do so, as Romulus the emperor did for his son, and showed him by examples how he should be aware of the world's deceits. Having said that Aesop translated into Latin for his master Greek fables he had found, she added that many wonder that such works should claim intellectual attention, but there is no frivolous fable in which there is no philosophy at the end which is the whole point of the story. In her Epilogue, she repeats that the book is called Esope, who had it written and turned it from Greek into Latin, from which it was turned into English by the much-loved King Alfred, and which she has now versified in French as exactly as she can. Here is expressed: the duty of the learned to preserve and *vulgariser* the wisdom of the ancients; the usual apology for taking seriously the foolishness of fables; the sense of the Aesopic tradition, cloudy and ignorant; high patronage for the fable, and its value for the introduction of the young to the ways of the world.

The 'Romulus Anglicus', the Latin of the English version Marie translates, shows a far greater interest in the story than the original 'Romulus' based on *Phaedrus*. The story is commonly twice as long, sometimes three times or more. Marie seems to have followed this closely, as she claims. Mostly, the story is left to speak for itself in both. Marie sometimes makes a specific application to contemporary oppressors, as in 'The Wolf and the Lamb' and 'The Wolf with a Bone in his Throat'. A long one, 'The Wolf who was King', carries a moral closer to the political philosophy of Locke (or Aquinas) than to 'the divine right of kings'.

The story of the two mice, perhaps of all fables the one that most invites telling, is told here with economy and psychological realism. In this version, the shock of the disturbance at the feast is reflected in disillusionment at misplaced confidence: the town mouse has misled her country friend, advertising all that was good in her way of life, concealing drawbacks; bruised confidence remains, not rural self-congratulation.

Economy combines with liveliness in 'Del chien e del furmage'. The action of the Dog is presented, rather than related:

> En l'ewe saut, la buche ovri,
> E li furmages li chei;
> E umbre vit, e umbre fu,
> E sun furmage avait perdu.

> (In the water he jumps, mouth open,
> And the cheese falls;
> And the shadow is there, and the shadow flees,
> And he has lost his cheese.)

This has the ring of a nursery rhyme, appropriate to the visual mime as it is.

In the striking fable 'De l'asne ki volt juer a sun seignur', the Ass anticipates what is to come by reasoning on his superiority to the little dog in giving pleasure to his master: he has a stronger voice, he knows better how to leap up and fawn on him with his feet; he will therefore easily outdo his rival. The anticipation doubles the painful sequel.

'Del leun e del vilein' is a longer version of the Man and Lion travelling together and disputing who is the braver and superior, man or lion. The Man takes the Lion to a house in which there is a wall-painting of a man who has killed a lion. This obviously is no evidence; a man can paint what he likes. The Lion then makes the Man an eye-witness of prisoners thrown to the lions, and takes him into the desert, where a stranger lion proposes to dispose of him as their natural enemy. The Man's companion will not allow the friend in his care to perish through him. Demonstration has disposed of argument, as the Man amply acknowledges. Marie de France tells this story in medieval terms, and it has grown from a mere wisecrack of the Lion on subjective judgements, in early forms, to a form in which it can show that experience is superior to carving or painting or fable in the demonstration of unpalatable truth. Psychologically, it is on the move in the direction that leads to *Candide*. This is truly a fable with a sharp point, but there are others which are nearer to *fabliaux*.

(ii)

An interpolation is needed here on the relation between fable and *fabliau*. The name is applied to narrative poems composed mainly in the thirteenth century, comic tales of some incident which might, with less exaggeration, take place in ordinary life. They were intended for recitation, rather than reading. The connection with fable is not only in name, but also in some features. They might be said to be bastard offspring of the fable; the earliest seem to have followed Marie de France, and to have been imitations of fables in which the characters are human. Some were oriental in origin and there were Indian fables that would provide a model, such as the one of a judge and his son who frequent the same harlot. They are bastard in the sense that they are not legitimated by the serious purpose of fables; any formulation of what is to be learned that may be tacked on is trivial or ridiculous. They are for amusement simply, elaborations of a joke or a proverb, bawdy or tall stories. The characters are conventional types: the infatuated lover, the jealous husband, the erring priest, the unfaithful wife. The story is carried forward with circumstantial detail and plenty of dialogue. Some few have the same theme as authentic fables and are virtually the same stories; for example, 'D'un preudome qui rescolt son compere de noier', about a fisherman who grabbed a boathook to save a man from drowning and, in thrusting it to him, accidentally blinded one eye. He is sued for injury. There are several fables which warn against doing good to the ill-disposed (Perry, 640; again, oriental in source).

As an example, it is tempting to recall 'D'Aristote et d'Alixandre' or 'Lai d'Aristote', another Eastern tale which seems to have been widely popular in medieval Europe, and is in the *Gesta Romanorum*. Alexander, with his army and retinue in India, becomes infatuated with a girl, to the total neglect of everything and everybody else. This goes on so long that his staff become seriously worried and it falls to Aristotle, his tutor, to bring him to his senses. Alexander is downcast; the girl asks the reason and is told that his knights blame him and his master has reproved him. She says that, artless as she is, she will prove more than a match for the greybeard his master, as the king will see with his own eyes on the morrow. Next day at noon, her toilet artfully artless, she goes into the orchard below the windows of the apartments occupied by Alexander and Aristotle, picking flowers to weave a chaplet to decorate her hair, and singing. Aristotle, at his books, attracted by the singing, goes to the window and is ravished by the appearance of irresistible maiden freshness. He returns to his books, disturbed and amazed; and after reasoning with himself and against himself, concludes that it is necessity – an answer arrived at earlier and differently by his pupil: 'Vielt Amors vivre par devis?' As her singing comes close under his own window, he returns to it, and calls down to her and confesses that he has fallen for her. She replies that it will not do; she is involved with the king, who would deal severely with anyone who tried to dally with her. Aristotle tells her not to mind all that, for he stands first with the king in all his retinue. She stipulates that he must first indulge her in a caprice: she has taken it into her head that she would like to take a ride across the orchard on his back. Aristotle submits, carries a saddle down to the orchard and has it put across his shoulders. She mounts and he crawls over the grass, whilst she sings in a loud voice:

> *Ainsi va qui amors mainent.*
> Bele Doe ghee laine.
> Maistre musart me soutient.
> *Ainsi va qui amors mainent*
> *Et qui bon' amor maintient.*

(Thus goes one who wages love.
The Master secretly me upholds.
Thus goes one who wages love
And who good love upholds.)

Alexander, who has been looking on from his window, shouts down
to ask if he is out of his mind. Aristotle looks up shamefaced, and
yields him the *a fortiori* argument: if someone of his age can fall . . .
He confesses that all he has learned in a lifetime has been undone by
Amors in an hour. The king bursts out laughing, and the performance ends. It is a delicious anticipation of the researches of a later
sage, and a greater maker of philosophic myths than Aristotle's own
master. The naughty story was so greatly enjoyed that it is found
celebrated in carvings in churches, and may be seen in Exeter
Cathedral.

The company on the road to Canterbury heard a literary version of
a canonical fable from the Nun's priest and a famous *fabliau* from the
Reeve. Both fable and *fabliau* are in the mainstream of the literature
of the period, in a low style, but one has better breeding and prospects. This is a class distinction, and a lower class has rights and
merits of its own, perhaps equal rights and equal merits; but there
remains a sense in which it is lower.

(iii)

Earlier than Chaucer, in the thirteenth century, there are two fables
in English verse regularly noted in histories for their literary merit,
'The Owl and the Nightingale' and 'The Vox and the Wolf'. The
latter is a spirited recital in couplets of the story which is the subject
of Branche IV of *Renart*, with caustic allusions to the idleness and
gluttony of monastic life.

'The Owl and the Nightingale' is a poem of 1794 lines in octo-
syllabic couplets, written in the southern dialect and attributed to
Nicholas of Guildford, who at least figures in the poem and gets a
plug for preferment. It has been extravagantly praised. W.P. Ker
calls it 'the most miraculous piece of writing . . . among the medieval
English books', meaning the most unexpected in accomplishment,
still more in its temper of detachment, humour, and irony; so that it
is 'a true comedy', with an urbanity he compares with that of Horace
or Addison (*English Literature Medieval*). At least, this startling
dislocation wrenches the poem out of the medieval context of compulsive allegory and allows it to stand on its own, and for delight.
This is not a fable; it is of a type that may be one, the verbal context,
which has a tradition that goes back to Akkadian literature, although
of course not maintaining the strict stylization of their convention.
William Dunbar's 'The Merle and the Nightingale' is a short poem in

the form of a contest between a champion of the courtly service of Love, and the Nightingale who represents the devotional cult: 'All love is lost but upon God alone'.

John Lydgate, in 'The Debate of the Horse, Goose, and Sheep', remarks that disputations settled by an independent judge was an ancient custom in law, and that he saw the subject of his poem painted on a wall: Horse, Goose, and Sheep before Lion and Eagle – symbols of royalty, the source and agent of justice.

> The processe was not to profounde nor deepe,
> Of their debate, but contryved of a fable;
> Which of them to men was most profitable.
>
> Of many strange uncouth simylitude,
> Poetis of old fablis have contryvid,
> Of Sheep, of Hors, of Gees, of bestis rude,
> Bi which ther wittis wer secretly apprevid,
> Undir covert tyrantis eeke reprevid
> Ther oppressions and malis to chastise
> Bi examplis of resoun to be mevid,
> For no prerogatiff poore folk to despise.
>
> Fortunes cours dyversely is dressid
> Bi liknessis of many othir tale;
> Man, best, and fowle and fisshis been oppressid
> In thir natur bi female or bi male;
> Of grettest fissh devourid been the smale,
> Which in natur is a full straunge guyse,
> To seen a kokkow mordre a Nityngale,
> An innocent brid of hattreede to despise.

In these few lines Lydgate domesticates man with all other creatures in the same situation, exposed to similar hazards and vicissitudes, men and others equally victims of predators, in need of justice and succour; so that the similitudes of the beast fable represented the human case, and could be used to bring home to tyrants the wrongs they do, arraign them before their conscience. The oblique political vocation of fable is recognized, and employed. 'The Horse, the Sheep, and the Goat', printed by Caxton in 1478, had a second edition. Caxton printed also another fable of Lydgate, 'The Chorle and the Bird', an elaborated variant of the story of the nightingale who gave her captor three precepts for her freedom (Perry, 627). This also had a second edition. Lydgate did his own versions of some of the Aesopic fables, which are among the happiest of his verses. As usual, a legendary Aesop appears in the Prologue:

> Unto purpos the poete laureate
> Callyd Isophus dyd him occupy
> Whylom in Rome to plese the Senate,
> Fonde out fables, that men might hem apply
> To sondry matyrs, yche man for hys party,
> Aftyr ther lust, to conclude in substance,
> Dyverse moralytees set out to theyr pleasaunce.

Chaucer was born a generation earlier than Lydgate, although his craft is immeasurably more mature. His one fable, 'The Nonne Preestes Tale', 40 lines in Marie de France's version, 454 in *Renart*, is expanded to 626. This 'Chauntecleer and Pertelote', supposed by Dryden to have been Chaucer's invention, is indeed that. Although a refreshing taste in English of the original *Renart*, it is inimitable Chaucer in all the delights and delays of the telling, which comes to grips with the fable in the end in the ruefully reflective drawing of the moral by the beasts themselves, victims each of the other because victims each of himself. Chaucer's version may well be preferred to any other for the telling, but there is in it more of the occasion than of the fable.

The fable content is there, faithfully reproduced, but it is a denouement more gay than grave, one congenial to the poet who, one might suspect, preferred *fabliau* to fable. There is reference to fable to illustrate a point (e.g. 'The Knightes Tale', 11. 319–22), but no other fable in his works.

(iv)

Of all these vernacular versifiers of fables, Robert Henryson, the fifteenth-century Scottish schoolmaster, is not the least among the few who have made poetry of them in the thirteen he selected. His narrative is graphic, paced and inventive, his dialogue in character, his style familiar, but ready to break into a parody of courtly literature or to burlesque legal procedures or to deal with matters ironically; and with regular use of alliteration, occasional bursts of (mock) lyricism and, at one point, an heraldic pageant. In short, his sure and resourceful craftsmanship makes him reliably readable.

The force of his didacticism matches the vigour of narration. Although a man of the Renaissance, Henryson carries on in the Scottish context the medieval Christian tradition, with its unquestioned assumptions about the world, the flesh, and the devil, the fall of man and the destiny of heaven or hell. His *Moralitas*, separated from each fable under that head and ranging from three or four stanzas to a homily nearly as long as the fable in a couple of instances, is evangelical and biblical, warning against the snares of this world and the wrath to come. Nowhere in the history of fable is insistent instruction, spelled out so determinedly, yoked to amusing narrative. Unlike Lydgate, who puts men and animals on a level in their endurance of fate and the predicaments of nature and society, Henryson equates fallen man with animals in the sense that animality represents human carnality and depravity. His fables are chosen to bring this home. Henryson's Aesop is thoroughly allegorized with theological meanings, leaving little to speak for itself. Pressing the metaphor to destruction to make his point, he can take the life out of the story – save that it remains in his own telling of it to contradict him. Thus in the first, 'The Taill of the Cok and the Jasp', the Cock naturally does not see that the gift of grace is any use to him, which shows how to destroy fable with allegory. Fortunately, this is followed by 'The Taill of the Uponlandis Mous and the Burges Mous', the least a preaching text. Henryson, with Horace, is among the few who have done it with fine touches of their own. His country mouse is not introduced as enjoying a desirable state:

> This rural mous into the winter-tyde
> Had hunger, cauld, and tholit grit distress.

But, her adventure over, she returns to her den:

> Als warme as well, suppose it was not greit,
> Full beinly stuffit, baith but and ben,
> Off beinis, and nuttis, peis, ry and quheit;
> Quhenever scho list, scho had aneuch to eit,
> In queyt and eis, withoutin ony dreid;
> Bot to hir sisteris feist na mair scho yeid.

The movements leading to this satisfactory finale are beautifully arranged: the city manners and squeamishness of the elder sister, untouched by solicitude for the other, reared with her and welcoming her with open heart; the lightning bolt to security within her hole at home when the butler appears and later the cat, leaving her helpless sister to be seized and played with by the cat, to escape behind the furniture by the merest luck. The fright is frightful, the foreign conditions intolerable, let the moral be what you will.

'The Taill of the Wolf and the Weder' is at a hotter pace, the Wether hounding the Wolf, eager and dogged in pursuit, hard on his heels, so that he fouls himself in fright, driven over bank, across bog and through bush and brier, till a brier catches in and tears off the dog-skin, exposing the truth. It is impossible not to feel how greatly the reverend headmaster is enjoying himself in virtuoso performances of the old school exercise, for which he would get high commendation if he were not himself the dominie, and giving the inimitable lesson of literary creation. His selection of the thirteen examples could hardly have been single-minded in strict regard for their *moralitas*, with no side glance at room for spinning the yarn. Five of them are from the *Renart* cycle. In his Prologue Aesop had appeared to him in a dream, a very impressive person who had declared himself to be a native of Rome, where he had studied civil law. The dreamer is delighted, and greets him as poet laureate.

Reformers and poets

(i)

As a prudential maxim for the conduct of life the proverb is akin to fable, but depends for its effect on epigrammatic formulation, not on graphic action. It may be as metaphorical: 'Night is the mother of counsel'. It may depend on a fable: 'To be shot with one's own feathers'. It may sound paradoxical: 'The half is more than the whole'; 'To offer much is a kind of denial'; 'There are those who despise pride with a greater pride'. Two of these examples are recorded by Erasmus, who amused himself, and made his first reputation as an author, by collecting 'Adages' from classical sources. He recognized both the likeness and the distinction between his adages and fables, and the contemporary addiction to fables. 'Some writers have attempted not only to force the fables of the past into line with Christian allegory, but to mix new fables with them and expound these to us allegorically, as if truth could never be learned without an admixture of falsehood.' He did not recognize how thoroughly confused with allegory fable was at the time. He intended his collection of adages to be used like the classical compendia 'for conferring beauty and distinction on all kinds of speech writing', the vocation of the humanists as formerly of the sophists.

In successive editions of this most successful venture (27 during his lifetime), Erasmus both increased the number (from some 800 to more than 4000) and developed the purpose, making it a vehicle of social criticism. This was particularly true of the 1515 edition, which followed another successful venture, his satirical *Encomium Moriae* (The Praise of Folly), which owed something to Lucian. In this edition the collection is used as a political resource, to make war on war, and in other matters of Church and State. 'The *Adages* went on from this point as a dual-purpose work, throwing off minor features on both sides like a catherine-wheel: the purely literary or school book aspect of it was often reproduced in Epitomes up to the seventeenth century, the longer political essays were in some cases printed in pamphlet form. The book itself . . . went on growing till Erasmus died.'[12] The longest and most famous of these essays, 'Dulce bellum inexpertis', familiarly called 'Bellum', was printed many times, first in 1517 and then in twenty-one Latin editions and in translation, and reprinted as late as 1953. Erasmus consistently thought of war as the most monstrous of human iniquities, 'nothing more wicked, more disastrous, more widely destructive, more deeply tenacious, more loathsome, in a word more unworthy of man, not to say of a Christian'. Unimaginable to sober reflection, yet accepted as customary, 'It must have been a gradual process which led to such a remarkable state of insanity': a fanciful account of the aetiology follows (Phillips, p. 317).

Of special interest in this study of fable is another long essay in this collection, 'Scarabeus Aquilam Quaerit' (The Beetle searches for the Eagle), which was also printed separately, in 1517 and in three later editions. This is simply Erasmus's retelling of the revenge of the Beetle on the Eagle for violation of the asylum given to a hare (Perry, 3). Before Erasmus can embark on this epic, in a mock exordium he invokes the aid of the Muses in the manner of poets. And before he comes to the action, he provides a description of each of the protagonists. He shows why the Eagle is king of the birds by general suffrage, although he loves none and is loved by none. The portrait of the Eagle, point by point, is the character of kings as tyrants. He rounds off by listing the peculiar excellence of a dozen different kinds of birds, and concludes: 'but of them all, the eagle alone has seemed suitable in the eyes of wise men to represent the symbol of a king – the eagle, neither beautiful, nor songful, nor good to eat, but carnivorous, greedy, predatory, ravaging, warring, solitary, hated by all, a universal pest, the creature who can do most harm and would like to do even more than it can'.

Exactly on the same grounds, the lion is appointed king of the animals. The poetic and emblematic glory of this beast is then ironically displayed. After this expression of intensest detestation, there follows a skilful build-up of the beetle into a credible opponent of the imperial bird. The two are well matched in the number of proverbial sayings and allusions, that is, in reputation.

Having portrayed the generals, Erasmus turns to the occasion of the war and recounts the fable, with his own elaborations, at leisurely length, embellishments that include a parody of lines from the *Aeneid*, allusions to other fables, and characteristically stinging comments: 'At this point the beetle, powerless to avenge himself, yet showed something regal in his behaviour . . . it was extermination and utter ruin that he was turning over in his mind'. Thus Erasmus turns this fable which comes rather casually to his attention into a *jeu d'esprit* which is perhaps the most bitter and biting exposure of tyranny ever written.

He defines the proverb 'Ollas ostentare', to make a show of kitchen pots, as 'to bring forward something which is ridiculous and squalid, but also of great importance', and likens it to the use of fables, which he defends, with that reference to Aulus Gellius mentioned above (p. 5). He then brings up his own *The Praise of Folly* as a jest which he threw off, without books, in a week, and which has won the full approval of people who know something about good literature. 'They say that as well as the fun of the jest there are many things in it which do more for the improvement of morals than the Ethics and Politics of Aristotle.' Like the fable as literature, this famous piece has the power to charm and please which feathers the arrows that fly to their targets. This piece and the *Colloquies* show the affinity of Erasmus with Lucian. He and More are, as it were, Renaissance friends and colleagues of Lucian, fellow-humanists. They translated him, and adopted his manner and method as part of their own literary equipment. (It is interesting that on the Louvain

Index of 1546, a list of permitted books includes *Fabulae Aesopae* and the works of Lucian; on the Louvain Index of 1550, the works of Erasmus are banned.) It is important to say here that Lucian did not have to wait for the Renaissance, and More and Erasmus, for a European public. He was much read and imitated in the eleventh and twelfth centuries. There is an anonymous satire of the mid-twelfth century, 'Timarion', modelled on him. Timarion descends into the underworld, and meets among others literary figures recently dead.

(ii)

In what sense, if at all, is *Utopia* (1516) a fable? The question has to be raised here because More's book excited great interest and was an example for more of the kind; and because modern images of a society – *Erewhon, Brave New World, Nineteen Eighty-Four* – will be treated as fables later in this study. It would be gratuitous to suppose that More owed his idea to *The True History*, for all his admiration of Lucian – whom the Utopians also enjoyed, when this was among the heap of Greek books which Master Raphael threw in on his fourth voyage; but it was Lucian's 'merry conceits and jests' they were delighted with. Indeed, there is something anti-Lucian in *Utopia*, because of More's earnest desire to carry conviction by verisimilitude in the setting of the tale; so that, as Chambers says, 'we can understand how the Vicar of Croydon came to take *Utopia* seriously' (R.W. Chambers: *Thomas More*, p. 123). The kind of incredible adventures which Lucian ridiculed in his fable are con-temptuously summarized to be dismissed in a sentence as of no interest, to underline the serious concern of the tale with good government, as practised elsewhere.

Portrayal of a society ideally constituted, a model, is a natural temptation in a literate and reflective culture. There were classical examples in Plato's *Republic* and Cicero's. Recovery of the New Learning and discovery of the New World at the time of the Renais-sance gave a new prompt and new credibility to a new kind of venture. *Utopia* was followed more than a century later by J.V. Andreae's *Christianopolis* (1620), Campanella's *Civitas Solis* (1623), and Francis Bacon's *The Fable of the New Atlantis* (1627). Andreae wrote a story in which Truth wanders round naked, complaining of ill-treatment at the hands of those whom she would like to assist. She is given advice by Aesop: 'Clothe your form in fable and fairy-tale, and you will be able to do your duty by God and man'. Since in most

of the hundred chapters of *Christianopolis*, after describing an aspect
of affairs as ordered in the city, he ended by making a violent contrast
with the world as he knew it, there was some reason at that time for
pleading fantasy; and there is a genuine use of fable for concealment.
But in the case of *Christianopolis* that hardly settles the point. There
is a sense in which *Utopia* was a 'Utopia' to end all 'Utopias', for the
concluding paragraphs indicate the conditions on which a 'commonwealth' in the literal sense, as described, could be a model: a society
without money or human beings without pride. More ends reasonably: 'I confess and grant that many things be in the Utopian weal
public, which in our cities I may rather wish for, than hope after.'
Andreae tackles the point head-on, but naively. Christians ought to
be different from the world around them, and the Gospel requires a
different government from that of the world: 'this merely denotes a
lack of serious attempts and a correct constitution of government,
since man is not really an untamable animal'. This implies that the
Kingdom of God can and should be established by good government, and is not what the Gospel suggests, not of this world.
Christianopolis is a village of about 400 citizens, under strict discipline wholly bound up with the belief, practice, and promise of
evangelical Christianity of a Protestant complexion (with hints from
Geneva). That is, it is written in a cause; and it is not the cause
of 'a correct constitution of government'. It is a 'Rosicrucian'
document.[13]

In sum, 'Utopias' are fantasy, not fable. The ironical general truth
they expose to thought is their impossibility. Bacon's *The Fable of
the New Atlantis* – never mind the title – is a special case, partly
because it was not completed as a portrayal of the constitution and
life of a community, and especially because of its practical influence
in connection with the foundation of the Royal Society. It has been
said that in many respects Bacon copied *Christianopolis* and, to more
purpose, that Andreae's ideas on education and plan for a college (the
centrepiece of *Christianopolis*) formed the foundation on which
Comenius built his 'Pansophia', with the idea of intercommunicating
colleges devoted to the promotion of universal learning. The basic
idea is in *New Atlantis*, but it was a different idea. Samuel Hartlib,
chief among several associates of Comenius in promoting these ideas
and tentative schemes, had written his own Utopia, *A Description of
the Famous Kingdome of Macaria* (1641). To systematize and
organize universal learning did not mean the same thing to Bacon and

to these others: they were at cross-purposes. Bacon's preoccupation was pre-eminently philosophic and methodological, with a long-term view to cumulative progress in basic research, 'to the relief of man's estate'. More than any other he was the progenitor of the Royal Society, and the revered forerunner to whom the *philosophes* of the Enlightenment looked back. The other group had a religious inspiration and orientation. They continually referred to natural science, for it dealt with the one divine cosmos, but they believed in illumination and in the teaching function of angels; and their methodologies had to do with immediate access to secret knowledge and belonged to an esoteric tradition, altogether other than Bacon's prospect of patient collaboration in the establishment of provisional, corrigible, progressive sciences.

Margery Purver, in her history, *The Royal Society* (1967), gives sixty lines to Bacon in the Index, which far exceeds any other entry; and she cites from *New Atlantis* Bacon's goal for his scientific society for collaboration:

> The End of our Foundation is the knowledge of Causes, and secret motions of things; and the enlarging of the bounds of Human Empire, to the effecting of all things possible. (p. 61)

Dr Frances Yates has stated that *New Atlantis* is full of Rosicrucian influence, and that Bacon's philosophy was largely drawn from the Renaissance Hermetic tradition (*Shakespeare's Last Plays: A new approach*, 1975, p. 103). Surely, this is a misunderstanding of Bacon's position. John Webster (1610–82), a Puritan writer who professed to follow Bacon in an attack on the Aristotelianism of the Universities, was himself one of those who wanted to combine the 'New Philosophy' with alchemical, astrological and occult ideas and practices, derived from medieval and contemporary writers, but he failed to understand the significance of Bacon's innovation (Purver, p. 65). He was like Comenius, who had turned to Bacon for the formula that would unlock nature at one stroke (the dream of the alchemists) and found only a method for systematic but laborious and age-long research (Purver, p. 207). Certain key Aphorisms in *Novum Organum* make Bacon's all-important insights clear: LXXXII and XCV–CVI, in which he outlines the method of moving from observations to axioms to be tested by devised experiment, in order to establish a hierarchy of axioms supporting one another. In four other

Aphorisms (LXXXVII, LXXXV, XLVI, CXVI) he makes very clear his own view of the claims of the occult sciences, of their limited successes, and of the reasons for their persistence; and states his own lack of interest in the speculative beliefs and extravagant hopes of the occultists. It is an explicit dissociation. In LXXXVI, he uses the fable of the father who bequeathed to his sons gold buried somewhere in a vineyard to account for actual discoveries and inventions of Alchemists. Nothing could more sharply distinguish such incidental finds from his own proposals for methodical and systematic production. He mentions the fable again in a judicious appraisal of 'astrology, natural magic, and alchemy' in the early part of *The Advancement of Learning*. More contemptuous is his rejection of occult sciences in the Second Book, and he likens the difference between them and empirical science to the difference between the story of King Arthur of Britain and Caesar's Commentaries. He adds this: 'Of this kind of learning the fable of Ixion was a figure, who designed to enjoy Juno, the goddess of power; and instead of her had copulation with a cloud, of which mixture were begotten centaurs and chimeras. So whatsoever shall entertain high and vaporous imaginations, instead of a laborious and sober inquiry of truth, shall beget hopes and beliefs of strange and impossible shapes.'

Dr Yates says that the truths of alchemy were thought to be hidden in the fables of the poets, especially Jason's Fleece and the Garden of Hesperides; and that the alchemical interpretation of myth was worked out in great detail by Michael Maier, the German Rosicrucian (p. 111). Bacon, in his interpretation of the myths, *De Sapienta Veterum*, follows in the main the well-established tradition (Macrobius, Boccaccio, Fulgentius). 'He wavered between thinking that the myths were so ancient, and sometimes so odd, that they must contain hidden meanings such as he discovered, and believing that the allegories were foisted upon them' (Charles W. Lenmi, *The Classical Deities in Bacon*, 1933). His empiricism is unmistakable in his interpretation of 'Pan':

> for that is the true philosophy which echoes most faithfully the voices of the world itself, and is written as it were at the world's own dictation; being nothing else than the image and reflexion thereof, to which it adds nothing of its own, but only iterates and gives back . . . That the world has no issue is another allusion to the sufficiency and perfection of it in itself . . . As for the little

woman, Iambe, Pann's putative daughter, it is an addition to the fable with a great deal of wisdom; for by her are represented those vain babbling doctrines about the nature of things, which wander abroad in all times and fill the world; doctrines barren in fact, counterfeit in breed, but by reason of their garrulity sometimes entertaining, and sometimes again troublesome and annoying.

In 'Proserpina', he explicitly repudiates Alchemy and its interpretations where they seem most plausible. In this game, there is not myth, allegory, nor fable.

Dr Yates and colleagues at the Warburg Institute have enabled students to appreciate the complex of ideas and ideals that inspired and informed a number of Renaissance thinkers, following Ficino and Pico in Florence; and to revalue their influence in successive phases of this period. In particular, Dr Yates's contribution to the history of ideas has been outstanding, and timely; but, as she herself admits, this has not involved a philosophical analysis of those ideas and their implications, which would expose incompatibilities where she tends to see compatibility, if not identity. Her repeated assimilation of Bacon to the movement she has studied so closely is not understandable: 'Francis Bacon's movement for the advancement of learning was closely connected with the German Rosicrucian movement, having a similar mystical and millennial outlook.' This is preposterous, or entirely baffling, for the two bodies of ideas belong to different universes of discourse. The concept of knowledge in the two is irreconcilably different, and so are the methodologies. Central to the difference also is the perception of imagination: cardinal in occult practice; outside the province of knowledge and utility in Bacon's classification. In sum, the empiricism of the one and the theosophy of the other are incompatible in presuppositions and in structural properties, and derive from different sources. Further references and observations are given in References and Sources for this chapter, under Renaissance Thinkers.

(iii)

Edmund Spenser has been shown to have been among those who were deeply influenced by Renaissance Neo-Platonism and its Cabala accretions. Recent detailed studies, using this background information, have provided clues to passages in *The Faerie Queene* that had always baffled literary historians; and sure-footed under-

standing of the making of Spenser's outlook and purpose in the
poem.[14] Before coming to Spenser's use of fable it is useful to turn to
another of his circle, Sir Philip Sidney, and consider his theory of
poetry. The *Apologie for Poetrie* (1595) has the extravagance, shrewd
insights and searching ideas of Shelley's *Defence*. Sidney's 'poetry' is
not merely verse, but mainly imaginative writing in its concreteness:
'that fayning notable images . . . with that delightful teaching which
must be the right describing note to know a Poet by'; a definition
which would include the Aesopic fable, as he recognizes. History, he
says, is tied to the particular truth of things from which there flow no
necessary consequences, not to the general reason of things. 'The
poet coupleth the general notion with the particular example . . . he
yieldeth to the powers of the mind an image of that whereof the
philosopher bestoweth but a wordish description which doth neither
strike, pierce, nor possess the sight of the soul so much as the other
doth'. Poetry is invention, not a borrowing imitation: 'the Poet
onely bringeth his own stuffe, and dooth not learne a conceite out of
a matter, but maketh matter for a conceite'. Again, fable is within the
scope of this. But the force of a similitude, he says, is not to prove
anything to anyone who would dispute it but merely to explain
something to a willing hearer. And the concreteness he is extolling is
ancillary in Plato, the philosopher he praises for his invention of
dialogue, the circumstantial detail of the encounters, and the inter-
laced tales and myths, as the one of Gyges' ring. There is, indeed, an
underlying contradiction. Poetry is the true and effective delightful
teaching of philosophy: 'it pleased the heavenly Deitie, by Hesiod
and Homer, under the vayle of fables, to give us all knowledge,
Logics, Rethorick, Philosophy, naturall, and morall'. On the other
hand, poetry is the skin, philosophy the inside. There is perhaps a
clue in the kind of philosophy by which Sidney, with Spenser and
others, was most influenced. For these Neoplatonists, both poet and
magus worked through images operating within the psyche, and
both attributed to imagination a divine function. Sidney says: 'those
most properly imitate to teach and delight who borrow nothing of
what is, hath been, or shall be: but range onely rayned with learned
discretion, into the divine consideration of what may be, and should
be'.

This philosophy had a pervasive and intensive concreteness, for it
was structured in terms of analogies and correspondences inherent in
the cosmos and reflected in architectural proportions and musical

harmonies, as in man and universe, microcosm and macrocosm. Its adepts deployed notations of numbers and of letters. Imagery was the basis of memory, assigning facts and ideas to places in some location. Condensed imagery, using emblems, symbols, diagrams, mandala packed into a single representation, as in John Dee's *Monas Hieroglyphica*, formed a 'magic parable', enabling the instructed concentrated mind to apprehend the cosmos in immediacy; or rather, to make the gnostic ascent to the One. Like ritual acts, this imagery was operational, a means of transformation and of manipulation. Thus the sensible image of the poet or other artist should reflect the immaterial world, correspond to and represent something in the cosmic structure. This defined the poetic or artistic vocation.

It is not to be supposed that Sidney was fully conversant with all this. His *Apologie* is a discursive statement, impressionistic and not thoroughly thought out – not philosophic. But some influence of the background thinking in the circle in which he moved is to be expected. His own attachment to the concrete was far from esoteric:

> for conclusion, I say the Philosopher teacheth, but he teacheth obscurely, so as the learned onely can understand him: that is to say, he teacheth them that are already taught, but the Poet is the foode for the tenderest stomacks, the Poet is indeed the right Popular Philosopher, whereof Esops tales give good proofe: whose pretty Allegories, stealing under the formall tales of Beastes, make many, more beastly than Beasts, begin to heare the sound of vertue from these dumbe speakers.

It can be added that fable is alien to the esoteric cosmic lexigraphy sketched above because of its essential perceptive and conceptual independence, truly philosophic.

(iv)

It is remarkable that Spenser, his imagination impregnated with allegory, a 'poet's poet', his language sensuous and passionate, inventively cadenced, his temper intensely serious, should have been the one English poet to produce a sustained fable, *Mother Hubberds Tale*, that recalled the forgotten *Renart* and carried the developed beast fable into the eighteenth century. He showed appreciative understanding of the comic satiric spirit in literature in 'the Teares of the Muses' (1591), in the voice of 'Thalia'. In *The Shepheardes*

Calendar, the 'Argument' for the month of February begins: 'This Aeglogue is rather morall and generall, then bent to any secrete or particular purpose' (which seems to be explicit recognition of the main difference between fable and allegory). The theme is scorn of the young for the old. 'To which purpose the olde man telleth a tale of the Oake and the Bryer, so lively and so feelingly, as if the thing were set forth in some Picture before our eyes, more plainly could not appeare.' The old shepherd who tells the tale feigns that he learned it from Chaucer, but, as noted in the Glosse, 'it is cleane in another kind, and rather like to Aesop's fables', providing an 'Icon or Hypotyposis of disdainful younkers'. The fifth, for May, is an argument between two shepherds who represent ministers of Protestant and Catholic persuasions. Piers, the Protestant, clinches his case against fellowship and trust between them with the fable of the Fox and the Kid, told by his mother not to open the door whilst she is away, but amended in this version to show what comes of yielding to plausible pretences. The Glosse gives a typically medieval allegorical detailed interpretation:

> By the Kidde may be understoode the simple sorte of the faithful and true Christians. By hys dame Christe, that hath alreadie with careful watchewords (as heere doth the gote) warned his little ones, to beware such doubling deceit. By the Foxe, the false and faithlesse Papistes, to whom is no credit to be given, nor fellowship to be used.

In 'Visions of the worlds vanitie' (1590), Spenser invents in ten stanzas separate images of ways in which the strong, the beautiful, the proud, the content, the rulers, the world's elect, come to grief at the hands of the weak, the small, the despised, the world's disregarded; all shown in what might be termed miniature elliptic fables, each an 'Icon or Hypotyposis', a vivid description to expose the differences of great and small in a true perspective and compose a meditation on that underlying pattern of things. In the fourth stanza the Eagle is outwitted and tormented by the Beetle, in lines which absurdly conflate two entirely different Aesopic fables, deforming both, when 'The Eagle and the Beetle' alone would have served the purpose perfectly.

The strange narrative which precedes the 'Visions' is 'Muiopotomos: or The Fate of the Butterflie'. This transforms a Greek myth of metamorphosis into allegory, to interpret the metamorphosis of Arachne into a spider by Athena as Arachne's self-transformation by envy and hatred into an ugly and venomous creature that plots destruction of the beautiful – a manoeuvre that allegorizes the myth by new invention, combining in practice the two senses in which 'allegory' is used, to interpret and to express.

Spenser's personal dedication, and the cast of mind formed in him, are intensely felt in the 'Fowre Hymnes' (1596). The last two were written to retract and reform the two more youthful hymns in honour of Love and Beauty, idealized although they were. The pair of pairs might be termed Platonic and Neo-Platonic. The last, 'An Hymne of Heavenly Beautie', although set in the fervent language of Christian redemption in Protestant terms, introduces *Sapience* in the bosom of the Deity, to wear the crown and bear the sceptre of sovereignty. This startling appearance is an intrusion into the Trinity of *Noûs*, second of the Three Initial Hypostases of Plotinus (Ennead V.1.7.10). In another poem, Spenser identifies *Sapience* with Apollo's wit, progenitor of the Muses. (Apollo, the one god whom Pythagoras is said to have worshipped, was in name, according to Plotinus, a symbol among the Pythagoreans of the negation of plurality, the One, V.5.6). This allegorical *Sapience* in so different contexts manifests that syncretic aspiration of the Renaissance theosophic movement inspired pre-eminently by Pico and his studies, in which Spenser and his friends participated, and had a more general precedent in the medieval practice of using Greek mythology to express concepts of Christian faith.

The puritan moralist had also personal grievances and strong political views, all three reflected in heroic couplets of 1388 lines, *Mother Hubberds Tale*, revised and published in 1591. The fable is an independent invention, influenced by the *Renart* stories (probably in Caxton's translation, *The History of Reynard the Fox*), and in manner by Chaucer. He adopts a 'low' style, suitable to the 'matter meane', after the brief opening frame story.

The Fox and the Ape, resolved for want of better fortune to live by their wits, set off on their travels – a picaresque theme. It is a perfect partnership in villainy, like linked with like, but with complementary aptitudes in mischief: the schemes and devices of the Fox get them into and out of trouble; the Ape plays the parts he is given with his own shallowness and effrontery, indulging his appetites and caprices. After deceiving and plundering a farmer they go on flagrantly to despoil a parish, as priest and clerk. Then, encountering a Mule, they are advised to try their fortune at court; in which they succeed well enough until Reynold overreaches himself and is banished. The Ape cannot shift for himself with any countenance and success, and is derided 'Like as a Puppit placed in a play,/Whose part once past all men bid take away.' He runs away and rejoins the Fox. The fable then takes a new turn. They discover the Lion asleep in the shade. He had laid aside his crown and sceptre, and his skin, all quietly usurped by the pair. It is soon settled which shall wear the crown, since by nature the Fox provides the shifts and pulls the strings, and on these terms Reynold is prepared to let the other ape the monarch. He remarks in the brief dispute that the Ape is counterfeit man in shape, the Fox in wits. (The Fox or Ape is the image with which the counterfeit philosophers are to be branded in Lucian's *The Fisherman*, above, p. 29) There follows in the forest an interregnum of outrageous arbitrary rule, until Jove is moved to intervene. Mercury awakens the sleeping Lion, who returns to his court. The chase secures the Ape, who loses his tail and has his ears cropped – which ends the fable with a parody of aetiological myth.

Although the fable gives scope for 'secret and particular purposes' political and personal, including the plight of court suitors like himself, and seventy-six lines are devoted to his portrait of the ideal Courtier, the general theme is exposure of behaviour in response to conditions at Court and in Church and State. At the core, and throughout the narrative, the characters and relations of Fox and Ape represent personal characteristics which in combination can be plausible and corrupting, and with opportunity can make the rules and apply the sanctions in a regime of total spoliation and terror. This is authentic fable. However insignificant may have been its direct practical effect – and it seems to have worsened his own fortune and prospect – as a literary performance it made an impression, and was not forgotten.

(*v*)

Some two years later a narrative poem was published of comparable length, incomparably different, which can also be considered as a fable. Shakespeare's *Venus and Adonis* is generally considered the first public performance of a poetic virtuoso, the story a mere excuse for the poetry. Closer examination may justify a different judgement, and one that is shared. Without calling it a fable, J.W. Lever, in a paper on 'Shakespeare's Narrative Poems' (*New Companion to Shakespeare Studies*, ed. Kenneth Muir and S. Schoenbaum, 1971), uses a term uniquely descriptive of fable, 'fictional paradigm'. 'Ovid's tales', he remarks of the new interest in them of the Elizabethan poets,

> presented a virginal world without history or morality. It was inhabited by figures who were creatures of impulse embodying divine or natural forces, archètypes rather than many-sided human beings. Their pursuits, flights, ardours and recoils not so much reflected as prefigured the behaviour of social man . . . In this realm of myth the springs of human experience could be descried and mapped out with a clarity no other medium could provide.

Perhaps this applies to Spenser's use of myth in 'Muiopotomos: or The Fate of the Butterflie'. But to construe Shakespeare's poem as allegory fails because of the generality of reference. Commentators have noted and stressed, as Coleridge did, the poet's detachment, his contemplative stance, the cognitive orientation, the ironic incongruities, culminating in Venus's identification with the boar, the embodiment of destruction:
He thought to kiss him, and hath kill'd him so.
  In form the poem is an aetiological myth: the Queen of Love in ultimate frustration lays a curse on love. The poem is a representation, not an explanation, but it is as an aetiological myth that it can be used to make a representation of the antinomies of love. Venus embodies the unrestrainable biological force in its human and transcendent form, speaking for itself and abiding no refusal. Adonis is the foil, in two senses. His horse expresses the masculine and animal form of this force, and recalls the *Georgics* and Lucretius. The boar is Time, and events more deadly and indifferent than that. Venus's curse or prophecy foretells the story of love in all human experience. If this myth, so handled, prefigures rather than reflects the behaviour of social man, it also prefigures Shakespeare's treatment of and responses to the antinomies and ambivalences implicit in the themes of human experience handled in the 'living labour of a play'.
  The continuous freshness of the poem in the smooth flow of poetic eloquence absorbs the reader in delight and covers the structural build-up of an image of polar tension within the human experience of love, exposed in the unresolved opposition between the obsessive

vehemence of Venus and the counterforce in the words and acts of
Adonis and the event that robs her of him altogether: a crystal
generality, rudely splintered by Venus in her prophetic curse. All this
makes the suggestion that the story is a mere excuse for the poetry too
hasty to take seriously. It is not a human story; it is the human story.
As a fable it is unique, within no convention and without precedent.
The myth on which it depends is disregarded for the myth it is, and
adapted for a special purpose. The young poet, for the ages to come,
breaks the medieval mould of the Allegory of Love, the courtly
masque.

The mask

Applying her studies of Renaissance Neo-Platonism, and the Rosicrucian movement in particular, to a consideration of Shakespeare's
last plays, Frances Yates asks: 'Dare one say that this movement
reaches a peak of poetic expression in *The Tempest*, a Rosicrucian
manifesto infused with the spirit of Dee, and using (like Andreae)
theatrical parables for esoteric communication?' Or elsewhere: Prospero is a symbol of the magical Renaissance philosophy; 'Its bold
affirmation of that philosophy makes *The Tempest* almost a Rosicrucian manifesto' (*The Occult Philosophy in the Elizabethan Age*,
1979, p. 171).

What dare one say about *The Tempest*, indeed? In traditional form
it is a romantic pastoral tragi-comedy, but there is little that is
traditional about it. Critics have been forced to say that it is extraordinarily secretive, deliberately enigmatic, truly 'Delphic', that it
invites conjecture. Accordingly, it has been a gigantic metaphor, a
latter-day myth, an allegory; or else autobiography – or a Rosicrucian manifesto. Others have been moved to take up its unfinished
business, or play their own game with its images or dramatis personae. The play cannot be taken merely as a play, a bout of entertainment, because it contains also ideas essential to the action and the
text, and a concentrated design and construction not necessary to the
amusement and illusion of the boards. If one stays with the play, one
is not merely invited but mainly forced into conjecture. Involved is
not only what Shakespeare meant, but also what the possibilities of
the play are.

It has been felt to have some of the character of an allegory. In that case, the text is assumed to have an esoteric meaning, coded or unconscious, and the interpretation is anybody's game; since it is not manifestly an allegory. It has been felt to have something of the character of a myth. The invention of Caliban, the supernatural agencies on the island, the compression of the plot: such elements as these might suggest the making of a myth. But the play could not function as a myth unless what it represented had a popular hold, which all the legacy of puzzlement consistently denies in the most positive practical way.

Arguments on similar lines might be used against a claim that it is a fable; and in any case it is a dramatic work, not narrative. However, it is fiction, apparently invented for a serious purpose, and the chief agents of the action are in no sense ordinary. Anyhow, to try to analyse it as if it were a fable might be instructive. The plot is the first thing to attend to in a fable for its indication of the central reference, the area isolated for exposure to thought. The plot, as distinct from the action, begins with the usurpation of the dukedom by Prospero's brother, and ends with Prospero's prospective restoration. Or the plot begins with Prospero's absorption in the acquisition of his Art, and ends with his renunciation of it. The action begins with Prospero's deployment of his Art in the tempest which brings into his hands his destroyers and his benefactor, and initiates the project to be enacted on the island, which he rules *de facto* since cast away from the realm he ruled only *de jure*. The action ends with the consummation of this project. Two counter-projects are initiated, the intention of Antonio and Sebastian to kill and supplant Alfonso, Caliban's conspiracy with Stephano and Trinculo to kill and supplant Prospero: both foiled in the light of Prospero's 'simultaneous knowledge of all that happens' on his island. Jung has likened dreams to a theatre in which one plays all the parts, and is responsible for the script and the direction: all the material and the machinery of the production is one's own. (Compare Addison's 'On Dreams', on 'that wonderful power in the soul . . . She is herself the theatre, the actor, and the beholder'.) Prospero the magician is almost the dreamer, and the play a dream, but not quite: the counter-projects are not of his devising. Subject to all his powers, the natures and will of others remain their own as Deity itself requires for a terrestrial plot. The island is a bewildering mixture of dream and reality, as all the newcomers find.

With the usurper and his confederate so completely in Prospero's hands, restoration of the dukedom is *ipso facto* achieved, the story is ended. However, the project is a moral one: to bring the wrongdoers to penitence, face to face with themselves, so that with restitution reconciliation and renewal are also possible. To this end, they are to be teased and tried. The pattern of response to this almighty mobilization of spirit powers is a moral commonplace: the better part of human nature, and the worse, do their work. Prospero's intervention on his own behalf, as if distanced by his studies and become disinterested, enacts within the hours of the action an anticipation of a theodicy: 'The powers, delaying, not forgetting . . .' Prospero identifies himself with this divine providence, shares in that power, and dispenses it. Gonzalo delivers the moral outcome in saying that all of them have found themselves, 'When no man was his own' (V, i, 212, 130).

However, here the enigmas begin. Prospero's usage of Caliban is harsh and predatory, justify it as he does. Caliban's wretched conspiracy becomes a sorry farce; he and his degraded agents are tricked and teased, harried and hounded, baited and plagued, exposed in a squalid operation in which Prospero is himself directly active. Prospero consistently overreaches himself: as Duke of Milan, as brother, as father, as master; even as mage, he is choleric or peevish (the 'bad-tempered giant-magician' of fairy-story). This could be the brittleness of aspiration to absolute ideals, in Prospero to spiritual knowledge and power. There is no innocence, neither in nature nor in pre-eminent virtue. Prospero's project is achieved, but there is disillusionment: in Prospero's speech that abruptly dismisses the masque, and in the Epilogue, which he speaks.

The moral project is the core of the action, motored by magic. Prospero and Caliban outstay the play. 'Caliban has not yet been thoroughly fathomed', remarked De Quincey more than a century ago. Imaginative operations on both parties continue. The setting deserves equal attention with the actors. The time was the eve of colonization, a time of encounters with strange peoples, subject of speculations and experiment. 'Colonization and transatlantic adventure meant much to the writer of *Utopia*' (Chambers, p. 142). Touched off by Gonzalo's fancy of what he would do as colonizer of the isle (II, 1), there is implied reference to a stock source, Montaigne's essay 'Des Cannibales' (I, xxx). More relevant to the realities of the relation between Prospero and Caliban is Bacon's essay 'Of Plantations'. His knowing schoolmasterly manner in this piece is in character; less so is the want of open-eyed perception of the facts of life, as in matters he did know about. The natives are to be taken into partnership, and leavened with an elect few who should be brought to see for themselves their fortunate destiny in the mirror of the motherland. This copybook conclusion is at a safe distance from the contagions and compulsions on location. On the island, Prospero and Caliban brew immiscible elements of human nature and culture, in prophecy of plantations to come.

Prospero, in line, assumed the title of lord of the island on which he had set foot, the usurped usurped. Caliban its inhabitant, at first the welcoming and admiring hospitable native, becomes in the sequel a resentful outraged slave, once his own king. Prospero, frustrated as missionary, is anyhow master, and becomes dependent for services (his magic has no efficacy here within the artifice of the plot): 'we cannot miss him', and 'he serves in offices that profit us'. Caliban, continuously and vehemently unwilling and rebellious, coerced and punished, conspires to end it and regain his liberty: in the dream of that emancipation, he cries 'Freedom! Freedom!' a word that cannot be denied. Of course, Caliban has grossly offended, and has justified suspicion and safeguards, but his nature and his lot are locked in incongruity and inevitability that anticipate the pastoral tragi-comedy of colonial exploitation: the mutual enslavement through double dependence, ultimately destructive, ultimately productive, the tangled theme of colonial history, still unfinished business.

Prospero's magic raises other questions, extraneous to the theme of this study. Perhaps, because of extravagant claims, it is worth remarking on the discrepancy between those early studies of the liberal arts for 'the bettering of my mind' to which he dedicates himself to the neglect of 'worldly ends' – and the responsibilities of his office – and the 'rough magic' on the island, which is dispensable when it has served to accomplish his project – more like the magic of Lucian's fiction.

In sum, *The Tempest* is not an insubstantial pageant that dissolves and leaves not a rack behind: it transcends the theatre. As Anne Righter says of the Epilogue, at the end of her Introduction to the Penguin edition: 'The effect is to suggest that the play goes on beyond the formal limits of its fifth Act, that it runs into and shares the reality of its audience'. It will continue to serve, and slip, many minds in production and on the page. To say that Prospero's relationship with Caliban sets up outside a model that prefigures the colonial future, a model that concentrates for thought inner necessities in the way things are: to say that is in effect to excerpt from the play a fable, probably not intended, but implicit in a perceived truth. In some support, the final sentence of Jan Kott's essay 'Prospero's Staff': 'If on Prospero's island the history of the world has been performed, then Caliban's history is a chapter from the history of mankind'.[15]

(ii)

Ben Jonson's *Volpone* (1605) is first and last a stage play, but the fabric is dyed in Aesopic juices and the pattern a Lucianic theme, which gives some colour to a mention in a study of fable: at least, the play is witness to the fable in literature.

The Aesopic fable is a continuous background, not merely reflected in the names of the chief character and his would-be heirs, and in direct allusions; for in these and other ways it remains the source for an image of human behaviour infused with the idea of non-human predators, vulpine and vulturine behaviour. The metaphor is enacted. The initial situation of feigned sickness of the Fox to get his prey into his power borrows from, or resembles, one of the most famous of the fables. A beast fable abstracts the portrayed behaviour from its human form and context to remove it from human associations and complexities. In *Volpone*, the 'clients' Voltore, Carbaccio, and Corvino are human beings, with professions, a son, a wife, but they behave simply as birds of prey, devoting all their human attributes and social resources to their common preoccupation with the pickings to be theirs with the rich carcass. All the others have some human traits, although Lady Would-Be, another hopeful, is described by Volpone as a she-wolf. The action of the three is abstracted from its human context by the extreme inhuman courses they are driven to by their lust for the Fox's gold; and by the shadows of their names which follow their words and deeds. The Fox himself maintains in his comments a reminder of the Aesopic background. He sets the scene:

> Now, now, my clients
> Begin their visitation! Vulture, kite,
> Raven, and gorcrow, all my birds of prey,
> That think me turning carcase, now they come;
> I am not for them yet.

He asks Mosca, his dependent parasite, what his first visitor has brought.

MOSCA: A piece of plate, sir.
VOLPONE: Of what bigness?
MOSCA: Huge,
     Massy, and antique, with your name inscribed,
     And arms engraved.
VOLPONE: Good! and not a fox
     Stretched on the earth, with fine delusive sleights,
     Mocking a gaping crow?

At the end, in the last Act, when he has disillusioned his predators and pursued them in the streets in disguise to mock and savour their chagrin ('Oh, I will be a sharp disease unto them'), he taunts Corvino:

A witty merchant, the fine bird, Corvino,
That have such moral emblems on your name,
Should not have sung your shame, and dropt your cheese,
To let the Fox laugh at your emptiness.

The Fox himself is an indolent sensualist, and the ruses and cunning are all the work of his parasite, Mosca. (Why keep a dog, and bark yourself?) But if Volpone lacks the resources of Renart, and the attraction, he is essentially an old schemer and revels in discomfitures above all. As he says at the end of the first scene, 'Letting the cherry knock against their lips,/And draw it by their mouths, and back again'. It is his prime delight to mock and jeer, to frustrate and deride. He is as preoccupied with this perversity as his predators with theirs, a predator of his own sort. The fox in the fable usually has the laugh, as he did on the gullible crow. The Fox in the play will give or risk anything to have the laugh.

Samuel Richardson, in his *Aesop's Fables* (1740), remarks in his Reflections on 'A Man turned into a Pismire': 'By the poetical fictions of men turned into the shape of beasts and insects, we are given to understand, that they do so effectually make themselves so, when they degenerate from the dignity of their kind: So that the metamorphosis is in their manners, not in their figure.' A gratuitous remark perhaps in regard to an Aesop's fable; but it can be applied to

Jonson's play, to justify the sense in which it is shown here that Jonson was in business on a draft from Aesop.

Cultural conditions

From the seventh century, there were sporadic attempts by Christian scholars to preserve and reproduce what could be obtained of classical literature, and to cultivate the liberal arts. One of the more illustrious of these schools was the Academie palatine at the court of Charlemagne, promoted by Alcuin, the probable milieu for the recovery or production of the *Aesopus ad Rufum*, mainly a paraphrase of *Phaedrus* and lost source of the many medieval collections and versions. Medieval habits of mind, heavily dependent on images and concrete representations, would seem to make the climate of the time a natural habitat for the Aesopic fable. This was not really so, for two main reasons. The essential independence of fable was not generally respected; it was commonly allegorized to make it assimilable to the teaching and preaching of the Church; although the text remained in use for linguistic exercises in the schools. To make a collection deliberately available as a treasured legacy of ancient wisdom, as Marie de France did, was exceptional. Most important: in the contexts of the time, meanings were not mainly generated or conveyed by comparisons and metaphors as in poetry (or fable); rather, they were charged with and carried by symbolic references. The universe was a system of connections, correspondences, analogies, so that one thing represented or called up another, with a lack of distinctions or with reference to established symbolic structures. Allegory was the core of imagination, and mental operations and expression tended to be in terms of allegories and parables. The schools positively cultivated a passion for symbolism and scenic representation, so that pupils would continue their interest in learning through miracle, mystery, and morality plays and interludes. All this concreteness favoured the profusion of allegory that obtained: all was multiple and diverse manifestation of the one central divine truth. Fable, as novel representations initiating independent thought, had to wait its season for development.

The exception to this lack of opportunity was in the serio-comic adaptability of the Aesopic fable as it was developed in the *Roman de Renart*. A time of experiment in fiction has been more than once an opportunity for fable. The *chansons de geste* were near the end of the road in heroic verse and its themes, time for a mock version. The poets of the new romances have been called 'the sophists of medieval literature' (W.P. Ker), emancipated and enlightened, and it was such as they who could turn a hand to such an available subject as was offered by *Renart*. After that, Odo was able to invent and use fables to expose what was often in Church and State.

Of course, it would be crude to suppose that the population was sunk in mindless imagery and associated connections, incapable of entertaining and deploying ideas. By the end of the thirteenth century, philosophy had established an independent foothold in the University of Paris and in other seats of learning. There were historic achievements: the dialectic virtuosity of Abelard, the imposing architecture of Aquinas, permanently mined by Occam. These were altitudes. At more habitable levels there were common assumptions, general impressions, stock information, daily discourse, established platitudes of the age; and this was a climate in which allegory flourished. Also: 'No medieval thinker set out like Descartes or Kant to build from experience' (David Knowles).

It is now a commonplace of history that Middle Ages and Renaissance merge with far fainter distinction than was thought and taught when the term was the New Learning, or the Revival of Learning. All the same, the period is marked both by the Protestant division and disintegration of Christendom, and by a fuller apprehension and reworking of the classical models that made a new beginning and introduced new standards, but not everywhere, nor at once. The invention of printing enabled entrepreneurs to bring together in a few of the famous printing-houses intellectuals with different skills and interests under a form of patronage independent of court and university. (Cultural revolutions are brought about by a happy conjunction of independent developments–conspicuously in the Industrial Revolution.) Accumulated recent research on the movement initiated by the Florentine Neo-Platonists may tend to obscure the Neo-Aristotelian studies at Padua. More permanent than either was the humanism derived from an entirely other Pierian spring from which Petrarch drank deep in Cicero: the educational discipline initiated by Isocrates in opposition to Plato, a discipline in the art of discourse, and therewith in thinking, exercised on themes drawn from poetry, history, and moral philosophy. This humanism, inherited and practised by Lucian and taken up by Erasmus, was the lineage that produced Milton of the 'Areopagitica': 'Give me the liberty to know, to utter, and to argue freely according to conscience, above all liberties'; the liberty of prophesying that breaks dogmatic moulds.

It is in the broadest sense only that cultural conditions may be said to be favourable to fable, or unfavourable. For it is not a conventional form of writing, like pastoral, or indeed allegory. It is occasioned, and therefore occasional. What gives it identity and purchase, and links its examples, is not merely certain characteristics, but mainly its anchorage in the Aesopic fable, which is a convention. This is the stock resource, drawn on and developed in different ways at different times for different purposes, personal, public, and literary. This prototype and the several inventions it has inspired and aided are there when occasion demands this independent way of thinking and speaking. There has to be the liberty of prophesying. The fragmentation of Christendom, the need for toleration, the inspiration and example of recovered and studied ancient classics, brought this period of European history to that threshold.

3   Olympians at Play

Aesop used and abused

Samuel Croxall published *Aesop's Fables* (a selection of 196) in 1722.
He gave this justification for a new edition:

> Nothing of this Nature has been done, since Lestrange's time,
> worth mentioning; and we had nothing before, but what (as he
> observes) was so insipid and flat in the Moral, and so coarse and
> uncouth in the Style and Diction, that they were rather dangerous
> than profitable, as to the Purpose for which they were principally
> intended: and likely to do forty times more Harm than Good.

The purpose for which they were principally intended was for the
instruction of children, who, being as it were mere blank paper, are
ready for any opinion, good or bad, taking all upon credit; and 'it is
in the power of the first comer to write Saint or Devil upon them'.
Croxall endorsed this assertion, and all the more for that he abhorred
the odious principles L'Estrange had used his Aesop to instil: to
promote the growth and serve the ends of Popery and Arbitrary
Power. There was not one fable nor so much as a hint to favour such
insinuations, Croxall insisted, for Aesop recommends liberty and
abhorrence of Tyranny and all arbitrary proceedings. There was
therefore a wrong to be righted. His volume is dedicated to the infant
Baron Halifax, who at the age of four is capable of reading anything
in the English tongue, without the least hesitation:

> These fables, My Lord, abound in Variety of Instruction, Moral
> and Political. They furnish us with Rules for every Station of Life:
> they mark out a proper Behaviour for us, both in respect of
> ourselves and others; and demonstrate to us, by a Kind of
> Example, every Virtue which claims our best Regards, and every
> Vice which we are most concerned to avoid.

Such instruction will teach the noble lord to love and pursue Honesty
and Benevolence, to the great satisfaction of his country. And if the
Fables themselves should be insufficient, there are of course the
editor's own 'Applications'.

The 'Raptures' with which it is alleged the Ancients spoke of
Aesop, and with which the editor speaks of his fables, sound fainter
in the final 'Application to the Whole', by way of Epilogue:

> It is not expected that they who are versed and hackneyed in the
> Paths of Life, should trouble themselves to peruse these little loose
> Sketches of Morality; such may do well enough without them.
> They are written for the Benefit of the Young, and the Unexperi-
> enced.

Less than mindful of the principal intention of fables, and of his
special regard for the education of the infant Halifax, the author of
the 'Applications' is engaged with the manners and opinions of his
contemporaries from the point of view of an Anglican cleric and
Whig. In 'The Country-Mouse and the City-Mouse', the Country-
Mouse is honest, plain and sensible, and shows these qualities in
entertaining a childhood's acquaintance, now a spark of the town,
who cannot understand how his old playfellow can bear to listen only
to the chirping of birds instead of the conversation of the World, or
to look on the rude aspect of the wild instead of the splendour of a
Court. 'The Mice in Council' is applied against government by
coffee-house politicians. 'The Ape and the Fox', in which the Fox
grudges any contribution from his sweeping brush to cover the Ape's
bare behind, starts reflections on the lottery of the world, some
having more than they know what to do with, others less than they
need for a tolerable life, and all without justification in deserts. This is
the disposition of Providence, beyond our understanding, but to a
human way of thinking things obviously might be ordered better.
Thus the Archdeacon of Shropshire mounts Aesop to counter
L'Estrange, and bring support to juster opinions and nobler causes.

Some twenty years later Samuel Richardson gave his justification
for a new edition of the Fables, 240 of them. The title-page reads:

> *Aesop's Fables.* With Instructive Morals and Reflections,
> Abstracted from all Party Considerations, Adapted to all Capaci-
> ties; and designed to promote Religion, Morality, and Universal
> Benevolence.

Of all the many editions in English, he considered only two worthy
of notice: 'that of the celebrated Sir Roger L'Estrange, and that which

appears under the name of S. Croxall'. He then examines the Prefaces of these two predecessors. Sir Roger had begun with attention to the 'common school book, as it stands in the Cambridge and Oxford editions of it', proposing to turn 'an excellent Latin manual of morals and good counsels, into a tolerable English one'. In proceeding, he found he had to consult other versions, and to prune and amend the old school book. He ended with 383 fables, to which he made 'a considerable addition of other select Apologues, out of the most celebrated Authors that are extant upon that subject'. Having said that the fables are universally taught in school, but in a routine way, learning the words by heart without any application, or with one that is 'infinitely short of the vigour and spirit of the fable', and that several English paraphrases in prose and verse had not helped matters, he had shown that he intended his version to be a good English text, with the moral meant; and he left 'the whole world to take the same freedom with me, that I have done with others'.

Turning to Croxall, Richardson deprecated his depreciation of Sir Roger's work, which 'seems to be the cornerstone of his own building'. He doubted if Sir Roger actually was a Papist, but shared the objection to his politics, allowing the excuse of a different age. In the upshot, Richardson recognized and wished to preserve the English version of Sir Roger, and to do this in an edition which reduced the excessive and costly bulk of the original, and corrected the bias of his opinions by giving them a more general turn.[1]

Thus Aesop; rescued in school and kept in general circulation. There were other well-known editions, particularly John Ogilby's verse translation (1668), with plates by Wenceslaus Hollar, which Pope had – and of which there is a copy in the library of Hawkshead School, where Wordsworth was educated. Pope thought L'Estrange excellent in his fable-style. John Locke was one of the warmest enthusiasts for Aesop as educator (*Some Thoughts Concerning Education*, 1693), and he produced a version in Latin and English, interlined, as an easy introduction to the acquirement of either language.

Croxall showed how to keep the fables alive by using them to make political points or satirical comment, or to initiate a train of reflection. Richardson, anxious to rescue Aesop from the politician and the pedagogue, and restore generality to the fables, smothered 'the vigour and spirit of the fable' in long sententious Reflections. To make it safe, he would keep it from particular use. The generality of fable is in continual surprising and telling applications to topical particulars.

New numbers

Fables were invented for his own day and age by John Gay. In 1726, he undertook to write a volume of fables for the improvement of the young Duke of Cumberland. He was not more noticeably confined by this pedagogic purpose than his predecessors had been. His fables were popular, and a second volume was published posthumously. There were fifty in the first volume, seventeen in the second. They 'survey mankind' in the Aesopic tradition, but in the manner of Gay and bearing on the faults, failings, follies and complaints of the day, as Thurber was to do in his own manner in a later far different age. The verses are consistently smooth, with happy turns of thought and of phrase, entertaining the ear and the mind, whether or not the point is taken to heart. The early eighteenth century was more given to raillery and ridicule than to the weighty pronouncements of the previous generation. Fops and pedants were particular and equal objects of derision. Both were extravagant manifestations of what was socially esteemed, fashion and literature; and the fable was a homely vehicle that would conveniently carry ridicule. 'The Two Monkeys' divides the world into these two, fops and pedants, engaged in ridiculing each other, both sides equally conceited and self-deceiving; the moral is applied in the fable that follows.

Gay is particularly skilful with allegory, liable to be the most insipid device. Vice makes a match with a travelling juggler to beat him at his own game, the sleight of hand that deceives the eye. After watching the exploits of Vice, her victims of many kinds deceived by what they see and desire, the juggler sadly submits:

> How practice hath improv'd your hand!
> But now and then I cheat the throng;
> You every day, and all day long!

Most of the fables in the first volume are invented to make their point, and left to speak for themselves. In the second volume, the fables are longer and more in the Horatian and contemporary Augustan manner of familiar satires, then duly translated into or illustrated by a fable. Many of these are political, aimed at the new race of manipulators and managers and projectors, as well as arrogant and incompetent officials. But old themes reappear. Plutus, Cupid and Time encounter one another in the park and, after the usual compliments, walk together, conversing on various topics till they get on to 'what each has done for man'. The preface, before they are brought on, is taken up with every day's examples of the slow torture of boredom. The conclusion:

> That Time, when truly understood,
> Is the most precious earthly good.

This is deeply perceptive, and the whole piece is a refreshing variation on the old theme of contests in terms of 'what each has done for man'.

Another hackneyed theme of the fables, complaining of one's lot, is redeemed by Gay's own blend of lightness and pathos in one dedicated 'To a Poor Man'. A lively young dog employed as a turnspit runs off in the midst of preparations for dinner, and the distracted cook runs out and calls after him. He skulks out of reach, deploring his menial task and envying the employments of happier breeds. A great ox who overhears gives him a lesson: in his own case, he has to endure the goad and unremitting toil, with a prospect ('Perhaps the hour's not far away') that brings his fortune home to the unwilling little dog:

> You, by the duties of your post,
> Shall turn the spit when I'm the roast;
> And for reward shall share the feast;
> I mean – shall pick my bones at least.

Man as exploiter and destroyer on a great scale appears in these beast fables as the worst of animals, and hypocritical, consuming (though shepherd) vastly more sheep than the wolf. But the line is exposure, not judgement. This is Gay, not Swift.

The last of the Fables, 'Aye and No', is an ingenious little squib:

> In fable all things hold discourse;
> Then words, no doubt, must talk of course.

The two hostile particles are not concerned with the grammar of opposition, by which they are kinsfolk, but with verbal wars in Parliament, the courts, and ecclesiastical controversy, in which they are enrolled by convention. AYE sets it all forth in a disarming speech, and all ends with a hit at venal votes:

Thus AYE propos'd – and, for reply,
No, for the first time, answer'd AYE.
They parted with a thousand kisses,
And fight e'er since for pay, like SWISSES.

This fable, although the last of the posthumously published second volume, had been included in the Miscellanies in Verse which, with Miscellanies in Prose, were collected and published in 1727 by Pope, with the acquiescence if not collaboration of Swift. These collections of officially unpublished pieces by these two and Arbuthnot and Gay, the principal Scriblerians, put foremost *The Art of Sinking in Poetry*, which developed into the *Dunciad*, and was in any case the most grandiose project undertaken by or under the inspiration of Martinus Scriblerus, the Don Quixote of learning. This treatise on 'Bathos', with abundant specimens, reduced to rule the practice of pretentiousness and ineptitude in poetical composition, and was followed by four other exhibitions of the erudition of the great polymath. Gay's versatile talents were stimulated in this school of wit and high-spirited emulation among friends. His *Fables* are smoother in tone, if not in verse, and more generalized than the occasional pieces in the Miscellany. *The Beggar's Opera* is an inspired medley, which had been paraded in a ballad in the Miscellany 'Newgate's Garland'. The mafia-like interdependence of government and underworld was a topical relationship that modernized 'renardie'.

Swift appreciated the *Fables*, and wrote to Gay when they were published: 'there is no writing I esteem more than fables, nor anything so difficult to succeed in, which, however, you have done excellently well, and I have often admired your happiness in such a kind of performance, which I have frequently endeavoured at in vain'. Of course, he was not thinking of *Gulliver*, which had just been published, but of his adaptations and applications of Aesopic fables (for instance, 'The Fable of the Bitches', 'The Lion and other Beasts', 'The Faggot', 'Dog and Thief'); and particularly of his own inventions, such as the 'Tale of a Nettle'. His diffidence was not justified in regard to his re-telling of old fables to apply them seriously to issues of the day, but his own inventions for the purpose were less effective. 'Desire and Possession' is not much better than Addison's allegory of Pleasure and Pain; and the 'Tale of a Nettle' is as lame – in the 'Bitches' he had adapted a fable of Phaedrus admirably to the same purpose. The best and most characteristic adaptation is 'The Beasts' Confession' (from La Fontaine's 'Les animaux malades de la peste'). This is applied to a very different purpose from the original (which he reproduced in 'The Lion and other Beasts'), and has an involved ending – which might indicate why Swift's muse did not constrain him to stoop to the directness and single-minded simplicity of the Aesopic fable. The longer deadly game of prose gave more scope to indulgence of his sportive wit. Of his poems altogether, Warton's judgement holds; he picked out 'On Poetry: a Rhapsody' and 'On the Death of Dr Swift'; the first is a mock *ars poetica* and a little dunciad of his own; the second, a masterpiece of wry reflection, heading into a full-blooded *apologia pro vita sua*. This alone is enough to register his accomplishment in verse.

And millions miss for one that hits.

A scandalous triumph

In 1705, some 400 lines of doggerel were printed under the title *The Grumbling Hive: or Knaves turn'd Honest*. This was the nucleus of Bernard Mandeville's famous, often thought infamous, *The Fable of the Bees*. In 1714 Mandeville reprinted them with a Preface, two essays ('An Enquiry into the Origin of Moral Virtue' and 'A Search into the Nature of Society'), and twenty-one annotations upon lines of the poem, many of these 'Remarks' running to the length of essays. A second volume followed of 'Dialogues' in which he further expanded and justified the ideas broached in *The Grumbling Hive*.

Thus *The Fable of the Bees* is in fact two volumes of argument in prose, in which received ideas on morality and society are sharply examined and a contrary view put forward and supported. In particular, the argument of Shaftesbury's *Characteristics* (1711) was controverted – that man is naturally a social animal whose feelings and propensities are benevolent and whose sense of right and wrong is innate. However, the original verses were in the form of a fable, and Voltaire was inspired by him to write 'Le Marseillais et le Lion'. Mandeville's early publications show his interest in the form: *Some Fables after the Easie and Familiar Method of Monsieur de la Fontaine* (1703) and *Aesop Dress'd or a Collection of Fables Writ in Familiar Verse* (1704). In his Preface to the expanded edition of 1714, he apologized for his 'story told in doggerel' which was 'rather too long for a fable', and which did not pretend to be witty or satirical. It seems that he wanted to provoke attention to a serious view unlikely to be well received. Having got attention, he could in sober prose and at length devote himself to explanation and justification. Before his death in 1733 there were six editions, and publication and translation continued during the century.

Extreme definitions ('virtue' = self-sacrifice; 'luxury' = in excess of subsistence) obtain extreme consequences, and it becomes easy to show that a 'virtuous' society is beyond the reach of the strictest religious order, and that the greatest happiness of the greatest number in a populous industrial society is obtained by virtue of human vices. This may be dismissed as a game of words – Mandeville said that he expected to be taken ironically, and read between the lines. What remains, however, is the stubborn fact of dependence on vanity, extravagance, waste and self-seeking in such a society to keep the wheels turning (even at the beginning of the eighteenth century), and the amount of general profit that may be derived even from rank dishonesty and flagrant vice, when the concatenations of the economy are exposed. The upshot of his contention is that if we want to enjoy the benefits of a plentifully endowed consumer society, we have to put up with 'the unacceptable face of capitalism' and other ugly features of an industrial system based on enterprise. He offers an early and crude cost-benefit analysis, and an early and crude social psychology. If everybody lived as moralists say they should, or as a few idealists perhaps do, the social system would collapse, and masses starve. *The Grumbling Hive* is not subversive, except of received opinions. On the contrary, it follows the pattern of those fables in which Jove heeds the complaints of a discontented species to their own detriment. The author does not want us to change our way of living; he wants us to change our way of thinking and speaking, to give up deceiving ourselves. He is orthodox in government and in economics, and even in morality, but contends that no society ever rose to power and prosperity, and maintained itself in that state, without human vices, particularly avarice and prodigality.

The argument still has relevance, and perhaps should be required reading along with David Riesman's *The Lonely Crowd* (1950). Dr Johnson, who rejected the premises and must have abhorred Mandeville's materialistic convictions, recalled that when he read the *Fable* as a young man he was impressed and made to think. Today, 'private vices, public benefits' is a coin which on the face is good currency, on the back the reverse: conspicuous consumption and built-in obsolescence are good for trade, bad for resources. Parkinson's law creates employment that generates unemployment. The war brought an end to the slump; massive welfare brings one about. There is still paradox wrapped in the tangle of economics – as in other social forms of profit and loss (*Brave New World*).

Mandeville's writing is vigorous, graphic and perspicacious, enlivened here and there by vignettes of the daily scene, like the 'characters' of one of the best of his critics, William Law, but far sharper and to the life. He was too anxious to be taken seriously to risk being consistently satirical, but could not forbear occasional ironical sallies. One of the longest and most amusing comes in 'Remark (T)', where he professes himself unable to resolve the contradictions between what is publicly prayed for and what all privately do, and illustrates the incomprehensibility of it in a parable which is a preposterous take-off of general hypocrisy. The 'Dialogues' are skilfully composed to amuse and to bring his views within the ambience of polite discussion, and get them voiced by the very people who have armed themselves against his reputation.

That reputation, as a heartless cynic, might be mended in the mind of anyone who took the trouble to read 'Remark (P)'. 'I have often thought,' he writes at one point, 'if it was not for this tyranny which custom usurps over us, that men of any tolerable good nature could never be reconciled to the killing of so many animals for their daily food, as long as the bountiful earth so plentifully provides them with the varieties of vegetable dainties.' After several pages on the subject, including a fable which is a dialogue between a lion and a castaway Roman merchant on an African shore, he ends with a paragraph of graphic detail on the fatting and slaughter of bullocks, and a final sentence of smouldering anger: 'When a creature has given such convincing and undeniable proofs of the terrors upon him, and the pains and agonies he feels, is there a follower of *Descartes* so inured to blood as not to refute, by his commiseration, the philosophy of that vain reasoner?' Man as the greatest predator of them all, a recurrent theme of beast fables.

'Persian' tales

Fables of the ancient Indian convention in Sanskrit, filtered through Persian and Arabic translations, as described above (p. 16), had been translated in the late thirteenth century into Latin by John of Capua. Thomas North put into English a 1552 Italian translation of this in 1570. There was a French translation of a later Persian version in 1644. This famous collection had circulation and revivals in Europe during this time, and was available to La Fontaine. The Arabs' mastery of Greek philosophy and their own original research and discoveries contributed early to the revival of learning in Europe. At a popular level *The Dictes and Sayings of the Philosophers*, the first book printed by Caxton, was a translation by Earl Rivers of a French version of a Latin recast of an Arabic collection of the eleventh century, a pot-pourri of mainly Greek philosophical teaching, but workmanlike and useful. Reinforcement in the seventeenth and eighteenth centuries of acquaintance with the ancient Indian apologue through the Arabic connection was accompanied by a new interest in oriental narrative. This was awakened by the French translation of *The Arabian Nights* by Antoine Galland in 1704. Hundreds of editions have been published since in all European languages. At the time, the immense popularity produced the *Persian Tales* and then the *Turkish Tales*, which revived the ancient Arabic *Book of Sinbad*, derived from a Sanskrit original.

In Spence's *Anecdotes*, Pope says: 'After reading the *Persian Tales* (and I had been reading Dryden's *Fables* just before them), I had some thought of writing a Persian Fable, in which I should have given a full loose to description and imagination. It would have been a very wild thing if I had executed it, but might not have been unentertaining.' This remark gives force to Professor Gibb's summing up at the end of a useful survey of the influence of Arabic literature in Europe (*The Legacy of Islam*, 1931). He suggests that the impact worked as a leaven at a time ready for experiment, a release of imagination in response to a new readership. But he is surely mistaken in suggesting that 'but for the *Nights* there would have been no *Robinson Crusoe*, and perhaps no *Gulliver's Travels*'. As far as Swift is concerned, he had Rabelais in his pocket and Lucian in mind. Addison and Johnson were among the hosts of imitators, though briefly, in the *Rambler* and the *Spectator*.[2] Although Johnson would not have thought of *Rasselas* as a 'fable', when he came to write it in haste and in need, it had been amply rehearsed in these occasional papers prompted by the vogue of the Eastern apologue and other oriental tales. It was Voltaire who by the occasions of his need restored the Indian fable to its ancient purpose, and instituted the modern 'conte philosophique'.

The Persian classic Sadi's *Gulistan* (1258) was translated into German in the seventeenth century, and was a stimulus to developments there. There was a Latin translation in the Netherlands in 1651. Although there was no English version in print, manuscript copies were in use as a common school book throughout the East India Company's rule, without regard to purity of text. It is studded with maxims and sayings comparable with the Wisdom literature of the Hebrews, with which it is linked by tradition, but set in the style of a Persian flower garden. The maxims are supported by similitudes and apologues, some animal fables. There is a reversal of common emblematic values: 'the burden-bearing ass is preferable to the man-devouring lion'; not only is the merchant worth more than the tyrant, 'oxen and asses that carry loads are preferable to men that injure their fellow-creatures'. 'Lucman, the fabulist and philosopher', is appealed to, as might be Aesop; and is likelier to turn the tables upon them than to meet their expectations. Or generally; 'They asked Lucman: "Of whom didst thou learn wisdom?" He replied, "Of the blind, who put not their feet forward till they feel their ground".'

There is a characteristic variant of the story of a discontented youth who leaves home against advice (ch. III, xxviii). He needs experience, he says. His father urges him to dismiss this absurd fancy. The young man counters with the wise sayings about the advantages of travel. The father instances five classes of persons who are likely to enjoy these advantages, with the reasons. The son trades back wise saws, and persists in his intention. After a series of adventures in which his life is all but lost on several occasions, by good fortune he is in extremity rescued, and reaches home. The son claims to have proved his point. The father replies that he has survived only by a stroke of fortune, and should not presume otherwise; and clinches the point with another similitude. The narrative represents complex relations between wisdom, experience and fortune, and leaves them to reflection. The general work of fable in this convention is reinforced, or overburdened, by constant recourse to maxims, a kind of stylized discourse. But the counter-thrust of opposed maxims contributes with the action to unsettle opinions and promote new thinking.

Allusive and elusive

(*i*)

Boswell tells a story of Goldsmith, who thought he could write a good fable, and observed that in most fables the animals seldom talk in character.

> 'For instance, the fable of the little fishes, who saw birds fly over their heads, and, envying them, petitioned Jupiter to be changed into birds. The skill consists in making them talk like little fishes.' Whilst indulging himself in this idea, he noticed Johnson shaking with laughter. 'Why, Dr Johnson, this is not so easy as you seem to think; for if you were to make little fishes talk, they would talk like WHALES.'

This esteem for the fable, and itch to write one, whether a 'Persian Fable' or a real-life beast fable, was prevalent at the time. Not only Goldsmith and Pope and Swift and Gay, but also Dryden and Addison, and in his own way Johnson, were taken with the virtues of fable.

Croxall, to match the high esteem in which Aesop and his fables were held by the Ancients, cited Addison to represent a measure of equal esteem among the Moderns, especially in paper 183 of the *Spectator*, 'On Fable'. Addison says that Fables were the first pieces of wit, and had always been valued, and his first paragraph ends:

> As Fables took their Birth in the very infancy of Learning, they never flourished more than when Learning was at its greatest Height. To justify this Assertion, I shall put my Reader in mind of *Horace*, the greatest Wit and Critick in the *Augustan* Age; and of *Boileau*, the most correct Poet among the Moderns: Not to mention *La Fontaine*, who by this Way of Writing is come more into Vogue than any other Author of our Times.

What these writers of our Augustan age understood by 'fable' is a question. When Goldsmith speaks of his little fishes or Addison of La Fontaine, it is clear that they refer to the Aesopic convention. Even when Pope speaks of a 'Persian Fable', it is a specific reference which leads back to another convention, the Indian similitudes which were a second source of the fable as it developed in European literature. But in this essay Addison goes on to take in allegory as another class of fable, with ancient and modern examples that include the Italian poets and Spenser, an altogether different tradition. After this preamble the purpose of the paper turns out to be an allegory of his own devising, to follow up the suggestion by Socrates in the *Phaedo* that 'a man of a good genius for a fable' could represent pleasure and pain as inseparably joined. Poor Addison was not 'a man of a good genius for a fable', and the result is embarrassingly banal, although considered by Croxall as 'most beautiful'. 'The Fishermen' (Perry, 13), in which the dragging net gives joyful notice of a heavy catch and brings up a load of stones, spells the sisterhood or neighbourhood of grief and joy in a way which no laboured allegory by Addison, or another, could match: it is a difference between imagination and fancy, conception and conceit, experience and reverie. The touchstone is practical.

Addison has six papers in the *Spectator* on Wit (58–63), and concludes the series with 'Allegory on Wit', as tediously fanciful and pointless as it is likely to be. However, he shows a discernment in these matters in the last of his five papers, 'True and False Wit – Mixed Wit'. He cites Locke on the difference between wit and judgement: wit is prompt to seize resemblances; judgement delays to discriminate distinctions, quite contrary to metaphor and allusion. Addison concludes:

> Mr Locke's account of wit, with this short explanation, comprehends most species of wit, as metaphors, similitudes, allegories, enigmas, mottoes, parables, fables, dreams, visions, dramatic writings, burlesque, and all methods of allusion: as there are many other pieces of wit (how remote soever they may appear at first sight from the foregoing description) which upon examination will be found to agree with it.

Here there is a simple dichotomy on philosophical grounds between 'all the methods of allusion', which depend on resemblances, and

methods of 'direct and close description', which depend on distinctions. The *Dunciad* is saturated with allusions, but hardly in the sense
intended here, which refers to different ways of making one representation stand for another. That might comprehend the whole
domain of fiction, but a tendency to greater realism in narrative
fiction brings it near to direct and close description.

(ii)

Dramatic and heroic and other poetical compositions were governed
by rules and rulers, from Aristotle to Rymer (and Dryden) and from
Horace to Boileau, but other fiction lacked a clear-sighted Lucian to
give it sure-footed experimental freedom, and reasonable relations
with credibility. Johnson allows himself this office in the *Rambler*
for 31 March 1750, in a piece headed by a quotation from the *Ars
Poetica*, rendered by Creech: 'And join both profit and delight in
one'. He says that the works of fiction coming into favour, 'such as
exhibit life in its true state', make a kind of writing 'to be conducted
nearly by the rules of comick poetry'. Just because the writers of this
fiction have abandoned tales of fanciful invention which have no kind
of application to the reader's life and self, it is incumbent upon them
not merely to be accurate in their descriptions, but mainly to select
for description the best examples only. 'If the world be promis-
cuously described, I cannot see of what use it can be to read the
account: or why it may not be as safe to turn the eye immediately
upon mankind as upon a mirror which shows all that presents itself
without discrimination.' For, 'These books are written chiefly to the
young, the ignorant, and the idle, to whom they serve as lectures of
conduct, and introductions into life.' Critically crude as these words
sound today, they perhaps enunciate rules which could be applied to
such a novel of the times as *The Vicar of Wakefield*, which Johnson
himself brought into the world by taking and selling it to a bookseller
to relieve Goldsmith's distress, having looked into it and discerned
its merit, although he did not think it would sell – and publication
was delayed until Goldsmith's reputation had been made.

A modern critic has called *The Vicar of Wakefield* 'a fable of the
values of the pastoral myth', the natural virtues and blessings which
constituted until recently the norm of Anglo-American realism in
fiction ('Realism in the Anglo-American Novel'. The Pastoral Myth,
John W. Loofbourow in *The Theory of the Novel*, ed. John Halperin, 1974). This does not mean that *The Vicar of Wakefield* was or

is any kind of fable, but that, looking back, it can be seen as a
paradigm of this type of fiction, in a tradition that has come to an end.
The values for which it stands appear the more distinct for the
remoteness of the narrative from reality – a mere two-dimensional
sketch, but animated by Goldsmith's own absurdities and engaging
simplicities. It is as unrealistic as pastoral myth, but if *Tom Jones* was
heir to the epic, the *Vicar* may be allowed heir in prose fiction of the
pastoral poem. It was just that it should have been Johnson who
carried it to the printer, if it was indeed prototype of the kind of
fiction he was recommending.

(iii)

Johnson's recognition of the direction in which fiction was moving
forward to prosperity was not matched by recognition that allegory
was a chronic disease in the Middle Ages, and seldom anything but a
literary blight in his own polite age. On the contrary, he was partial
to it. He remarks in the *Rambler* (21), on the dangers of imitation:
'To imitate the fictions and sentiments of Spenser can incur no
reproach, for allegory is perhaps one of the most pleasing vehicles of
instruction'. Another paper, 'An Allegory on Criticism', begins:
'The task of an author is, either to teach what is not known, or to
recommend known truths by his manner of adorning them'. From
this platform he launches into the allegory, a preposterous and
pointless parade of stark Personifications. 'The Voyage of Life' and
'The Garden of Hope – A Dream' are other examples of congested
and tedious allegory. On the other hand, the *Rambler* paper 'An
Allegory on Wit and Learning' has a stronger story-line gracefully
followed: the careers of these two daughters of Apollo and the
interplay of their virtues and vices are related as an aetiological myth.
This is a model of its kind, lightly amusing, unencumbered, perceptive, and to firm purpose. It tends to show that a *jeu d'esprit* was
more likely to achieve the wit and wisdom admired and aimed at in
Augustan allegory, than 'the nicety and correctness of the moderns'
in their similitudes and allusions, now that 'the rule of observing
what the French call the *bienséance* in an allusion, has been found out
of later years' – which was the opinion of Addison, given in his paper
'On Genius' (160).

In 'On Giving Advice' (512), Addison makes Johnson's point that
the whole purpose and art of writers is to vie in skilfully overcoming
the reader's reluctance to receive instruction; and after reviewing

devices for this purpose, he concludes: 'But among all the different ways of giving Counsel, I think the finest, and that which pleases most universally, is *Fable*, in whatsoever shape it appears'. His argument is that the fable is read for the story, and we draw the moral as our own conclusion, thus advising ourselves:

> It is no wonder therefore that on such Occasions, when the Mind is thus pleased with itself, and amused with its own Discoveries, that it is highly delighted with the Writing which is the occasion of it. For this reason the Absalom and Achitophel was one of the most popular poems that appeared in English.

His nomination of Dryden's poem, covered by 'in whatsoever shape it appears', shows the loose use of 'Fable', and recalls the comprehensive list in the category 'all the methods of allusion' in his discussion of Wit.

Dryden's *Fables* (1700) were not fables as Gay's were. They were fables in Addison's phrase 'in whatsoever shape it appears'. The title page reads: 'Fables Ancient and Modern; Translated into Verse, from Homer, Ovid, Boccace, & Chaucer: with Original Poems'. Pope said he had 'sixpence each line for his *Fables*', which suggests need, and this was his last publication, in the year of his death. Whatever the circumstances, it turned out a labour of love, under an ambiguous title.[3]

Of the apologue as an Aesopic fable Johnson had a strict notion that echoes Archilochus, before Aesop, and being archaic, ignored developments and confused function with form. In his 'Life of Gay', he says:

> His Fables seem to have been a favourite work; for, having published one volume, he left another behind him. Of this kind, of Fables, the authors do not appear to have formed any distinct or settled notion. Phaedrus evidently confounded them with *Tales*, and Gay both with *Tales* and *Allegorical Prosopopoeias*. A *Fable* or *Apologue*, such as is now under consideration, seems to be, in its genuine state, a narrative in which beings irrational and sometimes inanimate, *arbores loquuntur, non tantum ferae*, are, for the purpose of moral instruction, feigned to act and speak with human interests and passions. To this description the compositions of Gay do not always conform. For a Fable he gives now and then a

Tale or an abstracted Allegory; and from some, by whatever name they may be called, it will be difficult to extract any moral principle.

These words, mindful of lexicographical practice and critic's rules, both have point and miss the point. All the 'fables' of Phaedrus and Gay – and La Fontaine – are not strictly fables. A short fable easily slips into mere anecdote or story, perhaps with a moral, more likely with more wit than principle, as in the fabliaux. However, it is how the material is used, not the material itself, that makes a fable. Also, the action represented is not to be compacted with a particular moral by which the fable is indexed. The story does not necessarily yield a moral principle; it serves its purpose by exposure to thought.

From definitions and rules to concrete contrast in ethos: compare Addison's best-known allegory, 'Vision of Mirza', with Lucian's 'Charon Sees Life'. They both show a view of human life in the world seen from a high point, with the help of a guide and interpreter. Both turn on the perspectives. Resemblance ends with the abstract theme. The 'Vision' follows the characteristic course of life in a sequence of physical images, and lightens the gloom that gathers on an earthly view by a switch of scene to the blessed isles that loom *sub specie aeternitatis*. Charon, professionally occupied with the fact and facts of death, is brought to see the lives of others preoccupied with their own affairs: one for whom only death counts looks at those who do not count on death. The temporal perspective is dislocated: on the one hand, totalized; on the other, ignored. Neither is justified. Imagination is seized by the incongruity of the conception, and the sequence of scenes and comments picks out and points to the absurdities and ironies forced into view by the conjunction. Perhaps neither piece would give anyone noticeable pause, but the 'Vision' fades into inanity, and the jest provokes as much amusement and reflection today as when it was written. The one is a parade of fanciful images, the other enacts an imaginative conception that jolts experience. Judgement is by effect. Addison's *bienséance* is outplayed by Lucian's *malséance*, roughness. That is usually how it goes with allegory (eighteenth-century vintage) and fable.

(*iv*)

In Germany also, 'fables' of one kind and another were popular in the first half of the eighteenth century. Indeed, not only was allegory and the like in poetic vogue, but the Aesopic fable was brought into the focus of the discussion of poetics. Goethe has given an autobiographical account of this phase of the discussion in *Poetry and Truth* (Part II, Book vii). The argument concentrated on images, and the line of it recalls Sidney's gropings in the *Apologie*. Abstract doctrine has no hold on the mind, to which metaphor and imagery have natural entrance. Sidney's 'delightful teaching', reappearing in the formulas of this discussion, was declared by the Swiss theorist Breitinger to be most perfectly achieved in Aesop's Fables,[4] mentioned with mirth by Goethe. He goes on to say that this conclusion did have 'the most decided influence on the best minds', and names some of the many who applied their talents to this species of poetry, including Lessing. It was Lessing who eventually liberated Goethe and his contemporaries from the aesthetic confusion of the time with his *Laokoon* (1766). Meanwhile, some seven years earlier, Lessing was revising his youthful fables in verse, rewriting in prose those he did not reject. More important, he wrote an essay on fable, refuting current theories – including Breitinger – and producing a theory of his own.

He dissociated fable from poetry, and poetry from didactics. He distinguished the action in fable from the action in drama or epic, where inner conflicts are also actions or part of actions. Motivation of the action in a fable is implied and is simple, and is not a separate dimension. He distinguished between fable and allegory. A fable is not necessarily an allegory; it is one only if it refers to a particular real case. In itself, it is not an allegory, because it represents a general truth. The general application of the individual instance represented in the fable must be instantly recognizable. The action is both specific and obviously general, and this concreteness reinforces the meaning of a generality that is mere possibility. Fable roots the general in a particular that is seen to be general.

Thus a fable is a story that represents a particular case that is immediately recognizable as a general principle. Animals as agents are useful because they may conventionally stand for behavioural characteristics. The 'sour grapes' story is made simple and convincing because the fox is accepted as representing shrewdness and vanity. If the object of a fable is to offer a graphic perception of a moral truth, the action that represents it must be disengaged from human sympathies, which it is the object of most fiction to engage.

This piece of analysis and construction, in the light of a critical refutation of a range of contemporary theories of fable, making a definitive separation of the Aesopic fable from general poetics, was unprecedented and was accomplished by one of the best minds in Europe, the pre-eminent aesthetic theorist of his age. There was nothing of the kind in English; and without Lessing, probably would not have been in Europe. The analysis was focused on the Aesopic fable, and assumed a concern with moral truth, which was an unnecessary limitation; but it was basic, and sufficient at the time. Lessing had disciplined himself in concise epigrammatic statement, a lifelong cultivation, and he admired the clarity and brevity and finished precision of Aesopic narrative, which had for centuries lent itself to linguistic exercises. Lessing applied his rules to his own fable compositions at this time when he was revising them, aiming as well at graceful brevity. But he fully recognized that he was not himself 'a man of a good genius for a fable', and that his were inspired by critical judgement and reflection.

A fable lost

(i)

In Dryden's Preface to his *Fables*, he excludes from his intention anything 'which savours of Immorality or Profaneness', and asserts that he has 'endeavour'd to chuse such Fables, both Ancient and Modern, as contain in each of them some instructive Moral'. He selects for special mention 'The Flower and the Leaf', then attributed to Chaucer, 'with which I was so particularly pleas'd, both for the Invention and the Moral; that I cannot hinder myself from recommending it to the Reader'. This was a strange and interesting choice for one who allowed that the vigour and crowded variety of the action in Homer had a vehemence suitable to his temper. For this tale is of the gentlest nature, '*after the manner of the Provencalls*', that is, courtly and lyrical. It purports to tell 'Of mystique Truth, in Fables first convey'd', and is indeed an allegory, although the celebration or adornment of the moral objects of allusion in descriptive imagery and loving language leaves a general impression of 'all *Elysium* in a spot of Ground'. However, the vulnerability of pleasures to the climate of the world is duly enacted in the exposure of one party to the violence of a sudden storm; to be succoured with graceful kindness by the other party, their 'enemies', secured against such chances by adherence to enduring qualities. They are of course the parties of the Flower and the Leaf, knights and ladies all. 'The secret meaning of this moral Show' is at the end explained to the author of the Vision, and a declaration of allegiance invited. The poem as a whole is an allegory used to insinuate a morsel for reflection; an allegory rich in the telling, used as a mild fable. Dryden had reason to respect its quality.

(ii)

Dryden's longest poem and one which shows the maturity of his metrical mastery, 'The Hind and the Panther' – an ambitious endeavour – was 'a constitutional absurdity', said Johnson in a damning phrase. He asks rhetorically: 'What can be more absurd than that one beast should counsel another to rest her faith upon a pope and council?' If you have brought animals to life simply to carry on a theological argument already begun in your own voice, and which would be exactly the same if the interlocutors were called Petra and Henricus, there is nothing to rebut 'a constitutional absurdity'.

Dryden did anticipate ridicule, in the opening lines of The Third Part; where he says he has been led by the great examples of *Aesop* and *Mother Hubberd*:

> If men transact like brutes, 'tis equal then
> For brutes to claim the privilege of men.

That is a specious twist, but Dryden did, it seems, truly believe that the sectarians were made savage on principle (*Religio Laici*, 400 f.). To denominate them Bear, Hare, Ape, Boar, Reynard, Wolf, was but to refine and define this perception of them. By contrast, in the same order of human dignity, a 'Milk white *Hind*' was seen to be different, not a predator, a thing of purity apart. And with the Panther, 'sure the noblest, next the *Hind*', a special relationship must be seen that curtly excludes the rest. With this literary tradition in his mind, and his violent view of the distinct characters of the parties, he was led to cast the poem in this form. But it was a disastrous misconception. The sects are satirized and dismissed under their tribal names in the shortest First Part, and have no part in the dialogue of the Hind and the Panther which occupies the remaining two thousand lines of the poem, save for the interpolation of two dependent fables or 'Episodes', 'distinct Stories of themselves', introduced in the Indian manner. The hinge of fable is an action, and there is hardly a plot in this plain attempt to set out and justify a position. The moment of action is the moment of rest which comes at the end of The Second Part, when the Panther accepts an invitation to stay the night, prudently avoiding the dangers of the road after dark. A reader who remembers the seat of the Roman Church might be astonished by the 'mean retreat', no less than the Panther:

> The silent stranger stood amaz'd to see
> Contempt of wealth, and wilful poverty:
> And, though ill habits are not soon controll'd,
> A while suspended her desire of gold.

There follow in three delicious lines the physical symptoms of a carnivore restraining her appetite. But the staging of the poem has committed it to total absurdity, since there is nothing other than argument.

Voltaire had a narrative talent admired by Dr Johnson, but when he used it to stage an argument, as in *Histoire de Jenni*, the story is a clumsy contrivance of a dialogue to discredit atheism and fanaticism. Lucian knew better and used the direct Socratic dialogue, with none of his devices and no narrative, when he intended to mount an argument in which his point of view would prevail, as in *Hermotimus*.

Therefore, this longest, most serious, and metrically skilled poem of the venerable Dryden invited and deserved the ridicule of the young Matthew Prior and Mr Montagu in their burlesque *The Hind and the Panther Transvers'd to the Story of the Country and the City-Mouse*. This is not the simple parody advertised. It is a skit, in which a few lines of parody are introduced by the egregious Bayes, with a load of fustian that out-Bottoms Bottom, interrupted and twitted by two wits; so that the poem is pilloried and pelted, form and content, in scraps of parody strung out between heckling interchanges that expose and insult every absurdity and ineptitude. Thus the introduction of all the extras with no part to play – the Bear, the Boar, the Wolf, the Fox, the Hare, the Ape – provides due fun. The authors were of course against Dryden's religion and politics, and the piece is a shot from the other side. But it is made clear that it is a response to the literary impropriety of the poem. Prior was the real author, and he had some sense of the fable tradition. As they say in the Preface: 'What can be more improbable and contradictory to the Rules and Examples of all Fables, and to the very design and use of them?'. The skit is worth noticing here for this notable recognition of the fable genre and its character. Prior himself could turn out a topical fable when he wanted to, but not to serious purpose. 'The Turtle and the Sparrow' is a smooth-running dialogue with the elegance and gaiety of one of La Fontaine's *contes*. He was not more successful than Dryden in his long poem on a serious theme, but not for the same reason.

Spence records that Dean Lockier said that Dryden was upset by this skit on his poem. 'I have heard him say, "For two fellows that I have always been very civil to, to use an old man in misfortunes in so cruel a manner!" And he wept as he said it.'

(iii)

Dryden was the only English poet of his time who had the interest and skill as well as the gifts to compose a masterly fable in verse – perhaps even on the religious theme. In terms of poetic equipment, he had grasped the comprehensive range of mind required by the poet's vocation and he had the seriousness of dedication. He had in a superior degree the poetic energy to collect, to combine, amplify, and to animate his material (Johnson). Intellectually, he inclined to a sceptical temper, in agreement with the age as he believed, evident in the investigative procedures of the Royal Society. What he liked was Socratic dialogue, 'sustained by persons of several opinions, all of them left doubtful, to be determined by the readers in general' (Ker, 1900, I, 124). He was acquainted with and had regard for the fable tradition, in its Aesopic and in oriental forms. Not least, he had read Lucian with attention more than once, as he said, and recognized a kindred mind. He contributed a 'Life' as a preface to translations of the Dialogues by several hands, published in 1711, a decade after his death. He had probably composed this appreciation in 1696. He was fascinated by the Dialogues, and by Lucian's satirical wit: 'if the pleasure arising from comedy and satire be either laughter or some nobler sort of delight, which is above it, no man is so great a mastery of irony'. He had imitated none, unless Aristophanes. He who had best imitated him was Erasmus in Latin, Fontenelle in French. Dryden thought that the art of dialogue in its several forms needed a study. He recognized Lucian's fiction as a special invention, trying to combine in dialogue grave discourse and the wit and fooling of a theatre, a project of his imagination. The philosophic detachment and seriousness, employing pleasing fiction with comic licence to stir up the reader to think for himself, as found in Lucian's model, appealed greatly to Dryden. The conclusion seems justified that Dryden was more thoroughly versed in the resources of this form of fiction, and competent to exploit them, than any other contemporary English poet. What was needed was the occasion.

Margaret Wiley called her study of 'creative scepticism' in seventeenth-century England, *The Subtle Knot* (1952). The title was meant to express the anomalies and antinomies in which thought and things are entangled, grasped intellectually in paradox, experientially in metaphors and relinquishments, a response to the complexity of things and of human beings. The dialogue is left 'to be determined by the readers in general', as Dryden said. Yet at the end of her study: 'Dryden was indeed the poet of the untied knot'. He was on the side of the Royal Society and plain language, the transition from pictorial to conceptual thinking. Thus 'The Hind and the Panther', which falls between stools.

It might have been otherwise. He might have brought the outcast beasts on stage to speak for themselves, with etched self-images and images seen by others. The 'action' could have been a Council to debate a proposal for the re-formation of Christendom, a plot with sub-plots. Theological fortress warfare anticipating the Last Judgement, with the Tower of Babel as a dependent fable. Or whatever. The apotheosis of belief, perhaps; not belief 'such as', argued belief, but belief as such: in a word, Dryden as the poet of 'the subtle knot'. The elements were there for a true fable as the last and lasting achievement of the author of 'Absalom and Achitophel'.

'The Hind and the Panther' is the evidence for and against the possibility. It is not merely nor mainly a literary question.

The Whale

If *Rasselas* (1759) was an impromptu performance, it was a fruit of Johnson's mature experience and reflection and practice, a ripe product; as well as perhaps his most popular work, and least regarded by the critics. By his own standards, it was true to form: 'Nothing can please many, and please long, but just representations of a general nature'. His habit of mind was to condense experience in generalizations, aphoristic in expression, too charged with particularity to be mere abstractions. Imagination and desire were boundless and obsessive; restraint and modification were feasible only by the experience generated in their pursuit. Unruly passions governed by reason, as horses by the charioteer, was a vain metaphor. The management was a detailed process, not the exercise of a trained faculty.

The opening paragraph provides an example of the promythium of a fable, a brief statement of its application. After this warning against the extravagances of hope, the story begins a quest for happiness born of a longing to escape from Arcady, the Abyssinian Happy Valley in which nothing is lacking, where there are no predatory beasts, where every gratification is immediately to hand, with oriental voluptuous refinements. For the Abyssinian Prince, the hero, gratification is not enough. He begins with contemplation; his meditations on escape put him on the road to active achievement; he dreams of service; he finds communication with Imlac, the poet, who relates his adventures in the outside world, and confesses that although he has a mind stored with images and memories to console him, it is a kind of death to be cut off from that scene and those accidents and events, and from the exercise of his acquirements. The Prince's own incipient enjoyment of human faculties and fundamental activities, reinforced by Imlac's tale, leads to a pact to attempt escape. On the point of success, they are discovered and joined by the Prince's sister, 'not less desirous of knowing what is done or suffered in the world'. Both, with their companions, set out to judge with their own eyes of the various conditions of men, and then to make deliberately their *choice of life*.

The story has no sustaining interest except as an ethical quest. In this pursuit, every way of life, every situation in and experience of the world, is explored as it is found, and reported on, and reflected on, and discussed, all through the media of highly idealized characters, even the Arab brigand. We are interested in the fortunes of these persons and the incidents and episodes of the plot only in so far as what happens leads to an answer to their questions, a resolution of their quest. The discipline of human desires through vision of their satisfaction or inability to fulfil them is what is represented. Improvement of the world or of the conditions of human life is dubious or impracticable. Let the Pyramids remain as monuments to the insufficiency of human enjoyments. To judge for oneself at first hand the various conditions of men, and then to make deliberately a choice of life, is proved vain. Whether or not this is the best of all possible worlds, the inextricable mixture of good and evil, fortune and misfortune, makes any attempt to straighten it out totally impracticable, even if one had the power to intervene in control of events. It is even beyond one's scope by prudent choice and avoidance to determine the conditions of one's own life, as the Epicureans maintained. The negative conclusions are made agreeable enough by the pleasing narrative in the course of which they emerge. The formulated aspirations of the parties at the end of their survey and innumerable discussions, their *choice of life*, are more their fancies than their decisions. 'Imlac and the astronomer were content to be driven along the stream of life without directing their course to any particular port.' The choices of the young people, experienced only in having scanned concretely the experiences of mankind, have no general significance. They are conditioned by birth and upbringing, by their aptitudes, tastes, and interests, and by promptings from what they have seen. In other words, they have learned nothing, unless that, delaying to make their *choice of life*, they have neglected to live.

One of the more perceptive writers on Johnson has applied to him a remark borrowed from Keats on Shakespeare: he 'led a life of Allegory: his works are the comments on it' (Walter Jackson Bate, *The Achievement of Samuel Johnson*, 1955, p. 62). In his published works can be discerned in graphic outline a representation of the stormy story of his inner career. Fables are not made in the pedestrian way in which Addison and often Johnson constructed their allegories. They spring from discernment of what is not obvious, seized and isolated and displayed under the light in a compelling graphic form that is never a formulation. In *Rasselas*, Johnson composed an action which represented his conception of the truth about the rational management of human life, ending with a 'Conclusion, in which nothing is concluded'.

The Peregrine

(*i*)

Voltaire seems to have been right in thinking that *Gulliver's Travels* (1726) would succeed simply as a story, by its unique fantasies and lightness of style, even if it were not a satire on the human race. It did not appear as an evident fable to Johnson:

This important year sent likewise into the world *Gulliver's Travels*, a production so new and strange, that it filled the reader with a mingled emotion of merriment and amazement. It was received with such avidity, that the price of the first edition was raised before the second could be made; it was read by the high and the low, the learned and illiterate. Criticism was for a while lost in wonder; no rules of judgement were applied to a book written in open defiance of truth and regularity. ('Life of Swift')[5]

Swift probably did not think of his fantasy as a 'fable', for he would have had the Aesopic model in mind for that. But there were the 'Persian' tales, there was *Mother Hubberds Tale*, with its link with *Renart*, and thereby with Aesop. And there was Lucian's 'True History' and his valued experimental fiction. These were influences on some of the fiction of this time when *Gulliver's Travels* helped to give fable a definitive modern form. The sense in which it was a fable, not merely fantasy, not mainly a satire, can be shown.

The frame story is an account of four voyages and the adventures which befell the author, soberly narrated in parody of the 'voyages', imaginary or otherwise, that were popular at the time. Throughout, there is close attention to detail, to mock this method of preserving verisimilitude in such narratives, to maintain a matter-of-fact low-key foil for the amazing events and descriptions, to build up the visual effect of a fable, and perhaps not least because Swift's mind was made that way. (Johnson relates that Swift found some fifteen faults in the behaviour of a footman waiting on table when he was dining alone with the Earl of Orrery). The first, second, and fourth voyages are integrated in internal structure. The third is itself a minor series of voyages, with descriptions of several strange lands, and is by way of a digression; and digression is much to the point of a comic writer, like Rabelais.

Gulliver in Lilliput basks in the esteem and importance given him by his singular position, undiminished even at the end when his political naivety suffers rude shocks. Enjoyment of gratified vanity is succeeded by 'mortification' on the second voyage, when he finds himself among the Brobdingnagians. He is reduced to a social toy or pet. He is put in the care of a child, his 'littel nurse', in place of her doll. He is carried round the country to be exhibited as a freak for money. He becomes the Queen's pet. All that he does or that happens to him becomes a source of amusement to the court. His being carried into the quarters of the Maids of Honour, and his treatment there, negate his very condition as a man. All his efforts to stand well turn against him. His account of his country to the friendly King, whose character and intelligence he deeply respects, is thrown back at him as childishly blind and partial. He has no useful role, and his offer to be of service in introducing superior modern weapons of war is contemptuously rejected. A final humiliation is his discovery that the King has in mind to obtain a woman of his size, so that he might breed his own kind for the diversion of the Brobdingnag people. The deflation of human dignity in all the kindness and indulgence lavished on this matchless pet is total. Esteem, including self-esteem, in being thus strictly related to comparative size, is itself devalued, reduced to 'an instance of the great power of habit and prejudice'.

(ii)

Part III, which takes Gulliver to Laputa and elsewhere, has most clearly the marks of the Scriblerian workshop, and Spence says as much, on the authority of Pope. This breaks the thread of the narrative. Written last, it specially pleased Swift, for it has more specific targets for his ridicule. The visit to the Academy of Lagado is a high-spirited Scriblerian piece on 'The Art of Being Silly in Experimental Philosophy' to match 'The Art of Sinking in Poetry'.

(iii)

Gulliver's experiences on his first two voyages had together undermined his self-esteem. On this last voyage, his ties with his kind and his own person become abhorrent to him.

As he learns to recognize his identity with the Yahoos, his revulsion becomes a fierce loathing. When he is embraced by the young female whilst bathing, it is traumatic. Only his attachment to the Houyhnhnms saves him from the horror of being swept into and assimilated to the horde of his own kind.

When he is forcibly repatriated he cannot reconcile himself, first to the admirable Don Pedro, who treats him with such delicacy, consideration, and generosity, then to his wife and family, with whom he cannot bring himself to consort. Custom, of which he has learned the power, gradually strengthens his toleration, so that by looking at himself frequently in the mirror he learns to habituate himself to the sight of a human being, and can bear to permit his wife to sit at dinner with him, 'at the farthest end of a long table'. Then the bird strikes. He can endure the sight of fools and rogues and incompetents and betrayers: 'this is all according to the due course of things: but when I behold a lump of deformity and diseases both in body and mind, smitten with *pride*, it immediately breaks all the measures of my patience; neither shall I be ever able to comprehend how such an animal and such a vice could tally together'.

'As fierce a beak and talon as ever struck . . . belonged to Swift': Thackeray has in mind the image of a lonely eagle. But it is the Peregrine that is the master, the ultimate bird of prey.

This Fourth Book was inevitably a storm-centre of controversy. Swift was being intentionally offensive, as he told Pope, though Pope himself seems to have been diverted, by the verses he wrote on Part IV – which Swift did not much like. Was Gulliver speaking for Swift? More recently, the question has been: how do the ideas of human nature in *Gulliver* fit in with the assumptions and controversies of the time; are they for or against Shaftesbury or Mandeville; or do they reaffirm a Christian view? A great deal has been written on these matters.[6] I am concerned here only with *Gulliver* as a fable, which is to say that it is not an argument.

The business of a fable is to expose in a particular concrete representation a general 'truth'. *Gulliver* presents graphically several connected truths about the human condition. The first two voyages take Gulliver into quasi-human societies which differ from the human norm only or mainly in scale, by a factor of 12. He is in a society to which he cannot normally belong, but to which he is related. Comparisons are forced, and prompt reflection. All existents are members of a class of their kind. A human being is one among others, and this is a necessary condition of his/her self-concept. Gulliver's idea of himself is deranged by alien social contexts, beyond accommodation; it is hollowed out, and collapses. This is more specific than an exhibition of the relativity of things and 'the great power of habit and prejudice'. It is done by manipulation of the spatial dimension. In IV, elements of human vileness, savagery, and folly are dredged up, embodied, and encountered, without a redeeming feature. The product is recognizable enough to precipitate identification: 'I am that one'. This is the moment of truth. The total dominance of the vision persists after his repatriation, even in the bosom of his family. He remains alienated, from himself as from all others. If the extreme which is the truth but not the whole truth is not faced and accepted in the extreme way in which Gulliver faced and accepted it (and the metaphorical action is worked out in all its offensiveness), it is being played down, eroded, distanced, forgotten, denied, escaped or rebutted; and this also, and equally, is false and insane. The right of the justifiable extreme to be represented, to be taken intact, not rubbed nor robbed by any other truth, is implicitly proclaimed in the action. In the end, all right, people are not Yahoos, they are what they are. All the same, it has been shown that there is no reasonable ground for that italicized article *pride* – of person, of nation, of race. That is a prime and permanent target of extreme ridicule.

Why is the horse chosen as the foil to the human? Mr Crane argues that it is found in the Latin logic books when man is defined as a 'rational animal', as the example of an 'irrational animal', and that there is evidence that Swift had in mind this traditional definition in the school books. Professor Bridgwater says: 'The Houyhnhnms were obviously inspired by a passage in the Scriblerian *Essay Concerning the Origin of Sciences* where we read – in a variation of the mute philosopher theme – of a "philosopher" captured in Sylla's time who could not speak and "only showed his power in sounds by neighing like a horse".' This, at any rate, is close to home. On the other hand, Professor Hodgart argues plausibly that since 'the horse is the perfect symbol of upper-class culture', Swift, who was always uncertain about his social standing and reacted violently to snubs, produced in the Houyhnhms, despite his intention, 'a distorted image of the great gentleman in whose company he had lived but of whose caste he could never be' (in *Swift Revisited*, ed. Denis Donoghue, Thomas Davis Lectures, 1968). Unfortunately, the insipid nobility of the Houyhnhnms has none of the mettle of the creature trumpeted in the rhetoric of its maker in *Job*, nor the variety of the species worshipped in the many cults of the animal on earth.

The Serpent

(i)

Voltaire admired Swift, and called him the English Rabelais, but 'un Rabelais sans fatras'; and there is as much owing to *Gulliver* in *Micromegas* as to Cyrano de Bergerac. *Candide* (1759) is the consummate *conte philosophique* among more than a score which Voltaire wrote betwen 1747 and 1776, in the last thirty years of his life. Of far greater interest than the sources which Voltaire imitated or parodied in the tale are the siblings, so to speak, which were around in this family in the ten years before *Candide* was born: *Babouc* (1746), *Zadig* (1747), *Memnon* (1749), *Micromegas* (1752), *Scarmentado* (1756), to name the chief of them. The *contes* form a section of Voltaire's *oeuvre*, perhaps the slightest in his own estimation. Several were devised for private entertainment, and had their debut in the household of his hostess before their public appearance in print, rather like the tales of *One Thousand and One Nights*. Indeed, this example is the most general 'source', with the vogue of oriental tales of all kinds. With the occasion and demand for entertainment and Voltaire's readiness in response went his preoccupation with unanswerable problems of destiny or providence or the lot of man and the face of nature in a world ruled by an omnipotent and beneficent Master of all things. The 'Épitre Dedicatoire' to *Zadig* makes a prologue to them all, since it introduces 'un ouvrage qui dit plus qu'il ne semble dire', and announces itself as a translation into Arabic to amuse the celebrated sultan Ulugh-Beg at the time when the tales of the *Thousand and One Nights* were being written. Ulugh preferred *Zadig*, but his ladies the Arabian *Nights*.

> 'Comment pouvez-vous préférer', leur disait le sage Ouloug, 'des contes qui sont sans raison et qui ne signifient rien?' – 'C'est précisément pour cela que nous les aimons', répondaient les sultanes. ('How', the wise Ouloug used to say to them, 'can you prefer tales which are senseless and mean nothing?' – 'It is just for that reason that we like them', would reply the sultanas.)

That is the *conte philosophique*: it has a meaning, and is devised to mean more than it says; it is not like the tales in the *Nights*.

Voltaire's idea of fables was not quite the common confusion of myths, taken as allegories, and Aesopic or Eastern apologues. He instances the election of a king by the tree in Judges 9, and the Greek nature myths. Most of the rest, he says, are a corruption of early history (legend) or sheer fantasy; but there are old fables which are like modern tales, some of which are entertaining and have a serious moral, and some that are pointless. He supposed that the fable was invented in Asia by people afraid to speak openly to tyrannical rulers. But he allows that a natural love of images and tales may have encouraged such inventions for their own sake by people of intelligence. 'Les fables attributés à Ésope sont toutes des emblèmes, des instructions aux faibles, pour se garantir des forts autant qu'ils le peuvent.' (The fables attributed to Aesop are all devices to instruct the weak in order to preserve them from the strong as much as possible.) All nations with a little learning have adopted them. In *L'Ingénu*, the young Huron, making progress in his European studies, remarks with satisfaction on the naturalism of early Chinese history, whereas before Thucydides Greek history is tiresome fiction:

'Ce sont partout des apparitions, des oracles, des prodiges, des sortilèges, des métamorphoses, des songes expliqués, et qui font la destinée des plus grands empires et des plus petits États: ici des bêtes qui parlent, là des bêtes qu'on adore, des dieux transformés en hommes, et des hommes transformés en dieux. Ah! s'il nous faut des fables, que ces fables soient du moins l'emblème de la vérité! J'aime les fables des philosophes, je ris de celles des enfans, et je haïs celles des imposteurs.' (ch. xi)

(Everywhere there are apparitions, oracles, prodigies, sorceries, metamorphoses, dreams interpreted that settle the destiny of the greatest empires and the smallest States: here are animals that speak, there animals that are worshipped, gods changed into men, and men changed into gods. Ah! if we must have fables, let them at least portray the truth! I like the fables of philosophers, I laugh at those of children, and I hate those of impostors.)

This makes all clear. The same distinctions are made by the learned princess in the near-farcical satire on fables *Le Taureau Blanc*, which brings together a menagerie of fabulous beasts from the *Old Testament* conducted by the Witch of Endor, who leads by a chain the white ox that was Nebuchadnezzar. Eve's serpent is set on to distract the princess by amusing her with stories, and she tells him how boring the famous myths which he retails are to her 'qui ai lu *l'Entendement humain* du philosophe égyptien nommé Locke' ('who have read *The Human Understanding* of the Egyptian philosopher named Locke'). She says he will appreciate that a girl who fears to see her lover swallowed by a large fish (Jonah's whale) and herself to have her throat cut by her own father needs to be amused, 'mais tachez de m'amuser selon mon gout' (but try to amuse me according to my own taste), that is, 'pour achever *de me former l'esprit et le cœur*', (in order to complete the education of my mind and heart) (ch. ix).

(ii)

Candide is in some respects a revision of *Zadig* and *Memnon, Le Monde comme il va* (Babouc) and *Histoire des voyages de Scarmentado. Zadig* illustrates the vicissitudes of individual life; the hero is supremely deserving and cumulatively unfortunate, leading to a climax in which the cup of attainment is dashed from his lips. The happy denouement, prepared in the last chapter but one, 'L'ermite', recounting a famous fable, is not altogether a resolution of the moral problem of destiny. Experience yields a harvest of explanatory and consoling truths, 'Mais . . .' *Memnon* crowds the disastrous events into one day that dawns brightly with Memnon's dedication to the pursuit and practice of wisdom.

Le matin je fais des projets,
Et le long du jour des sottises.

(In the morning I make plans, and during the whole day do foolish things.)

Babouc's dream (Jonah and Nineveh) of a mission to Persepolis to report on whether its vices and follies merit destruction shows him veering for or against as he is appalled or touched or captivated by what he finds; and then having second thoughts about all his feelings. His report cannot be put into words. He submits a figure, a little fabrication of precious stones and common stones and metals, for preservation or destruction – a concrete metaphor. Judgement is not in the balance: the project of judgement must be abandoned. Scarmentado makes the usual voyage round the world, in which he tastes as well as sees the cruelties inflicted on each other by sects, factions, races in all parts of the globe, and concludes: 'J'avais vu tout ce qu'il y a de beau, de bon et d'admirable sur la terre; je resolus de ne plus voir que mes pénates. Je me mariai chez moi; je fus cocu, et je vis que c'était l'état le plus doux de la vie.' (I had seen all there is that is beautiful and good and admirable on earth; I resolved to see only my own place. I got married at home; I was deceived, and I saw that it was the most agreeable state of life.) The balance is redressed later in *La Princesse de Babylon*, a beautifully related parody of the fairy-tale which also traverses the world, in which new models of civilization are set off against remembered barbarities of the past. As a fairy-story it has its happy ending, but is freshened throughout with happy ironies.

Micromegas, more in the character of a fable, goes into space and finds people of astronomical stature. On Sirius, an able young entomologist of about 450 publishes a monograph which incurs a prosecution lasting 220 years, and banishment for 800. He sets out on an interstellar tour. On Saturn, he picks up the secretary of the Academy (Fontenelle), and together they set out again, visiting Jupiter and Mars and finally Earth. Nowhere, in spite of multiplied and superior endowments, are there people who do not have more desires than true needs, and more needs than satisfaction. In comments, the Saturnian is always rather behind the other, or more foolishly in front with rash statements and premature conclusions. Ingeniously, speech with the microscopic inhabitants of Earth is established. The visitors are now astonished, now disappointed by what they hear. They are most pleased with a Lockian spokesman, but this passage and the tale are abruptly broken off when a Thomist intervenes, firmly of the opinion that all is made for men, including the visitors and the places they come from. Homeric laughter shakes the human interlocutors off the fingernail of the Sirian where they had been accommodated.

(iii)

Dr Johnson claimed to refute Berkeley by kicking a palpable object, not perhaps recognizing that he was speaking in another universe of discourse, and missing the point, although he was offering the only refutation possible – a stubborn affirmation of animal faith; that is, a refusal of the argument. One may be inclined to think that Voltaire refutes the theodicy of Leibniz (*le Tout est bien*) in the same way by writing *Candide*. But Voltaire did know what he was doing; he was justifying abandonment of a view he had held. He was not arguing with Leibniz; he was protesting against such arguments, on the ground of invincible agnosticism in such matters; and, *a fortiori*, on the ground that the complacent declaration of this unintelligible doctrine insulted our human griefs. He was angry: from the blows he had himself suffered, the resentments he felt, the injustices and sufferings he saw, the accumulated experiences of life which had worn away and undermined the sanguine cosmic view he had cheerfully shared when younger. *Candide* is the explosion of that anger in ridicule, after the smouldering and crackling of the four earlier pieces.

Candide is a double mockery, of speculative systems and of stock romances and travellers' tales. Voltaire's mind was stored with his reading for *l'Essai sur les mœurs*, and he adopted or parodied themes, incidents, plots from the literature of the time. The selected ingredients have been traced, but there is no recipe for others to try their hand. The narrative gets off at a brisk canter, scarcely a sentence said with a straight face, saying 'plus qu'il ne semble dire', with irony or otherwise. Even the unspeakable is spoken of with imperturbable gaiety. But gaiety speaks in different tones, as the dance is a minuet or a tango, or the dance of shadows or of scorching flames. In Paris, Candide was told, everybody laughs, but in a rage; complaining of everything in bursts of laughter, even of the most detestable actions. Our author is more seemly, with everything under control. His characters are without independence; they are character traits that play required parts in an elaborate orchestrated performance, figures in a composition. But they have their human appeal, which starts with a story. Abominable misfortunes overwhelm the hero, his tutor, his love, and his friends, and therefore the gentle reader, who alone in the tumultuous seas remains buoyant on the knowledge that all is safely in the hands of the omnipotent author, and will be for the best in the end; dire events will be followed by extraordinarily fortunate coincidences, to work out this desirable fortuity. *Tout est bien* rules the world of romantic fiction, as of metaphysics; indeed, the one is justified by anticipating the other; and both respond to desires of the heart, in defiance of the head. To parody the fiction is to expose the philosophy: it is one and the same theme. The fortunes of Candide and Cunegonde are also the fortunes of Pangloss's cherished doctrine, which is the refrain of the composition and the intermittent argument pursued as Candide pursues Cunegonde. However, to bring a parody of romantic fiction to its predestined conclusion, with the lovers reunited and happy ever after, and to end mockery of a thesis with its reaffirmation, would parody the mockery and mock the parody. Reunion of the lovers is followed by disillusionment, boredom, moral deterioration, the very worst of calamities, until there is a marvellously realistic denouement brought about by the happy, and not unlikely, accident of the encounter with a market gardener from whom they learn that 'le travail éloigne de nous trois grands maux: l'ennui, le vice et le besoin' (work takes away three evils: boredom, vice, and need). Candide is impressed by the example and the precept. Pangloss starts to argue. 'Travaillons sans raisonner', dit Martin, 'c'est le seul moyen de rendre la vie supportable.' (Let us work without arguing, it is the only way to make life bearable.) When it works out, Pangloss is triumphant. He rehearses the train of events that has brought them to this reasonable issue, to show how all has happened for the best. 'Cela est bien dit', répondit Candide, 'mais il faut cultiver notre jardin.' (That is well said, but we must cultivate our garden.) He is liberated from the spell of the argument.

> Heureux qui, jusqu'au temps du terme de sa vie,
> Des beaux-arts amoureux, peut cultiver leurs fruits.
> (Voltaire's fifth 'discours sur l'homme')

('Happy is he who till the end of his life, devoted to the fine arts, can cultivate their fruits.')

In the course of the narrative there are several occasions for reflection upon comparative misfortunes, and for satirical comment on particular follies. There is also a paradox to match, Gulliver's paradox of a rational animal inflated with pride, ignoring all reason. The ridiculous weakness of wishing one were dead, and still wanting to live: 'car y a-t-il rien de plus sot que de vouloir porter continuellement un fardeau qu'on veut toujours jeter par terre; d'avoir son être en horreur, et de tenir a son être; enfin de caresser le serpent qui nous dévore, jusqu' à ce qu'il nous ait manger le cœur'. ('for is there anything more stupid than to want to go on carrying a burden that one wants all the time to throw down; to hold one's existence in horror and to hold on to one's existence; in brief, to caress the serpent that is devouring us until he shall have eaten our heart.')
However, there is a fable about that:

> Plutot souffrir que mourir
> C'est la devise des hommes.
> (La Fontaine, I, xvi)
>
> ('Better to suffer than to die'
> That is the human motto.)

The remarkable similarities in plan and theme between *Candide* and *Rasselas* made Johnson say that if their publication had not been nearly simultaneous, nobody would have believed that the latter had not borrowed from the first. In both, 'Human life is everywhere a state in which much is to be endured and little to be enjoyed'. In both, Eldorado does not satisfy human desires. The difference is in the questions raised. In Johnson, it is about a rational *choice of life*; in Voltaire, about the rationalization of experience by philosophers. Boswell was wrong in thinking that Voltaire meant to ridicule religious faith. Both fables expose vain uses of reason. Both intend liberation. The difference in tone could hardly be greater. If, as Dryden said of Lucian, 'no man is so great a master of irony', he had nothing to teach Voltaire. Irony ripples through the *contes*. In *Candide*, it is the musculature on the skeleton of the plot.

The Castalian fount

(i)

Voltaire would not allow top rank to La Fontaine. He thought that the *Fables* were excellent of their kind, but not in the same class as Racine or Molière's *Misanthrope* or *Tartuffe* or Boileau's *Art poétique*. Sainte-Beuve took account of the evidence:

> Apparently the least classical of the four great poets of the age of Louis XIV, was Molière; he was then applauded far more than he was esteemed; men took delight in him without understanding his worth. After him, La Fontaine seemed the least classical: observe after two centuries what is the result for both. Far above Boileau, even above Racine, are they now unanimously considered to possess in the highest degree the characteristics of an all-embracing morality. ('What is a classic?' *Causeries de Lundi*, III)

The phrase 'characteristics of an all-embracing morality' is a dubious literary award, but if that is the name of what La Fontaine does have, nobody doubts that he has surpassing skill in expressing it. When David Hume bought the *Fables* for the Advocates' Library in Edinburgh, and the Curators ordered its removal, he wrote to them: 'But this I will venture to justify before any literary society in Europe, that if every book not superior in merit to La Fontaine be expelled from the Library, I will engage to carry away all the remainder in my pocket'.

What made La Fontaine so special? In his Preface to his *Contes* (1665), stories retold from Boccaccio and others, he wrote: 'ce n'est ni le vrai ni le vraisemblable qui font la beauté et la grace de ces choses-ci; c'est seulement le manière de les conter'. (it is neither truth nor verisimilitude that makes the beauty and charm of these pieces; it is solely the way of relating them.)

In his Preface to the *Fables* (1668) he disclaims emulation of Phaedrus, whose simplicity and extreme brevity are beyond his powers, but claims to have added some novelty and gaiety to justify the retelling of familiar stories, not the gaiety of laughter, but of charm: they will be read with pleasure – like the *Contes*. However, in this case *le vrai* if not *le vraisemblable* will count as the reason why they should be read. As elementary definitions in geometry have led on to measurements of the earth and stellar bodies, so reasoning about human behaviour drawn from fables lays the foundation of judgement, conduct, and great achievement.

Thomas Gray, in his verses 'On a Favourite Cat, Drowned in a Tub of Gold Fishes', turns the piece into a mock fable if not by the tone, by the facetious moral tagged on. It would be absurd to suggest that La Fontaine parodied Aesop, but his playfulness sometimes brings him nearer to Gray than to Phaedrus. The patina on these old fables delights him, but he can use his respect for their archaic device as itself a device to keep his distance, and ever so faintly mock his original in using it to score his version of the same point, with a wit and grace and poetic economy beyond the reach of others. And as he goes on, he uses his independence with greater freedom. But the crude ore of earthy observation, proverbial wisdom, refined to the limit, remains authentic metal taken from the ground.

His first love, the *Contes*, to which he returned in the midst of the *Fables* (VIII, 13)

> J'avais Ésope quitté
> Pour être tout à Boccace
>
> (I have left Aesop
> To give myself to Boccaccio)

was an infatuation, regretted by many; but in retelling these old tales with novelty and charm, he was perfecting his art. He affected that they were not serious, he excused himself, but he took unaffected pleasure in them, because he was almost totally involved in their everlasting theme. They were stories told simply for pleasure, not moral tales, but they had their own philosophy, and La Fontaine could not keep out of that; as mediator rather than monitor, and often counsel for the defence.

Diversity was necessary to him, and his affection for Boccaccio did not mean that he was not also a professed disciple of Rabelais. And there was Molière. Aesop offered him a puppet stage on which to mount the human comedy diffused in a hundred Acts. Henri Taine, with the new sociological interest in literature, wrote a little treatise, *La Fontaine et ses Fables* (1853), to show that the *Fables* gave a complete picture of the social classes of the time, a Balzac in miniature. The tribute to the range of characters and types is deserved, and La Fontaine himself makes a little boast of the matter (IX, 1), but anything like a sociological view misses the central point, the author's self. It is his insinuation of his own humanity into his picture of mankind that is special. This is done all through and in many ways. It is shown as the ground-plan in the first of the fables dedicated to La Rochefoucauld, 'L'Homme et son Image' (I, 11). The follies of others are the mirrors in which we see ourselves. The poet is victim along with everyone else in this inquisition, viewing himself indulgently, painfully, disgustedly, contemptuously, ruefully, severely, amusedly, in one and another of these ancient tales. Self-scrutiny is the first and last moral, as it is indeed the last word, 'Le Juge Arbitre, L'Hospitalier et le Solitaire' (XII, 27): those in authority have most need of it for everybody's sake, and least opportunity, since they are fully occupied and, surrounded by flatterers, see neither themselves nor anyone else as they are. Identifying himself thus unreservedly with the objects of his ridicule, La Fontaine rarely administers the lash of satirical indignation. He does above all scorn the selfish calculation of avarice ('Le Loup et le

Chasseur', VIII, 27), and, more mildly, the failure to enjoy what one has at hand in greedy expectation of getting more or better ('Le Héron' and 'La Fille', VII, 4, 5).

Generalizing this self-scrutiny, he is uneasy at the use of animals in fables to represent human behaviour. Already, in his early telling of 'The Wolf and the Lamb', the Wolf works himself up into a state of indignation at his undeserved vilification. The protest is explicit in 'The Wolf and the Shepherds' (X, 6). In another, the serpent turns the tables on man; witnesses are called; the evidence is overwhelming; the man makes his case good by force (X, 2). Perhaps this is to take the story literally in this last case, but it follows the 'Discours à Madame de la Sablière' in which he vehemently contests Descartes's view of animals as machines, mechanical in constitution and behaviour. 'Hôtes de l'univers', they share with human beings of all conditions a basic sensibility.

(ii)

In these age-old, oft-told stories there is still room for his 'novelty' and his 'gaiety'. After all, for a very long time now there are no new plots and no new morals; but the reel does not end, nor discourse cease. 'The Cock and the Pearl' (I, 20) is given instead of a moral a practical turn, and paralleled in a modern instance. 'The Ass and the Lap-dog' (IV, 5) is turned into a comedy of manners. Instead of a violation of the harsh regime of station and duty, there is an understandable but ridiculous solecism. The weakness that succumbs to flattery is exhibited more to the taste of Paris in the seventeenth century in 'The Obsequies of the Lioness' (VIII, 14) than in the primitive 'The Fox and the Crow' (I, 2). In 'The Pig, the Goat, and the Sheep' (VIII, 12), the realistic pig is not allowed the last word. What La Fontaine does to make them his own in this way may sledgehammer the point, 'Lion takes all', or may make a new fable, or drag in his marvelling at the grand madness of the Spanish soul, in which he rejoiced exceedingly (IX, 15).

His intervention is sometimes direct and forceful. Scornful of avarice, he is angered by charlatanism, the claims of astrology or alchemy (II, 13; VI, 19; VII, 15; VIII, 16); as by the puritanical rigours of an anti-human philosophy (XII, 20). In contrast, the achievements and pursuits of science interest and excite him (VIII, 18; 26). This is not Aesop. All the *Fables* are steeped in La Fontaine's Epicurean humanism, his passion for liberty, for friendship, for the arts and sciences, and the peace in which they flourish; his view of the human condition, his rejection of fatalism and acceptance of fate. No wonder Hume loved him. And there creeps in the poet's own elegiac note (IX, 2; XI, 4). This is not Aesop; but La Fontaine remained loyal to his respected source (as in the *Contes*), and happy with the device that had given him his puppet stage, a device like the Wooden Horse which succeeded at once after years of vain heroic prowess. Epics will not turn men into heroes, but fables may make them a little readier to know themselves. Towards the last, in 'The Companions of Ulysses', there crop out underlying ambivalences that perhaps put all in question, without seeming to do so. Following this transfusion of blood into the Aesopic fable, producing 'l'éternal chef d'oeuvre du genre', La Fontaine had many imitators, of whom Florian (1755–94), a protégé of Voltaire, was chief.

(iii)

The characteristics of Gray's verses on the favourite cat, the 'pensive Selima' are such that William Cowper might have written them. Among Cowper's miscellaneous pieces are some dozen slight poetical fables. He has one called 'The Dog and the Water-Lily No Fable' because it recounts a true incident. One called 'Pairing-Time Anticipated A Fable' is perhaps as good as any. In 'The Flatting Mill An Illustration', he makes a parable to illustrate the difficult skill of combining pleasure with instruction in poetry, overcoming reluctance to receive unwelcome truth. His playfulness combined ill with the morbid religiosity that got hold of him, so that he tended to sermonize ('The Poet, the Oyster, and the Sensitive Plant'). The moral comes best when it is his own case ('The Needless Alarm A Tale'). The slightest are the happiest ('The Lily and the Rose'). One of his last literary efforts was to translate into Latin three of Gay's *Fables*. He had the parts for a delightful minor fabulist, but not the constitution.

Wordsworth did not have the turn of mind. 'The Waterfall and the Eglantine' is rather silly. The piece that follows, 'The Oak and the Broom A Pastoral', is the same fable as La Fontaine's 'Le Chêne et le Roseau', which he is said to have considered one of his best. Both poets follow the contours of the story, but they do not compare. After the neighbourly dialogue of the two, which he prolongs a little, Wordsworth's narrator passes on into the diminishing monochrome of observation and report. La Fontaine presents in thirty-two lines the event itself, soberly, with an irony that is not the poet's, the incongruity of survival. The soaring majesty and solid anchorage of the monarch are evoked in the last two lines, the instant of crashing upheaval. Wordsworth gives the old fable a local habitation, associates it with the genius of a place; the story passes into the company of his pastorals of the hills. La Fontaine gives us once for all the genius of the fable itself.

Fable in the Age of Reason

This most literary and self-conscious period of European history, in which the cultivated looked back to Augustan Rome and thought with satisfaction that a comparable level of civilization had been achieved, had come a long way since the Renaissance, the historic looking back. This distance could be documented: from, say, Petrarca's apologia 'On his own ignorance and that of many others' (1368) to d'Alembert's Discours Préliminaire' to *L'Encyclopédie* (1751); from Pico's 'Oration on the Dignity of Man' (1486) to Condorcet's 'Esquisse d'un tableau historique des progrès de l'esprit humain' (1795); from Vives's 'A Fable About Man' (1518) to Diderot's 'Le Neveu de Rameau' (1763). In about one-sixth of this time lapse, it has been said, 'La majorité des Français pensait comme Bossuet; tout d'un coup, les Français pensent comme Voltaire' (Paul Hazard, 1935). Institutionally, as it affected authors, the move is from courts and patrons to coffee-houses, clubs and coteries, and to booksellers – at worst, Grub-Street. In literary forms, epics and pastorals are on the way out, superseded by the novel and short story. These shifts, seemingly revolutionary, are a prelude to accelerating social change, which in our retrospect does bring together the Age of Augustus and the Age of Anne as a common civilization, from a literary point of view.

In this Europe of the eighteenth century, the fable as known and used in the ancient world of Greece and Rome and of India achieved a consummation in the hands of La Fontaine, of Voltaire, of Swift, and of Johnson. Moreover, the general looseness about what was meant by 'fable' was sorted out by Voltaire, and settled in a disciplined examination by Lessing. At the same time Lessing, and Johnson in his own way (*Preface to Shakespeare*), dispelled the traditional cant about 'delightful teaching', and broke the tyranny of rules, in a more

comprehensive and a more realistic critical outlook. With this consummation of fable in ways that broke its archaic moulds, and with
this general emancipation of fiction, it may seem that the fable as
known was due to expire as outmoded. So it did seem. Fiction writers
in the nineteenth century had no use for it. Modern theorists have
made the judgement explicit. Examination of that conclusion must be
deferred. But the germ of the answer is discernible in these mature,
and very different, achievements themselves.

Voltaire, without that intention, provided the collective moral of
La Fontaine's Aesop in one of the opening sentences of his Dictionary article 'Tolérance': 'Nous sommes tous pétris de faiblesses et
d'erreurs; pardonnons-nous réciproquement nos sottises, c'est la
première loi de la nature'. (We are all formed of weakness and error;
let us pardon each other's follies, it is the first law of nature.) His own
Candide had a background in the voyages of his earlier *contes*, which
had a background in the voyages of the time in fiction that discovered
alternative societies, with a footing for the imaginative destruction of
the author's homeland. Voltaire's own variations on this popular
theme were like the beliefs of Socrates, who believed in the gods of
the city in whom his accusers believed, but not as they did. In
Rasselas, Johnson was not kicking Berkeley's imperceptible external
world, but the moral philosopher's *summum bonum*, more accessible to demonstration. *Gulliver* exposes in the moment of truth the
paradox of truth, that it is never the last word. In short, these fables
are the achievement they are because they reach and touch the human
condition – at some point. Fable is a way of thinking concretely
about the way things are. Not about the way things are in general,
sub specie aeternitatis, but some aspect of the way things are, *sub
specie aetatis*, forced into prominence by the form and pressure of the
age. The authors of these fables do not think with their generation,
nor against them, nor (consciously) for them. They do not think
geometrically nor mystically, nor romantically; but playfully and
soberly, with the concreteness of fiction and mindful of the general
bearings of what they show. A vehicle with this capability is not due
to be taken off the road.

4 Modern Instances

The Greek Aesopic fable, the use of fable in the Indian classics, and Lucian's comic dialogues were ancient forms of fiction turned to modern account in three masterpieces: La Fontaine's *Fables* (1668), *Gulliver's Travels* (1726), and *Candide* (1759). In 1871, *Erewhon* ('the best of its kind since *Gulliver's Travels*', said Augustine Birrell) carried over the tradition, with a glance at the future that foreshadowed utopias as nightmares. Samuel Butler picked off in his own way the absurdities of a race clever enough accidentally to supersede itself.

Also in the eighteenth century occurred another anticipation or contributory source of modern fiction. Laurence Sterne had the six volumes of his *Tristram Shandy* sent to Denis Diderot as a present. Diderot was at once struck by the way the story is told. He was set off on a train of thought that eventually produced *Jacques le fataliste*. The author keeps intervening in the narrative to involve the reader in the way things are to go, and uses different levels of meaning to get nearer to the way things actually are – in the world, not in the 'realistic' novel. Whatever earlier readers may have felt, modern critics reward Diderot with delight and respect.

In these ways, the eighteenth century leaps over the age of the novel to land in 'the mess of contemporary life', with fiction facing all ways. This chapter of representative modern instances of the fable is intended to show how it holds its own, true to its orientation, in the mass of contemporary fiction.

Offbeat poets

(i)

Emery is not likely to be compared with emerald, nor Thurber with La Fontaine; but some of his fables invite the comparison. 'In the great and ancient tradition',[1] he tells once again 'The Fox and the Crow', the archetypal Aesopic fable, in his own best manner, with the flattery cunningly transferred to the Crow's own mouth. Four variations follow, which complicate the theme by bringing in a new figure, the farmer with his gun; a new situtation, the cheese is stolen; a new question, who shall be blamed – and shot? But before that there is a simpler variation: the Crow is shamed into dropping the cheese. Then come the three other tries, in which the Crow out-foxes the Fox twice, leaving the Fox with one to crow about.

But it is not this exercise in virtuosity on one string that invites comparison. Take 'The Philosopher and the Oyster' along with 'L'Huître et les Plaideurs' – although there is nothing in common except the Oyster on the sand as an object of envy/desire, and that in the upshot both passions are confounded, with incidental mockery of two classess of men, philosophers and lawyers, leaving ordinary people, envious or litigious, to heed if they care. 'The Bluebird and his Brother', like 'Le philosophe scythe', scornfully damns the wicked waste of asceticism and genially blesses the healthy flow of natural energies, but heeding the sanctions, not the sanctities. There are two interesting confrontations: 'The Human Being and the Dinosaur' and 'Le Paysan du Danube', both cumulative rhetoric, exalting/degrading man in the adumbration of his exploits or his exploitations, leaving the last smile with the Dinosaur and the Establishment – or with the reader. Lion takes all, repeats La Fontaine, beaming a light on the scene or, once or twice, turning away with a shrug ('L'Etat, c'est moi'). It is not as simple as that nowadays, says Thurber ('The Lion and the Foxes'), authority is caught in its own traps. He also introduces the Tiger to challenge the supremacy of the Lion, and succeed – to the holocaust ('The Tiger who would be King'). Thurber's gadabouts don't return: 'The Wolf Who Went Places', thrown out of college, goes smash in a big way that flattens himself in the finish, and others. The climate is harsh. Domestic scenes are abrasive or noisy, with pocket characters who spring to terrifying life-size. But compare 'Le mal Marié' or the almost Thurberesque 'L'Écolier, le Pédant, et le Maître d'un jardin'.

Of course the vast difference predominates – in temperament, in times, in style and method. In Thurber there are more sardonic residues of contempt, less evidence of feeling included in the unflattering panorama of the cussed species. No doubt he shared the humanist values of La Fontaine, but his positives are negatives, scraps that can be saved to eke out a living in a hard world, like freedom from tyranny or rudiments of decency and toleration. La Fontaine, having declared in his Preface that the moral is the soul of which the fable is the body, seems slightly embarrassed by the incubus, and escapes very often by using the writer's licence to please. He more than frequently leaves the story to speak for itself, and occasionally and engagingly takes the opportunity to dissent for himself ('Le Renard et les Raisins'; 'La Mort et le Malheureux'; 'L'Oeil du Maître'). It suits Thurber's book to revert to the moral unassimilated, as an additional resource in facetiousness which does not always come off. Sometimes it is plain, sometimes savage, sometimes mocking; not consistently anything except not sententious, not moralizing, but not afraid to point a moral, and occasionally perfectly simply apropos: 'Where most of us end up there is no knowing, but the hell-bent get where they are going' ('The Wolf Who Went Places').

Of course, both fabulists are male chauvinist pigs, redeemed here and there, charmingly by a touch of kindred nature in 'La Laitière et le Pot au lait', dubiously by a bouquet in Thurber's very first, 'The Sea and the Shore', which, however, may be booby-trapped. Anyhow, it matches the last in title, 'The Shore and the Sea', which tells a plain story plainly, and appends a sober moral soberly, to bring the series to an end with a grand, but vague, gesture as good as a lecture.

Fewer than fifty in number, these fables seem roughly divided between alternatives on traditional themes in Aesopic form, and modern inventions. 'The Rose and the Weed' is a facetious modern version of the oldest kind of fable. 'The Trail of the Old Watchdog' brings 'The Wolf and the Lamb' up to date, in the sense that the deed is hypocritically justified by grotesque forms of injustice cynically concerted. 'The Magpie's Treasure' is an indulgent version of 'The Cock and the Pearl', in a social setting. 'Ivory, Apes, and People' is a business deal that prematurely counts chickens, like the milkmaid or the clergyman. Oliver, the wise Ostrich, is alone among his kind to see their follies, like the wise owl and swallow that gave their warnings. The fox's flattery of the crow is egregiously represented in 'The Lady of the Legs', when a Parisian restaurateur induces a frog to swoon with joy in anticipation of being served up with delectable additions to a celebrated *bon-vivant*. The great and ancient tradition of 'Three Wishes', always a trap, snaps-to unexpectedly to flout the godfather bountiful. The voice of the sceptic is heard in this as in any other land: and may prevail ('The Turtle Who Conquered Time), not without regrets – 'Oh, why should the shattermyth have to be a crumplehope and a dampenglee?'; or may not ('The Goose that laid the Gilded Egg') – 'It is wiser to be hendubious than cocksure'; or may upset the clan, and be silenced ('The Peacelike Mongoose') – 'Ashes to ashes, and clay to clay, if the enemy doesn't get you your own folks may'; or may be the voice of the sole survivor ('Oliver and the Other Ostriches'; 'The Shore and the Sea'). 'Two Dogs', Plod and Plunger, bloodhound and police dog, show how simple a theme could be in the classical days of 'The Hare and the Tortoise', how unstraightforward in our tangled times: 'Who would avoid life's wriest laughter should not attain the thing he's after'.

His inventions on modern themes, if there are such, turn out a fable or two as good as any. 'What Happened to Charles' – the cart-horse who was merely led away one morning to be shod, at which a garrulous duck started a rumour that he had been led away to be shot, at which the whole barnyard was in commotion; the picture deftly and comically brings into focus the multiple aspects of a simple truth. 'The Chipmunk and his Mate' is a checklist of a housewife's neurotic night worries, repeated in her successor: 'A man's bed is his cradle, but a woman's is often her rack'. 'The Bat Who Got the Hell Out' is the familiar case of the young who are bred up in an old and cherished tradition and take it into their heads that a different one is superior, and after much anguish and futile discussion have their way and go their way, to suffer sharp disillusionment and return to carry on and hand on. The formula here is applied to exorcise a revolting prevalent form of spiritual vulgarity: 'By decent minds is he abhorred who'd make a Babbitt of the Lord'. The device succeeds here by its very outlandishness: that a bat should be shocked, and so shocked that its dreams are annihilated and it rushes back single-minded to embrace the beliefs and customs and tasks from which its thoughts and feelings had been alienated, is quite preposterous, but quite convincing; the kind of spirituality depicted could work such a miracle. A cheeky modern mouse, by good luck and the exceeding caution of a cat living in dangerous times, gets away with utter folly. 'The Bachelor Penguin and the Virtuous Mate' is the epitome of a short story, including embellishments and asides – the not unfamiliar story of the seducer enslaved, and told sufficiently in 612 words. There are other such miniatures, on timeless and not so timeless themes.

Accompanied by the clowning of line drawings, these fables bring the beast fable back to the popular ground of its origins, if suburbia takes the place of the village; and there are broad hints of what happens when it leaves literature for the journalism of the strip-cartoon, the resourceful new vernacular. Meanwhile Thurber retains, and extends, the developed resourcefulness of the literary device. He is articulate; he uses language as well as line – and much better. He brings to the genre the craftsmanship of a journalistic humorist, high-class of course, like Robert Benchley and *The New Yorker*. Whether he does really bring this contribution to the development of the fable, or merely borrows the device as a new ploy in his game with his own public, is a nice question, but neither here nor there. Literature can be made by one of the players as well as by university wits. Emery and emerald: comparison, where there is comparison, means perhaps little more than Aesop, awakener, can be reborn to some purpose even in this crazy, too-awakened age. Thurber, humorist, not poet, yet some kind of poet, is not ready to be found in anthologies of these you have loved, well-thumbed and therefore at hand, but not near enough to bite or scratch. He is still at large, and dangerous. But the cue is, and really is: laugh. The hilarious and the alarming have never been strangers.

(ii)

The words 'fantasy' and 'nightmare' are freely used in reference to Kafka, perhaps too freely. They express an impression, dominated by memories of *The Trial* and *The Castle*, of a world engraved in detail like *Bleak House* yet peopled by phantoms, where everything that happens is a sinister non-event; but far from the haunted house tradition or any version of the horror story, even the most ingenious. Joseph K is arrested one morning whilst still in bed on a charge unspecified, but not taken away. His case is reflected first in his scorn, then in his self-harassment through feeling the prosecution secretly encroaching upon him and touching him to the quick, and finally in his helpless submission to an unheard sentence of execution, carried out with a bizarre ritual. To be alone with manifold uncertainties, brittle in all their forms, is not fantasy if it pictures a truth, not a nightmare if it is an awareness to which one is awakened; as a narrative may not be telling what happened, but what is. The legal system which K is up against and by which he is enveloped is of course preposterous, but every anomaly and absurdity is given reasons, and many aspects are not far from parody of familiar systems. Is the charge 'original sin'? Is the system the Church (or religious establishment), with its far-reaching claims, beyond all certainties, administered with all the corruption of a vested interest? So that a sensitive person might be involved in the claims of the institution, of the transcendent, and of reason in the most confusing ways (think of Kierkegaard). In the conversation between K and the prison chaplain in the Cathedral shortly before the end, the priest cites a parable about access to the Law by grace; what follows reads like a parody of scriptural exegesis. One deep uncertainty indexes reference to others: the uncertainty of a political prisoner, the uncertainty of one who cannot get access to the faceless official in whose hands he is, the uncertainty that hollows out the self, the uncertainty of one lost in the maze of all this unintelligible world. The same image does not fit all such uncertainties equally, but all such uncertainties make human existence homeless.

That Kafka was fable-minded is evident in his short stories. In several of them he uses animals, not in the Aesopic tradition, perhaps; rather, because he did not have to approach them with deep-seated feelings of apology and reparation; they could be felt as closer than his fellows. Thus they might be said to have insinuated themselves into his stories, to bear with him the human condition.[2] *Metamorphosis* is the most celebrated of the stories, and the most frightening; it goes back to 1916. The story begins abruptly with the transformation, with no attempt at explanation: 'As Gregor Samsa awoke one morning from uneasy dreams he found himself transformed in his bed into a gigantic insect'. Everything follows from that, for the gigantic insect (of no known species) remains after all a son and a brother and, for all the complications, has to be treated as such, and is so treated (almost) until his death, which changes everything for the family, and for the better. At the outset this is a comic situation, but your smile is frozen; rather, it does not occur. It would be natural to take this metamorphosis as an allegory of the transformation of a personal identity by an incurable and long-drawn-out illness, with its burden on all. But the metaphor is taken literally, not allegorically, and its consequences pursued faithfully as the consequences of an hypothesis. David Garnett published *Lady into Fox* in 1922, and Kafka knew of it later when young Gustav Janouch mentioned it.[3] This story, too, starts boldly, after faint attempts at justification to get going. The transformation is sudden, and then gradual: the separated wife becomes by stages a wild animal, tamed. The metamorphosis is a plot, with consequent developments. Given the plot, new views, thoughts, recognitions, insights follow. The transformation has no evident connection with the previous character or behaviour of the person; it is a predicament or fate, and attention is focused on the effects on others. In Kafka's story what has happened has happened to a family. He called the story an indiscretion, as though it said something covert of his feelings about his own family situation. That this was deeply painful and embarrassing to him is exposed in the 'Letter to his Father', written in 1919 and published in 1953 (*Wedding Preparations in the Country* and other posthumous prose writings, tr. Ernst Kaiser & Eithne Wilkins, 1954). But *Metamorphosis* is a compelling story which creates a memorable image that has general force which cannot be confined to any particular application.

Two other fables in the Penguin collection of Kafka's stories in translation, which contains *Metamorphosis*, are 'The Burrow' and 'Investigations of a Dog', both first published in 1931. 'The Burrow' is a highly-strung monologue by an animal unspecified. It contains, as it were, the same volatile gas as *The Trial* or *The Castle*, but agitated in a confined space. In some 38 pages there are only 13 paragraphs. It is just possible that the idea for the story came from the Indain fable 'The Crow, the Tortoise, the Deer, and the Mouse', in which the Mouse, who is old and learned in science and policy, able to foresee danger in the distance, lived in a hole with a hundred openings, for he was in continual apprehension of danger. The animal of 'The Burrow' is likewise fearful, and getting on in years. In early life he lived in constant peril in the wild. Now he seeks to live the serenely peaceful life of a hermit in the burrow he has created, a self-sufficient domain, the result of careful design and assiduous work: it is not only a safe retreat but also a work of art, a storehouse, a commodious structure providing many conveniences, a possession aesthetically and intellectually satisfying as well as comfortable and useful. The animal has invested himself in this creation, and is identified with it. Yet he feels impelled from time to time to leave the peace and plenty of his retreat for the freedom of the wild. Then he becomes afraid to re-enter, lest he call attention to the entrance. He needs to be within and safe, and outside and watching, at the same time. His solitary self-dependence in an intensely hostile world is borne in on him. He wants to live the serenely peaceful life of a hermit in the burrow he has created, where he has everything, yet he is restless and self reproachful. His peace of mind is finally undermined by his hearing a distant and persistent whistling sound which he cannot satisfactorily account for. What has been his secure and proud retreat, meeting all his needs, suddenly becomes too many-sided: too late, it should have been built as a fortress, solely for defence. The monologue breaks off in the midst of a continuous train of reflection and speculation, merely perpetuating uncertainty and irresolution.

To reproduce these tangled orbits of satisfaction, aspiration and anxiety on the plan of an animal and its burrow is a drastic simplification, but the product is not simple. What seems immediate and practical twists into problematic knots without warning, like a cramp, paralysing or diverting action. The everyday routine gets blown up into a phantasmagoria of the gratuitous. This is merely a neurotic fever, of course. But the prescription 'Snap out of it' offers no cure. Sooner or later, more or less; it is a permanent liability of the human condition – from which animals are exempt.

'Investigations of a Dog' is another monologue. An old dog, withdrawn and solitary, reflects upon his life, which has been vexed by a vain pursuit of ultimate questions that has separated him from his fellows by an invisible barrier. They are frightened, and alienated, by the questions that preoccupy him; he can attend to nothing else, and feels that the collaboration of all is required for success. Yet sometimes he is overtaken by the doubt that he may have 'got it all wrong': they are perhaps after all enquirers like himself, as unsuccessful as he, and for that reason either silent or garrulous to no purpose. He has had strange experiences, and twice he has made prolonged attempts to reach the truth by prayer and fasting, with an exhausting and barren outcome. It is an instinct for freedom that keeps him from adopting and adhering to the methods of science and scholarship in his researches, a freedom that is a condition of the ultimate science to which he aspires.

Why this metaphor? An allegory, to bring together all the troublesome phenomena, more or less secret, of a perplexed and baffled inner life? The disablement caused by the slow poison of unanswerable questions does not kill.

My questions only serve as a goad to myself; I only want to be stimulated by the silence which rises up around me as the ultimate answer. 'How long will you be able to endure the fact that the world of dogs, as your researches make more and more evident, is pledged to silence and always will be? How long will you be able to endure it?' That is the real great question of my life, before which all smaller ones sink into insignificance; it is put to myself alone and concerns no one else.

This great question is unfortunately the one to which he does know the answer: he will endure to the natural end of his canine life; the questions will grow weaker, and he will survive them; it is the malice of physical endowment.

'The Great Wall of China', one of the best-known of the stories, is not an animal fable. It is perhaps an allegory; building the great wall is building communism, piecemeal. But that is too simple. This short story has in little the baffling complexity of Kafka's longer works, one theme raising another, one vista opening into another, through connections and parallels deeply worked. The fable itself, if it may be so called, has within it several explicit parables.

Kafka's art is for the most part a kind of terrorism that operates, like dreams, from a base beyond the reach of ordinary conceptions, and infiltrates the heartland of the domain of reason, creating disturbances, but with no revolutionary plan. He was professedly not a prophet.

No confident tomorrows

(i)

'This little book, about as long as *Candide*, may fairly be compared with it as a searching commentary on the dominant philosophy of the age.' This opinion from the review in *Punch* of Orwell's *Animal Farm*, reprinted on the inside cover of the Penguin edition (1951), suggests a misconception of both fables. Neither is an argument – but 'searching commentary' can stand. *Candide* is conceived as a liberation from the argument, and the philosopher besotted by it is made a figure of fun. *Animal Farm* was conceived as an exposure of the 'Soviet myth', the belief that the USSR was an example of socialism, and that every loyal socialist should stand by it and justify every action of its rulers. It is not a judgement of revolutionary socialism, nor of 'the dominant philosophy of the age', presumably Marxism; explicitly, it was not even a judgement of the Soviet Union.[4]

The fable, at first rejected for publication because Russia was an ally, very soon after publication was misused in the propaganda of the Cold War. The story shows a revolution going full circle, to a conclusion implied in the direction taken by the leaders in their first steps. This is not a critique of views but a display of behaviour, the same in kind as the Aesopic fable 'The Wolves and the Dogs' (Perry, 342), in which the Wolves, having persuaded the Dogs to quit their servitude to men and join the brotherhood of the free, make them their first victims. Georges Lukacs, the Hungarian Marxist, writing in 1947 after the collapse of fascism, likened intellectuals outside Russia who cherished their own ideals of socialism, and turned away from the Soviet Union, to a mother who boasted of her maternal love, but could not love her child 'parce qu'il a les oreilles décollées' (because his ears stand out).[5] This was a grotesquely simplified image intended by a great critical intelligence as a reasonable rebuke to shake thinking opposition to an uncritical allegiance. Orwell's image is also a drastic simplification, but concentrates on the essentials for contemplation and consideration, intending, not like Lukacs to shame, but like Aesop to awaken. The animals defrauded of the benefits of the revolution are victims of their own stupidity, their credulity, their unthinking or craven compliance, or of cynical detachment. The exposure is total. The image says: it can happen like that; perhaps it has happened like that; if it happens, it is allowed to happen. Not: it must happen like that.

On the title page, *Animal Farm* is described as A Fairy Story. This justified without more ado what happened after Mr Jones locked the hen-houses that night. But Orwell was interested in the fairy-story as a genre, and he adopts the style of uncomplicated narrative about uncomplicated characters, lifelike enough to engage strong sympathies, and conducts his parody of life-and-death matters in a tone of reassurance, as if it were after all merely a nursery tale, even if it does not end: 'And so they lived happily ever after'. As stated in the Introduction, what makes a fable is not the form of the material, but its orientation and the use made of it. A fable may use a myth or fantasy or fairy-story to 'picture its truth'. In this case, *Animal Farm* is not really a fairy-story used as a fable; rather, it is a fable which borrows the name and tone of that kind of nursery narrative for its device. (See Introduction, pp. xiv–xvi and Chapter 5, 'Particular distinctions', (iii), pp. 188–9).

The initial description assembles a remarkable complement of characters, bringing together all the required traits that play allotted parts in the development of the action, which is the denial seriatim of the set of laws ordained by Major, the venerated sage, to govern the revolution of his prophetic message. The system thus inaugurated is 'worked' by those who are looked to for leadership in making it work; and the devices and techniques by which this is done are brought out one by one as the surprising events and turning points that make the plot. A Law that is categorical and infallible is of course bound to generate hypocrisy and evasion, but the necessity of modification which accuses the system does not excuse arbitrary changes made to augment the spoils of power. The whole spectacle – now enraging, now nauseating – is bearable as parody, although this sometimes overreaches itself, because the tone of the narrative makes it so. The economy of line makes a picture whose leading lineaments are clear and coherent and memorable. (It started in Orwell's own mind with his seeing a small boy leading a cart-horse.) The image is more than any of the truths that it portrays, of which one is that in the particular case all animals are to blame, but some animals are more to blame than others; and in general terms, always and everywhere defences against government need to be continuously manned and perpetually devised. This 'Fairy Story' is only a prelude to the most terrifying fable ever written, without rival.

(*ii*)

Orwell conceived the idea of *Nineteen Eighty-Four* after the meeting of the Allies in Tehran. He was concerned about the political implications of dividing the world into zones in influence, and about the intellectual implications of totalitarianism. He wanted to show these implications unfolded to their full extent, and to expose them as integral to the notion of a theocracy with the claim to infallibility. This abstraction was conceived in the form of a naturalistic novel that was a fantasy of the future. The fantastic behaviour of the Nazi regime, which was the primary model, brought the fantasy near enough to realism for the purpose of fiction. In any case, there was the general example of science fiction and, more to the point, the particular example of *Brave New World*. The scene was laid a generation ahead, and the full accomplishment of Ingsoc (English Socialism) was pushed a further two generations on to 2050, when Newspeak would have superseded Oldspeak entirely, so that the past would have been definitively abolished, removing the possibility of independent thought: the implications would then be fully unfolded.

The simple construction in three parts builds the image of this infallible omnipotent theocracy. Part One steeps the reader in the circumstances of members of the Outer Party hierarchy, a uniformly grey environment, grim, grimy, dilapidated and generally nasty, including insufficient repulsive food and drink, a continuous five-fold offence to the senses; combined with drastic privation, under non-stop ubiquitous television surveillance – tolerable only to those who had known nothing better.

Part Two brings in an exposition of how the system works, the reasons for its stranglehold and its promise of permanence. Two forms of resistance and rejection are developed in Winston and Julia. Winston edges into a reasoned rejection of what he is engaged in doing in the Ministry of Truth, where he is adept at rewriting past leaders in *The Times* to bring them up to date in conformity with unforeseen events or changed policies: 'Who controls the past controls the future: who controls the present controls the past'. He recognizes that the further this goes, the further the possibility recedes of any criticism of the regime and resistance to it. Julia is indifferent to any general ground of resistance, and merely objects to interference with her own appetite for a good time, and her intention of having it at all costs. She defies the system by 'working' it to get what she wants.

Part Three brings retribution at the hands of the Inner Party, represented by O'Brien. Winston learns from O'Brien, whom he admires and loves as well as fears and hates, why the ruling elite devote themselves entirely to the unremitting control of all aspects of the lives of their subjects, at least those who are regarded as human enough to be members of the Outer Party: it is for the sake of power, and only for the sake of power, a transcendental ideal. It is here that the parody bites home. It is here that intellectuals who allow themselves to believe that the end justifies the means, or who try to justify the organized lying practised by totalitarian states of which they in general approve – it is here that they are mocked, and seared. Winston and Julia betray each other, not merely verbally by giving evidence, but mainly viscerally by wanting the other to suffer the worst they are threatened with, instead of themselves. They are thus drained of their humanity, and reduced to indifference to each other. They no longer have private or personal feelings. They are absorbed into the collective. Big Brother wins.

There is no story, properly speaking; no characters, no places, no plot. Rather, there is barely enough of these to provide the form of a story for the purpose of telling something else (almost the formula of a fable): to warn humanity of the danger of allowing any tampering with the condition of thinking and learning. Newspeak as the only language is the absolute zero of thought, when a continuously self-creating collective intersubjectivity, sealed off from contact with any external existence, extinguishes the concept of truth. This absolute zero is merely an ideal, an imaginary concept, a fiction, a parody; but approximation is so possible and so dangerous that intellectuals, particularly, need to have their attention focused on it, so that they reconsider the consequences of condoning or excusing the systematic misrepresentations and deceptions, the variety of deliberate falsifications, practised by totalitarian regimes.

The tendency to read into Orwell's works, or to read them for, signs of his attitude to or opinions of socialism misses the point. His analysis of James Burnham's book *The Struggle for the World* in 1947 (*CLEJ* IV, 313–26) insists that the important thing is the time factor; that the totally dedicated fanatical communists described by Burnham are a few million dehumanized people, not characteristic of the communists one knows; that there is no mass support when issues are forced; that Burnham is too fond of apocalyptic visions; that history never happens quite so melodramatically; that there is time to show that democratic socialism is workable. This evidence suggests that *Nineteen Eighty-Four* was neither an expression of disillusionment with socialism nor merely a venture into science fiction. The future was still open, but all depended on timely action, and the risks were real. What the analysis of Burnham does suggest is that his political ideas and ideals were more firmly based, clear-sighted, complex, and subtle than he is often given credit for. Probably he was not an instructed and dedicated socialist in the orthodox mould, but the point here is that to examine *Animal Farm* or *Nineteen Eighty-Four* for his socialist views, as even Raymond Williams does,[6] is a literary misconception of the nature and limited purpose of a fable. Orwell was a critically appreciative rereader of *Gulliver's Travels* from his youth.

(iii)

Brave New World, written at the beginning of the 1930s as a cynical *jeu d'esprit*, was taken more seriously by its author in his Foreword when it was reissued nearly twenty years later, partly because he was

himself no longer quite the 'amused, Pyrrhonic aesthete' who wrote
it, partly because there were signs that its prophecy could come true
in a time-span much shorter than the six hundred years projected,
partly because the dilemma posed (a choice between collective and
personal insanity) seemed less amusing when more pressing: there
could be an alternative, something like a version of 'small is beautiful'. The sceptical aesthete was more than ready to take part. The *jeu
d'esprit* was after all a philosophical fable.

Later still, in *Brave New World Revisited* (1959), the drift
towards the point of no return seemed even more menacing, documented in half a dozen topical works by leading sociologists and
psychologists. Overtaken by overpopulation, mankind is forced into
over-organization, which is the opportunity of power elites furnished with new techniques. The danger seemed at hand: within a
generation it might be impossible to speak of the integrity and value
of the human individual. Given escape from total destruction in
nuclear war, it 'looks as though the odds were more in favour of
something like *Brave New World* than of something like *1984*'. An
American-style rather than a Russian-style revolution loomed as the
shape of things to come and the fate of the world. Accelerating
technology brings a flux of change that dissolves society, and therewith personality. Human existence in such circumstances can survive
only by achieving stability under centralized totalitarian control, the
modern version of the historical resort to dictatorship in a state of
emergency. But central control is rather inefficiently maintained by
terror; it can be more effectively and permanently established by the
rewards and pleasures used for 'reinforcement' in the techniques of
social conditioning. Manipulation to this end is 'the ultimate, personal, really revolutionary revolution'. The totalitarian scientific
welfare state will put an end to the crudities and uncertainties of
political revolution. The shift of focus is from politics to science and
technology, and from the physical sciences to the applied sciences of
life, capable of instituting a definitive qualitative change in human
being.[7]

A thin chill wind is felt between the rather jaunty lines of the first
pages of the book, which set the scene and the tone. After 'the Nine
Years' War' (as we learn later) the World State was established, with
the motto 'Community, Identity, Stability', which means the
assembly of multiplied standard parts for designed functions. Progress towards unfailing repeated performance in the production of

these parts is safely in the hands of a dedicated scientific caste who, like all other castes, are decanted (born) socialized by genetic determination, awaiting only the conditioning which will induce lasting attachment to their own part. This is the melody heard in the first few pages. Thought is not discouraged, because prevented by avoidance of occasion from the beginning. For, 'Not philosophers but fret sawyers and stamp collectors compose the backbone of society'. In this bright, sterilized, shiny, sorted, safe, balanced, even perfumed, man-designed and fabricated world, cleansed also of contingency, the story can be only about this model of a stable collective, for there is no individual to be hero. But a hero, or anti-hero, is brought in from outside, an outcast from a primitive culture, to which he had striven in vain to belong; and brought up mainly by himself on an abandoned copy of *The Complete Works of William Shakespeare*, first used to practise himself in reading. The turning point is when, echoing Miranda's 'O brave new world that has such people in it', he leaves the Reservation to visit the great world collective. The second turning point is when he relinquishes the new world with the short-lived thought of redeeming it, but definitively in the futile attempt to live solitary.

Variations on the primitive inescapable theme boy loves girl are heard, but the principal one (occasion of one of the rare comic situations) is abortive, and finally fatal. Obscenity survives in rare references to the vile practice of viviparous reproduction, which fortunately belongs to the unremembered and unspeakable past, but obscenity also survives cleansed and utilitarian and unrecognized in frequent references to the 'pneumatic' properties of the female. More interesting than the characteristic features of this society, mainly the usual pleasures standardized and freely and permanently available, are the conditions of attainable stability. Most fundamental is the prevention of disinterested studies and pursuits. History goes with the past that is obsolete and worthless, viewed, so far as it is recalled at all, as comic and astonishing, useful only as reinforcement of the present. The technique of banishment relies less on systematic falsification, as in *Nineteen Eighty-Four*; more on the normal derision of thoughtless youth. The future will ever more closely resemble the present, until it is exact repetition, like ritual. Therefore science, the most potent source of change – as distinct from technology applied to practical problems of absolute control – is not forbidden, because unknown. The Alpha caste of scientific intelligences, bred and trained for the required specialities, have no leisure nor occasion to think. Their avocations outside the working hours of their occupations are exclusively the standardized infantile and juvenile amusements in which all are engaged. This is normal in any society, but whereas in developed societies there have been minorities who want to think for themselves and live their own lives, in the great stable world collective individuals who show such inclinations are early shamed out of them, and the very few who persist are eventually eliminated by exile, as are the two in the story. Therefore, there is no occasion nor opportunity for comparisons, for general questions, for thought. Minds are compartmentalized and sealed off.

The Alpha caste, individuals and not multiplied identities like the more specialized lower castes, are aware and proud of their privileges, and of their superiorities, but not of the world in which history and philosophy and literature and untrammelled enquiry have their being. They are intelligent, not intellectual; in the upper ranks, but in the ranks. By contrast, Mustapha Mond, Controller for Western Europe, is familiar with both worlds, and can discuss the rationale of the stable collective with the two dissidents and with the Savage, the rootless outsider, steeped in Shakespeare, but lost in confusion. Mond is like a sage Catholic Eminence of the past who seems to take a critic of the Church into his confidence: ' . . . industrial civilization is only possible when there's no self-denial. Self-indulgence up to the very limits imposed by hygiene and economics. Otherwise the wheels stop turning'. The logic of *The Fable of the Bees*. All that the Savage had consoled and exalted and tormented himself with in Shakespeare belonged to the old unhappy world whose rights had been taken away:

> the right to grow old and ugly and impotent; the right to have syphilis and cancer; the right to have too little to eat; the right to be lousy; the right to live in constant apprehension of what may happen tomorrow; the right to catch typhoid; the right to be tortured by unspeakable pains of every kind.

Perhaps it is unfortunate that this is a catalogue of human ills which though prevalent in this best of all possible worlds can mostly be avoided or remedied without recourse to the possibly impossible Brave New World. But the essential point remains that the measures which promise to remove definitively danger and dirt and pain and guilt threaten also to do away with all occasions of the classical human activities and virtues and ideals. A world made safe for gratifications only is as safe from the admirable as from the Holy Ghost.

The amused aesthete who thus satirized standardized man had made a reputation with his portraits of individuals in the world around him produced by human variability, particularly the very silly and the very clever. And he continued to bring forth out of the treasure of his Byzantine mind things new and old.

Little men

(i)

As a school text for nearly a generation, and after being eagerly and ingeniously interpreted, annotated, and written about by so many, *Lord of the Flies* has faded under the light. The original fable has been intercepted, not allowed simply to speak for itself. Since this has happened, and since the author has been drawn decisively into the discussion, and since he is technically interested in fable, has spoken and written about it as a literary method and has produced four other narratives that might be so described, there seems good reason to try to take to pieces this first book of his as an instructive modern example of the fable.

In an unpublished letter, Golding recalls that in about 1953 he said to his wife: 'Wouldn't it be a good idea to write a book about real boys on an island, showing what a mess they'd make?' She agreed, and he set about telling a true story about real boys.[8] By 'real boys' he meant boys as they are, not the boys idealized by Ballantyne in *Coral Island*; and as a schoolmaster and son of a schoolmaster, he knew about boys as they are. It is well to bear in mind this surface conception of the story, as intended to be about the mess they'd make, and an implied critique of *Coral Island*. For that remained the ground level at which the story is told; and it can still be read at that level – after all the scholia and the essays. And at that level it is compelling and convincing, as, for example, a television play on a similar theme, 'Blue Remembered Hills' by Dennis Potter (1979), although selected for award, is not. The play is too obviously trying to render the author's argumentative points, with the result that his children fail to take possession of the imagination, and he is left to offer an embarrassing fake for fiction that gives an experience, as Golding's does.

The boys, from six to twelve years old, finding themselves on their own on an island as a result of a wartime disaster and having recovered from their stunned feelings, with the resilience of their age are ready to have fun before they are rescued and carried back to the grown-up world. Some are old enough and sensible enough to recognize that if they are to be rescued in the end, they will have to make arrangements for survival and for communication; they will have to vest authority in someone, to make rules and keep them, and to carry out certain tasks, like lighting and maintaining a beacon, building shelters, hunting for food. Grown-ups are out of their way for a time, but they will have to imitate the ways of grown-ups for a time, whilst they have fun.

The idyll is very soon another kind of story. They are struck by an epidemic of irrational fears; indolence and the lure of fun leave rules and tasks ignored; the hunt for food falters and then dominates, when a taste of blood and of power supervenes, leading the successful hunter to rival, challenge, and overthrow the elected Chief, taking his adherents, by providing more fun, more to eat, and an exciting native style. At least two are killed, if partly by accident, by the tribe organized by the successful rival. The last act is a concerted hunt to kill the elected Chief. The island is set on fire in this manhunt, and before the kill the boys are rescued by a boat-party from a British cruiser, attracted by the pall of smoke. At the outset, the boys behave with all the recognizable characteristics of their age and upbringing, and at the end when they are taken off, after all the dark happenings, and surprised in a manhunt, they are suddenly little boys again, sobbing and ashamed before the puzzled naval officer, who assumes at first, when confronted by a pack of British schoolboys who have made themselves look like savages, that he has found them playing at tribal war.

Ralph is elected Chief at the beginning because he seems best to represent the adult society they know; but he distrusts himself because neither he nor any of them has the tradition or the experience of the authority he is aping. He is supported and aided by Piggy, the short-sighted, fat, bright boy from a poor home; and in the background by Simon, epileptic, withdrawn, inarticulate, despised or ignored, yet the most thoughtful and realistic of them all. Ralph's authority and the mirrored institutions they improvise soon lose their grip. Under the leadership of Jack, the skilful hunter, there is a regression to earlier and simpler social forms: ritual becomes important – to nerve endeavour, to quieten irrational fears, and to enforce concerted action when rules have ceased to bind. They are 'liberated into savagery' by adopting primitive devices. They learn to kill and to rejoice in killing, as well as in savouring the results. Ralph, Piggy and Simon, with only the twins as adherents, stand out against this reversion or this rediscovery; and the first two of these are compromised. Of the three, only Ralph survives: 'Ralph wept for the end of innocence, the darkness of man's heart, and the fall through the air of the true, wise friend called Piggy'. Ashamed as he stands before a grown-up again, he is more awakened than the uncomprehending naval officer, calm and capable, waiting to take them all back to the ordered and controlled society whose image Ralph had not been able to impose; 'the majesty of adult life' is brought back to them with the cruiser, engaged in a war infinitely more devastating and more respectable than the squalid affair on the island among miserable little boys.

There are details left out of this outline of the story which are essential to the meaning which, as it were, supervened in the writing of the fable. When Ralph calls a last general assembly, to rebuke them for neglect of the fire and other essential tasks, and to rally support, the defection sets in, with defiance and panic fear, a fear supported by report of a Beast that comes up out of the water. The meeting breaks up, leaving Ralph, Piggy and Simon feeling helpless, and longing for the reassurance of home, of the grown-up world.

Their vague looking for a sign from this quarter is answered in the night by the descent from the sky of a dead parachutist, quitting an air battle ten miles up, who gets lodged in the rocks close to their beacon, and there lifts and bows with the wind. There is now a visible Beast from the air, to scare them from their beacon and scatter their hopes of rescue. Jack, as part of his instituted rituals to contain the fears of his followers, has fixed the spoils of a kill, a great sow's head, on a stake as a propitiatory offering. Simon, confronting this head, this 'Lord of the Flies', with its cynical all-knowing expression, interprets its comment on the situation. He hears the head in the voice of a schoolmaster tell him he is a silly little boy, scold him for being apart on his own, and tell him to go back to the others and have fun. But in the midst of this he is also told that he knows that the unknown object of their fear cannot be projected outside them as a

Beast, to be propitiated, for it is a reality inside them; and that is why things are as they are. The climax of the scene is an epileptic fit. When he comes to himself and gets on his feet and climbs out of the forest, he sees the body of the parachutist and the parachute with its tangled lines, and recognizes what has happened. He is physically sick. When he makes his way down to tell the others the truth of the matter, they are in an orgy of feasting provided by Jack. When his figure emerges from the darkness they all take him for the Beast, and set upon and kill him in a frenzy of fear and excitement.

Golding portrays the boys' behaviour as an unparalleled mixture of the frank inconsiderateness of a schoolboy style of life with darker and deeper promptings; of fun and games with the raw lusts of survival and supremacy; of the rational fears of Ralph and Piggy with the irrational fears of an unknown Beast which is not there, but which cannot be escaped within them. Ralph clings desperately and falteringly to the one line of communication with 'the majesty of adult life' that can save them, a continuous and conspicuous smoke signal. The despised or ignored Simon comes down with a solution of the basic irrational fear which has tormented and twisted them, to be overwhelmed by that dark incomprehension in a concentrated frenetic tide.

Golding, in his essay 'Fable', and in conversations about *Lord of the Flies*, has recognized that the discipline of the form requires tight control of the narrative by a single-minded intention, and that it risks having characters or events run away with it if it is too rich in suggestion. Yet stimulation of the author's imagination, so that he goes on to make discoveries in the writing, even if it does confuse the original intention of the fable, is likely to bring out his most creative contribution, as in other forms of imaginative writing. Golding knew that the figure of Simon involved him in this way and that the boy's character and his private revelation, prompted by the indelible image of the knowing old sow's head perched on the stake presiding over the flies, threatened to be an irrelevance unrelated to the overt behaviour of the boys in the taut sequence of events, yet promoted to the presiding place – a climax, a clue, claiming attention in the tale's title. In conversation with Frank Kermode ('The Meaning of it All', *Books and Bookmen*, August 1959), he said he would prefer to have his novels considered as myths rather than fables; and in his aesthetic, fable is a preparation that can burst into the imaginative incandescence of myth-making or discovery. The symbolism with which

Lord of the Flies is studded, a study in itself, contributes to the same surplus of meaning. Yet it is possible, and reasonable, to ignore the superstructure for the mere image of the insulated life of boys under teenage, and its implied comment on 'the majesty of adult life' so relevantly present in the initial disaster, the visit of the dead parachutist, and the rescuing cruiser.

In a later novel, *The Pyramid* (1966), Golding seems to be offering a straightforward narrative in the form of autobiography set in a country town, and constructs an image of human shallowness, a pervasive meanness, with rather squalid episodes, nuanced but without any counterforce. This has the 'a truth' of a fable, not 'the truth' of faithful fiction; and therefore provokes resistances and resentments – 'things are not really like that' – which the author does not intend, and cannot use to his purpose. This is especially true of the episode in the middle, an operatic production in the Town Hall. The description is burlesque, but not funny; farcical, but not farce. As a novel, it seems to aim at the effect of a fable, and to fail to win acceptance because it leaves out too much. A fable offers a different contract, is a code with its own liberties and undertakings. It may be rejected, but does not allow the light dismissal: 'real life is not like that'.

(ii)

A fleeting comparison of *Lord of the Flies* with Jean Cocteau's *Les Enfants Terribles* (1929) may be worth suggesting. Of course, this is not a fable; rather, the 'Game' played by Elizabeth and Paul ritualizes the myth of eternal youth, and involves them in Nemesis, anticipated, with Greek resonances, as the Euclidean lines are drawn that will inevitably meet. The only ground of comparison is that the children are removed from the discipline and influence of parents and school; they are on their own, in this case self-insulated. Nothing is admitted to their world from the outside that has not been distanced and brought it on their terms as a valued part of their private junk or bewildering iconography; and only persons who feel themselves privileged spectators or collaborators. From the point of view of the author, it is a breathtaking vision of sustained innocence, in defiance of all the laws of man and nature. Their addiction is natural and self-engendered, yet the drug is in their blood stream, and they are doomed, bound to end their own improbable lives themselves when the laws of nature compel them to betray each other.

In this case, the children on their own attain a higher level of being than the average upright citizen, as in their different ways do Simon and Ralph in *Lord of the Flies*. The two stories could hardly be more different, yet both are finding in detached youth the rare and fragile, not merely the loose and lost. *Les Enfants Terribles* is an image of rare achievement, self-transcending. *Lord of the Flies* is more positive than it has seemed to some – excluding the author.

(iii)

Alex and his team in *A Clockwork Orange* (1962), all four, are in their teens, some three years older than Ralph and his fellows. Part One might be documented piecemeal from the New York papers or court records. But we have no information other than Alex, 'Your Humble Narrator', is pleased to tell us. Since this gentleman and his language are the invention of the very clever Anthony Burgess, and it is no authentic autobiography, what is the truth status of this fiction? In an Aesopic fable, an image of behaviour that is obviously foolish or vicious is easily recognizable as a prevalent kind of human behaviour; that is the truth of the story, which obviously has no other kind of truth. In this case prevalent adolescent behaviour, ostensibly as seen from the inside, is shaped into a masterpiece of detached iniquity, in defiance of all the laws of man and nature, as though it were the obverse of the masterpiece of detached innocence presented by Elizabeth and Paul. In the end the iniquity is seen to implicate us all, unexpectedly, unlike the timeless innocence – given by Cocteau the status of poetry – in which our part at best is admiration. The self-masterpiece of young Alex is equally doomed, and is eventually seen to be a *reductio ad absurdum*. Meanwhile, his story reads as basic realism. (Conceivably, the piece might be read as a parody of the romantic: Alex as a modern Werther, with all that would connote in comment on our world.)

In Alex's team there is Dim, the vulgar, loud-mouthed but in-articulate Yahoo, despised by his leader but valued for his heavy effectiveness and mastery of the blinding bicycle chain. Alex himself is a fastidious operator whose cleanliness is remote from godliness, with an eye for fashion and expensive clothes, ritualistic and a little sybaritic, with idiosyncratic compunctions and antipathies. His obsessive delirious joy in bloody violence is identical with his joy in classical music, with which he is as limitedly familiar as he is with the slick use of an open razor. He uses 'nadsat', teenage argot, for verbal currency, but can switch into his very polite gentleman's voice, when occasion requires, as easily as into a torrent of vicious abuse; or at odd times use a quaint mocking inverted turn of phrase. A notorious precocious maestro in his little subversive subculture.

His account in Part One of an evening out begins with a pepping up on large drinks of milk plus. Out on the streets, they mock and mug for a start an elderly man on his way home from a public library, tearing up the books, pulling out and smashing his dentures, stripping him to his underclothing, kicking and knocking him about. Having established an alibi by lavishly treating and bribing old ladies drinking in a bar, they rush out to replenish their pockets from the till of a nearby shop. Then there is a skirmish with a rival gang, interrupted by the approach of the police. They pick the best-looking car availabe and make out of town, running down anything that gets in the way. In a village on the outskirts, they select an isolated cottage named 'Home' and, putting on their masks, gain entry by feigning trouble and the need of help. Of the couple inside, the man is at the typewriter. The title of his script is *A Clockwork Orange*. He is heading a crusade against the attempt to impose a mechanical creation on 'a creature of growth and capable of sweetness'; reducing human beings to mechanisms, by conditioning techniques and the like. However, that is beside the immediate point, which is to abuse him and hold him down so that he may witness the rape of his wife by all four in turn.

Having made havoc, they jettison the car in a pond when they run out of fuel, and return to town by public transport, which also receives their attention. Alex begins to feel tired, there is school in the morning; but before he gets home there is a decisive moment in the milk-bar, to which they have returned. He strikes Dim in the mouth for an extremely vulgar mockery of a girl from a nearby television studio who has come in, singing a bar or two of an aria he knows and loves. This implants a deep grudge in Dim, and the others share the resentment. The night ends with Alex lying at home on his bed luxuriating in the sound of his stereo player and the violent fantasies the music accompanies.

The next morning he sleeps late and is ready with an excuse for not attending his corrective school till later, his poor parents being anyhow subdued to helpless pandering or courting to keep things bearable. He receives a cautionary visit from his weary and exasperated probation officer. In the afternoon, instead of school, he goes to his record shop for a purchase, encounters two giggling girls of about ten, listening to pop records, entices them back to his room to hear them properly, and there treats them to a seductive, then terrifying, sexual assault before turning them out. He then sleeps till past the time arranged for meeting the others for the night's programme.

When he gets down from the flat in the high-rise block, his mates are there, having come for him. He senses their mood, and re-establishes his ascendancy by a convincing exhibition of superior fighting power. His rival for the leadership has set his sight on bigger loot which a fence will take and dispose of for them. Alex does not like this, but goes along with it, and goes to his doom. He enters on their behalf through an upper window a large house occupied by an old lady who lives with a multitude of cats, and who is too canny to listen to their tale at the front door. She has called the police and, his friends having deserted him, Alex is found entangled with cats and saucers of milk and overturned furniture. He has knocked down the old lady, who subsequently dies. At the age of fifteen, he gets a sentence of fourteen years.

In the overcrowded gaol there are six of them in a cell built for three, and one Sunday, after he has been there two years, still another is thrust in among them, a most unpleasant character without a bunk of his own. He turns Alex out of his. His behaviour proves intolerable, he is set on by the others, and Alex is allowed to finish off the punishment. The unfortunate is dead, and Alex gets the blame. There is a visit from the Minister of the Interior, deeply committed to new ideas in penology that promise to solve the prison problem and deal with crime root and branch. Alex speaks out of turn in his politest voice in the presence of the Minister and is picked on to be, if he consents, a pioneer subject of the new conditioning technique. Promised unconditional freedom in a fortnight, he is only too ready to agree, in spite of the misgivings of the prison chaplain.

The therapy to which he is subjected consists in being made to watch, in a state weakened by drug injections, horror films depicting the kind of behaviour he had enjoyed, reinforced by films of Nazi and Japanese wartime torturing atrocities and accompanied by emotion-stirring music that includes some of his favourite compositions and composers. The results are prompt and dramatic, and up to the highest expectations: violence, as a propensity within or a spectacle without, induces extreme nausea; and so does the hearing of the music associated with it, including music he had revelled in. His identical obsessive joys are turned to dread. His reactions have been normalized. He is triumphantly exhibited to the prison authorities and the Minister of the Interior to show that in simulated situations he will react in ways opposed to his former behaviour, and lick the boots where he would have slashed the face. He is sent home reformed, 'inclined to the kindly word and the helpful act', if that can be believed. And in Part Three he arrives home, to find his place and room occupied by a repellent and aggressive lodger, who has proved a more considerate son. His parents are embarrassed. He abandons home, plans suicide, goes to the public library to look up the right drug, is recognized by the first victim of the original night in the story, and attacked by him and other old men around reading the newspapers. He cannot respond in the old way nor defend himself. Library staff send for the police, who recognize him and take him away as the troublemaker. Two of them are no other than Dim, his old mate, and the leader of the rival gang, who have found in the police service permanent and privileged scope for their talents and proclivities.

They take him out of town, knock him about, and leave him on the ground in winter dusk and cold rain. He makes his way to a nearby village, and finds himself knocking once again on the door of the writer of *A Clockwork Orange*, in a pitiable state, this time sincerely begging for help. Since he was masked on his former appearance, he does not fear recognition. He is taken in, and treated with tenderness and gratifying comforts. The writer identifies him from his photograph in the papers as the victim of the government's famous new technique for dealing with offenders. This is the run-up to a general election, and the writer has stepped up his campaign. He seizes the advent of Alex as his masterstroke. He cannot conceal his excitement, and brings in his colleagues to plan their tactics. Meanwhile Alex is taken off and lodged in a high-storey flat.

Waiting there, and locked in, he is driven beside himself by the loud playing in a neighbouring flat of some of the music he has been conditioned to abhor. When he fails in his panic to get out or to get it stopped he remembers his plan of suicide, and throws himself out of the window.

He is not killed, and finds himself in hospital, badly injured and recovering consciousness after some days under concussion. There is a visit from the Minister of the Interior, appropriating him as vindication of the new method of penal treatment and telling him that the author of *A Clockwork Orange*, who had recognized him after all and was determined to tear him to pieces, has been put away for the protection of them both. There is a visit from his parents, who tell him that the lodger has gone and he can come home. He tells his mother that he will kick her teeth in if she does not stop crying, which makes him feel better. He is photographed shaking hands with the Minister, and afterwards signs a document presented to him, when he is given a present of a record-player. He asks for the *Ninth*, and the end reads:

> When it came to the Scherzo I could viddy myself very clearly running and running on very light and mysterious nogas [feet], carving the whole litso [face] of the creeching [screaming] world with my cut-throat britva [razor]. And there was the slow movement and lovely last singing movement still to come. I was cured all right.

Alex's narrative constructs a multiple image of violence. There is common adolescent violence on the streets, from mugging to rape, from vandalism and car thefts to gang fights with all the variations and refinements, stimulated by drugs and emulation. There is the bored, contemptuous, routine brutality of police and warders, with plenty of extras when the fillip of provocation seems to warrant it. There is the frustration and exasperation of probation workers with their unhelpworthy charges, expressed in words or gestures of final rejection. There is the shrill revenge of victims when they get the chance. There is the complicity of the weak and fearful – parents, witnesses; or of the corrupt. There is the manipulation of others: in the name of law and order, in the name of personal reclamation, in the name of science, in the name of freedom and the inviolability of the person. This pattern of violence and retaliation is manifold and ubiquitous, O my brothers – to reiterate the refrain of Alex, which recalls Baudelaire's slyly malicious lines:

– Hypocrite lecteur, – mon semblable, – mon frère!

(Hypocritical reader, – my fellow-creature, – my brother!)
    It is fortuitous that in an earlier stanza there are the words:

un plaisir clandestin
Que nous pressons bien fort comme une vieille orange

(a secret pleasure
Which we squeeze very hard like a used orange?)

Within this multiplex image of universal violence, there is the self-image of Your Humble Narrator. The mock humility throws into relief his consistent sense of superiority. His fastidious contempt for Dim is lavished on his fellow-convicts, whether his cell-mates or the shambling crowd as they move along, barked at and driven with blows by the warders. The sight of them and the fear of becoming one of them after two years among them make him ready and resolved to get out at all costs. His contempt for the chaplain, whom he uses, is of a different order comparable with his contempt for his parents, arising from his perception of weaknesses, rather than from physical and moral revulsion. He is impressed by dress and accent and a grand manner, but with detachment, and an underlying reserve of contempt in store. There is really nobody in this world but little Alex, and the world is his oyster – thanks only to Ludwig van and his peers. He is born as he is, and the concomitants violence and music are his life; that is the way it is, that is how he sees it himself, and there is nothing else. There is no development, no growing up or settling down, no other theme or possibility.

His philosophy of life at fifteen is articulated after the visit of his probation officer that morning. He foresees a violent death in the end, but meanwhile will do everything to escape getting caught; and carry on in pursuit of his particular pleasures as others do theirs. If the authorities cannot allow such as he is to be what he is, well 'is not our modern history, my brothers, the story of brave malenky [little] selves fighting these big machines?' This heroic pose brings to mind Alan Sillitoe's 'Long Distance Runner', who feels that he is engaged unarmed in combat with authority that possesses a knife, simply in order to be himself and live his own life. But Alex, however he deceives himself, is not enduring oppression, still less the kindly-seeming oppression which embitters and isolates the Runner. He looks after himself, first and last, as the other is at last brought to understand he must; he is always ready to shout for consideration, if never to give it, and his grievances are rhetorical. The difference is between an authentic struggle for self-survival and a romantic contempt for all conditions, natural or social. In defiance of all the laws of man and nature, he lives in a solipsistic fantasy that depends on endless victims from the real world, a predator outside the economy of nature, a fantasy creation worthy of the beautifully absurd conception 'A Clockwork Orange'. He dimly recognizes that death is the only solution, albeit a romantically defiant death, blaming this wicked and cruel world for a ruined life. He does not die. He is an automaton: before the 'therapy' that reverses his reactions, and after the restoration which is the end of the story, incapable of growth, or death – an ingeniously constructed non-human agent. Perhaps he represents an automatic element in all violence.

Nadir

(i)

Thomas Mann's story 'Mario and the Magician' (1929), at least founded on an actual event and experience and in that respect least like a fable, is a story told to picture a truth. It works out a figure of speech for Italy enslaved by Mussolini's spell; it is a scenario of the inner drama of the nation.

Cavaliere Cipolla appears on the stage for an advertised conjuring show in the small resort of Torre di Venere. He is half an hour late, and the audience are impatient. All and sundry are there, including the narrator and his family, to please the children; and including Mario, a young, gentle and dreamy waiter whom they know at a café they frequent. Cipolla comes on attired in foppish old-fashioned evening outside clothes, looking like an eighteenth-century mountebank, with small black waxed moustache and imperial. He stands silent before the restive audience, holding attention by stage 'business', lighting a cigarette, taking off his gloves, pushing back his cloak in a theatrical manner revealing a frock-coat, not evening dress, and a riding-whip with a silver claw-handle that hangs by a leather thong from his left forearm.

Challenged by a loud voice from the back, the conjuror envelops the heckler with his peculiar patter and holds him in the circle of attention:

'You do what you like. Or is it possible you have ever not done what you liked – or even, maybe, what you didn't like? What somebody else liked, in short? Hark ye, my friend, that might be a pleasant change for you, to divide up the willing and the doing and stop tackling both jobs at once . . . For instance, suppose you were to show your tongue to this select and honourable audience here – your whole tongue, right down to the roots?'

This sets the tone and the tune for the evening. The young man does not will to do it, the contrary, but he does it, at the crack of the whip. There follows the magician's apologia, which excuses him as a cripple from doing his bit in the war, but identifies him with the glory of the Fatherland under the Duce's regime. He exposes the illiteracy of two young louts at the back by bringing them up to write on the black-board, and says that such ignorance shames Italy; and when the original heckler comes to their rescue induces him, with ironical sympathy, to double up with colic, releasing him by a crack of the whip.

Innumerable tricks are accompanied by ceaseless patter until Cipolla puts himself into the hands of the audience, to will him to do what they like – an unlikely sequence of actions. He carries on talking, to explain that whether they do his will or he theirs, it all comes to the same thing: the capacity for self-surrender; for un-conditional self-surrender, becoming a tool, is but the reverse of the power to will and to command. Commanding and obeying form together a single principle, comprehended one in the other, as people and leader are comprehended in one another. But what is *done* is in every case his, the leader's, whose person is the cradle and womb of both, and who thus suffers enormous hardship. (He frequently resorts to draughts of cognac.) So it goes on.

The interval comes, and nobody leaves. Among the tricks in the sequel, a colonel is unable to lift his arm when told he cannot, for all his confidence and struggle. People are made to dance. In the end Cipolla beckons Mario, the young waiter, who comes. Cipolla chaffs him about the girls, exciting rough laughter among young men at the back. He brings him on with gentle teasing and ingratiation, and says: 'Tell me, have you troubles?' To the absolute denial, Cipolla returns, 'You *have* troubles', and suggests love troubles, a particular girl, encouraged by a laugh from the back. He asks her name, and there is a shout. Silvestra! Cipolla ignores the interruption but takes up the hint and begins to enlarge on the attractions of Silvestra, and to soothe Mario: 'And she makes you suffer, this angel, or, rather, you make yourself suffer for her – there is a difference, my lad, a most important difference, let me tell you'. The magician soothingly persuades Mario of his comparative worth and deserts in the eyes of his beloved, and then casts himself for the part of the responsive girl: 'It is time that he should see and understand, my chosen one! It is time that you see me and recognize me, Mario, my beloved! Tell me, who am I?' The response: a public exposure of timid and deluded passion and rapture: ' "Silvestra!" he breathed, from the very depths of his vanquished heart.' 'Kiss me!' said the hunchback.

In that evil span of time, crowded with a sense of the illusiveness of all joy, one sound became audible, and that not quite at once, but on the instant of the melancholy and ribald meeting between Mario's lips and the repulsive flesh which thrust itself forward for his caress.

It was the sound of a laugh, from the young heckler. Then the denouement. The deluded Mario, staggering away amidst the applause and general laughter, turns and fires two shots at his tormentor. 'An end of horror, a fatal end. And yet a liberation – for I could not, and I cannot, but find it so!'

The story is of a particular event, dramatically self-sufficient; but it quivers with general meaning. The author intervenes with observations: 'It is likely that *not* willing is not a practicable state of mind; *not* to want to do something may be in the long run a mental content impossible to subsist on'. Negative resistance is swept away. As the nanny said to the child: 'You say you didn't mean to do it, but you must mean not to do it'. The most vulnerable are attacked first, and example is contagious. Those who have surrendered are seen to be enjoying the relaxation of irresponsibility. The audience is mixed in class and education and age, a microcosm of society. It is an evil experience: what has seemed most real – joy, security, faith, integrity, human dignity, the assumed and counted-on blessings of civilized existence – are seen as illusive, all eroded and washed away by the insistent suggestions, persuasions, impositions of a repulsive, defective, feeble but demoniac charlatan. All are degraded in the hours of their submission to the long performance of this degraded being.

(*ii*)

Heinrich Böll's *Absent Without Leave* (Entfernung von der Truppe, 1964), on the face of it a confidential narration in the first person in a frank conversational tone, is a masterpiece of indirection. In his first sentence the writer announces the date, in the manner of his date of birth, 22 September 1938, shortly before five in the afternoon, as the date and time of his marriage into the Bechtold family, 'a kind of rebirth'. It is also the date, we are reminded much later, of Chamberlain's historic mission to Hitler. Herr Schmölder, who married Hildegard Bechtold on that day, was studying masculine absurdity in a 'compulsory mutual fellowship camp' of the Third Reich as a labourer assigned to latrine duty 'to make a man of him', a mere 'arts student'. The camp was situated in the heart of the forest in which many of the Grimms' fairy-tales originate, and the officers spoke 'in the dialect which must have been spoken by the peasant woman who told the Grimm brothers the fairy-tales'. Schmölder gave Hildegard Grimms' Fairy Tales for a wedding present, and she read them a great deal, finding 'How the Children Played at Butchering' the most impressive, since the most topical. His own favourite was 'the one about the Singing Bone'.

The ostensible subject of the narration is the Bechtold family, to air a few secrets about the source of his own character, to celebrate innocence and love in an idyll, to construct a memorial chapel, with memorial plaques. The method of narration is an elaborate parody of modern approaches to fiction; above all, throwing back responsibility on the reader – nothing is done deliberately. The beginning is a provocative Lucianic avowal: 'Before coming to the actual subject . . . I would like to submit a few facts which I trust will be misunderstood and arouse suspicion'. There are the usual 'changes in the narrational level', regressions and digressions: 'Here I am seen at the age of 21, 23, I shall appear at the age of 20, and then not until I am almost 50'. In the modern manner the author takes the reader into his confidence, discusses with him what he is doing, explains, apologizes, reassures, gives him scope, absurdly – 'in place of the dual, triple, or quadruple levels of ambiguity which may be missed by some, I suggest multiple levels . . .' The model he takes for what he proposes to do is a child's colouring book in which there are shapes, outlines, dots, for the child to complete and colour as he likes for decorative effect. The reader can complete the author's offerings of this kind to decorate the brickwork of the memorial chapel with a fresco or a graffito, perhaps even a mosaic. In the middle are ten pages of literary collage, a collocation of news items from the past, 'some historical material all by itself'. Having filled in the commemorative tablets he has something to say about the surviving members of the Bechtold family, leaving till last those who will be used 'as keystones to the closing pages of this idyllic colouring book', those nearest in affection: 'I shall chip away at them a bit and stylize them, to make them fit in and look decorative'. Reassurance comes early: 'I solemnly promise that at the end of this work I will make a full confession and offer a readymade moral, as well as an interpretation which will spare all interpreters, from high school student to university professor, the trouble of sighing and wondering'. The indirect manner does not forbid sharp sketches of several characters in and around the family, with a glimpse of the new generation to whom stories of indelible horror in their own family would be vaguely seen as though it were about a film. His own experience forces him to restrain himself from plunging into the dark waters of the Rhine. 'Only my grand-daughter's hand holds me back, and the thought of my mother-in-law.'

The Postscripta, the promised confession, moral, and interpretation, are headed; 'A Jew by a bellow, a German by a kiss, a Christian by baptism'. Summary words which, however baffling, stand as well as any could for story, tone, and implied comment. The Moral in full reads:

> I urge everyone to go absent without leave. Defection and desertion I would advise in favour of rather than against, for as I said: there are idiots who aim to hit, and everyone ought to realize the risk they are running. Firearms are instruments completely lacking in humour. I recall Angel, and Anton Bechtold.
>
> To go absent without leave from irregular troops is particularly dangerous because this – most thinking people do not think far enough – gives rise automatically, as it were, to the suspicion that the would-be absentee wishes to join the regular troops; so, watch out.

In other words: Sit loose to society, which is liable to be organized crime, as well as glorified slavery. But all has been said somehow to similar purpose in the text, and the Postscripta are merely an additional tease.

The lightness of touch, the parody and irony and general indirect-ness, which creates space and the play of light and shade, with the villainous Nazi saga distanced and very close, makes this story a masterly statement of personal feeling from a centre which radiates spoken and unspoken thoughts of general import. All the time, smouldering, leaping into flame at one or two points, is the protest of a life against the imposition of unquestionable duty by the concerted pressures of a society: 'as a sharer in our national destiny and a member of that compulsory mutual fellowship whose uniform I was supposed to be wearing' (and which he had taken off for his mother's funeral), when the parson afterwards 'whispered severely: "Why aren't you wearing your country's uniform?" ' his considered response was: 'because of this remark I herewith dub him the most unpleasant character in this work'.

This playfulness, this transparent bafflement, this dissipation of attention, these devices deviously enforce concentration on an authentic image of the violation of a truth and the behaviour and sufferings of a generation entailed. This does the work of a fable, as *The Tin Drum* of Günther Grass certainly does not, to take an example from German fiction covering the same period and also written in the first person.

(iii)
Kurt Vonnegut's *Slaughterhouse 5* (1969) is an unpleasant little book unpleasantly written in a good cause. The writer's intention is to tell about the destruction of Dresden in the bombing raids of 1944, an intention made obsessively manifest from the beginning, the haunt-ing duty of a professional writer who was there, a duty procrast-inated over the years; for how can the felt enormity of an event be brought home when the measure of it and the rationale of it are fully evident on record? The solution is by way of indirection, and by that means grotesque filigreed incongruity: situations resolve into a series of ironic contrasts culminating in the survival of the enemy as prisoners of war consigned to sanctuary in an underground Dresden slaughterhouse. There is a long road to that destination and destiny, and near that point the road has become a river of humiliation, a Mississippi of tens of thousands of captured Americans drifting to the city – the dregs of America's enlisted infantry, teenagers, with all the beastliness of unhappy rejected children aggravated by the physical beastliness of dearth and filth in the collapsed order of a

doomed army. The butt of their resentful spite is the puniest of all, Billy Pilgrim, the anti-hero, a figure of fun but mildness itself, and by good fortune an American success story at home. A remoter figure among the prisoners is an educated older man, a volunteer of high ideals, destined to be shot, as an example, by a firing squad of his compatriots in Dresden itself.

The narrative is a temporal mosaic, since Billy Pilgrim, due to brain damage in a car accident and saturation in science fiction, shuttles back and forth within the time-scale of his forty-odd years, and outside that into the realms of space. Events may thus be arrested, preserved, recovered, juxtaposed. An image is etched of the puerility and pitiability of war, the real context in which the event occurred. The text incorporates expressed views of Dresden by two senior air commanders, American and British, the one justifying the bombing in the context of the war and the defeat of Nazism, the other lamenting it as a tragic mistake, and pointing up its comparability with atomic destruction. By contrast with both, the anti-heroic motifs that are warp and woof of the tapestry woven by the text supply a context in which the event is reduced by the measure of commoner happenings because men are as they are and do as they do – underscored by the irritating refrain: So it goes. One of the mental and moral casualties of the war, in the bed next to Billy's, says to a staff psychiatrist: 'I think you guys are going to have to come up with a lot of wonderful *new* lies, or people just aren't going to want to go on living'.

Take-off

(i)

When Robert Maitland, in mid-afternoon in April, leaves the motor-way in the exit lane in central London at high speed after a burst tyre and plunges unseen down the embankment to finish up out of sight under the roadway, there is an abrupt transition from a world in which he is successful and competent, and securely enmeshed, to an underworld in which he is isolated, impotent, and totally frustrated.[9] He is badly bruised and shaken, but not seriously injured. His first efforts to make his way back up the embankment to the roadway and flag down some passing car fail painfully and ignominiously. His separation and isolation become hourly more serious and challeng-ing. His familiar world is close at hand, visible and audible in the passing traffic, as close and as separate as life and death. Visually and topographically, the underworld in which he finds himself is also close yet remote, littered with the detritus of the world above – wrecked or abandoned cars, building refuse, domestic rubbish and foundations and vestiges of demolished dwellings and graveyard memorials, a landscape of the expendable and the abandoned, stretched below the concrete strides of the superlative urban amenity. This transition from topside to underside is matched by a psychological transition from unquestioning adequacy to impotent childish rage, when he fails to get himself noticed.

What follows in his preoccupation with self-preservation is an imperceptible weaning from his familiar world to which he has been wholly anxious to climb back without delay, and from his established self in that world. With immediate return blocked, his will turns to exploration and domination of his new environment. This is complicated when he encounters the ex-circus acrobat and the drop-out girl who have found their refuge from an alien world in this unlikely urban jungle. They both help and hinder. The burly mentally defective ex-circus tramp adds to his physical injuries; the girl brings food and nursing care and shelter. Ambivalent relations with both make him more self-assertive and self-confident; he must dominate them in order to survive and not become their victims, used by them, detained by them. At the same time, he experiences with them the outcast state, by sympathy and by new self-knowledge assisted by his relations and conversations with the girl in their enforced and spontaneous intimacies. Each of the three makes his appropriate exit from this strange and squalid urban refuge. The ex-acrobat swarms up modern mechanical tackle and is swung away and crushed to death, without any witness except Maitland. The girl is precipitated by the event into a decision to leave. Maitland is not ready to go with her. He is confidently coming to terms with the island and with himself; and with that, his return which had been so wildly difficult has become quite easy.

Obviously, this is not merely adventure fiction; there is too much of an inward story that goes with the outward events. There is perhaps a parody of the castaway theme, and irony in the proximity and distance of two worlds, both inner and outer. And the island is a self-image or myth, which is a fate, a haven, a paradise lost, and in this experience a therapy. Maitland's distance from others is also a distance from himself and from all attachments, so that he is no longer their victim, and therefore ready to return to them. He learns how to survive, in his real inner world space.

However, it could be added that a harsh climate of violence and aloneness pervades the story, beginning with the crash and the hero's ejection. The language insists on detailed gritty description, technical, severely topographical, combining immersion in the flotsam and jetsam of giant engineering and dependence on the garbage of civilized congregation with the aloofness of the ranging labyrinth of concrete structures, as though abandoned by the builders on a deserted planet. The struggle to scale the sliding mud of the embankment, the reckless exposure to random hits in the tide of traffic, the soaking rain, the hunger and thirst: these forms of struggle against a hostile environment give way to the conflict with competitors for possession of a refuge with scarce resources. The tramp is powerful and violent, the girl is inscrutable. Maitland responds with violence, and gets on top. The tramp dies a violent death. Maitland dreams of having the relationships in which he is enmeshed above ground on a contractual footing, with the best of the bargain. That is the ultimate of the survival theme, the ultimate violence, even if a fugitive thought. Whatever the moral, a sombre abstract hangs alongside the text, a shadow as a second epimythium.

(ii)

In roughly the same year,[10] another Englishman, Howard Baker, of roughly the same age and similar profession and family, sat in his car and accelerated violently, not in this case to be ejected into a void, to be without role or audience, but to be projected into the metropolis of the universe, into the plenitude of all possibilities, where space and time are not obdurate, obstacles can be pushed aside, and difficulties avoided, or overcome by talking. The story follows with pleasant stills and delightful sequences, delightful because take-offs of characters and scenes from Howard's past: his Hampstead social set; the team of talented young men he worked with, their back-room design office and their exuberant behaviour in running it; undergraduate jokiness and frolics; the publicity man; the film impresario; and the like. But the past is anyone merged in the present, for the friends in Howard's set have somehow found their way after him, and this elite of talent and privilege who were engaged in one way and another in running their country find themselves now engaged at the centre of things with the whole universe to plan and control and advise and entertain. It is liberating, and fun, and important. But Howard is a sensitive soul, and conscientious, and a bit of an amiable fool. He begins to see that his particular part in the operation is lethal, and he will have to give it up. Meanwhile, he goes on a mission to Britain to see for himself the consumer side of the business, and to consult. He has a good time, as always, and his report is seized on by media people and becomes the story for the scenario for the New Jerusalem, to be written by Howard himself. This is of course a frightful flop, but anyhow Howard has seen the light; he has discovered in the course of these transactions his own immoral capabilities – so his wife tells him – and that the system is the system whatever they do, and they are all implicated in deception and betrayal.

He turns his back upon the life he has led in this society. Its moral confusion disgusts him.

He resigns from the New Jerusalem. They sell up. They take the children out of school. They will live simply in the country.

They do. In rural surroundings, living daily from hand to mouth, he and his family, he dreams of the revolution that must come, the new order that cannot be imposed.

The universe which men will create for themselves, after they have thrown off the tyranny of Phil Schaffer, Roy Chase, himself, and the rest of them, will be a very different sort of place. He envisages it in a kind of ecstasy – a world made by man, to man's scale, for man to live in.

(It is a fatuous world, this vision.)

His friends track him down. He gets caught again in the publicity machine. He ends up as adjutant to God, whom he worshipped from afar at Oxford in the shape of a very superior person. All his friends gather round once more. And in the end he is back at the wheel waiting at the lights, left pondering and wondering, before he again steps on the accelerator.

The climate that pervades this story is agreeable and balmy, for Howard's set are a civilized lot who make fun of each other with affectionate malice. They can, of course, because they are in a well-provided world where there is room for them all to do well, and room for them all to do better than each other; either better at something else, or 'each secretly *thinks* he's the best . . . This is what we have achieved by extreme centralization and extreme specialization – a society so complex that everyone is winning the race'. No rat race. No struggle for survival. Sweet Dreams.

Just fun? Perhaps. However, the incomprehensible and intractable real world shows through the sweet dreams. It may not be the best of all possible worlds, but Phil decides that the best intervention is to do nothing. And Howard's own specification for an improved model is simply fatuous. All are deliciously mocked, and the benevolent ass Howard in the divine office is a supreme comic, partly because he really knows better, partly because he is a comic: 'old Howard Baker, everyone's friend, the slightly comic figure with the earnest expression leading the way down the street for the rest of his body, the man who innocently believes whatever he is told, and gets everything slightly wrong'. But whoever plays at God, and whatever is done that causes trouble, it is what each makes of it all as it is for himself, however it may be, that is humanly ultimate and is not the province of divinity. As for the struggle for survival, in a well-provided world nobody gets seriously hurt so long as a self-deceiving sense of superiority is an ever-available emollient.

Lift-off

(*i*)

J.G. Ballard is a distinguished writer of science fiction, who likes to use even a geophysical accident to launch a voyage into inner space: in *The Drowned World* (1962), Robert Kerans sets out physically like a scientific explorer at the end, but solely to make 'a devolutionary descent through archaeopsychic time'. When Howard Baker comes across his friend Phil Schaffer in the great metropolis, he is engaged in reading an ancient copy of *Amazing Science Fiction*. Neither *Concrete Island* nor *Sweet Dreams* is 'science fiction'. The one explores 'inner space' in a situation that borrows nothing from the future. The other plays fast and loose with the universe without benefit of technology. However, at this point the world of fable and the world of science fiction can be thought of together, and the question asked whether there is mutual exclusion or overlap, or how in general they stand to one another.

Science fiction is in general concerned with the future; not merely with possible inventions or discoveries, but mainly with the use that is made of them, and what follows. This future is the future of the environment, the biological future of the species, or the ultimate future, whether a cataclysmic end brought about by human behaviour or the physical death of the planetary system. This fictional future is shaped by extrapolation from present trends, or is even more speculative, with more or less tenuous connections with established science and technology. Probability corresponds to verisimilitude in traditional fiction. But the convention allows far looser adherence to probability than is allowed to verisimilitude in the novel. Speculation may be tacitly abandoned for sheer invention, which may be wild invention. This might make the story like a fable in appearance, but in so far as science fiction is merely an adventure story or a horror story, a tale of mystery and imagination, for excitement, it is not a fable; it has no application to present behaviour, to the human condition as it is known.

The advent of science fiction comes with an enlargement of what is relevant to the present. Whilst the conditions of social and personal life were relatively stable, the future could be expected to resemble the present and the past closely enough to be thought of in the same terms. Acceleration of the pace of change brought about by the explosion of knowledge means changes in the environment, possibly even in the species, which begin to be with us, which are near enough in the future to have to be taken account of now if there is to be reasonable hope of influence upon or adaptation to them. Minimum control and stability depend on accurate forecasts, and forecasting has to be built into present operations. To an extent, the 'speculative' becomes the 'realistic', and those who do not look ahead bury their heads in the sand. This extension of the present and all its concerns to the foreseeable future, and some way beyond that, gives the images of science fiction (some images of science fiction) relevance to present thought and action such as the fable has. Science fiction which says, 'Look out, something like this is what we are heading into', is comparable with the Aesopic fable which said, 'Take note, this is the kind of behaviour to which human beings are liable'.

This possible relevance of science fiction is brought out in the two following quotations from Brian W. Aldiss, historian of the genre, and one of the most respected names. They are from his Introduction to a collection of autobiographical chapters by some of these writers which he edited with Harry Harrison, *Hell's Cartographers* (1975).

Science fiction, to my mind, is not a matter of prediction, and never has been . . . Rather, it mirrors the present in such a way as to dispense with inessentials and dramatize new trends. In my own fiction, each decade would typically present some central image which differed from the one before: in the forties and early fifties, a bleak landscape cleared of people by some almost-forgotten catastrophe; in the fifties, men imprisoned in huge spaceships and technologies; in the sixties, men's minds altered by drugs or engines.

. . . our fiction gained its power by having as unspoken topic one of the great issues of the day: the sense that the individual's role in society is eroded as society itself becomes wealthier and more powerful. This is certainly so with novels as unlike as Pohl and Kornbluth's *The Space Merchants*, Silverberg's *The Time Hoppers*, and Knight's *A for Anything*. Harrison and Bester, in their most characteristic fiction, allow the individual more latitude; their heroes can save worlds or defeat the solar system; but nobody who ever meets them is likely to forget the oppressions of the decadent society in *Tiger! Tiger!* or the hunger-line crowds of *Make Room! Make-Room!*

The stripping down and abstraction, the creation of a central image, the unspoken serious topic: these are phrases which could apply equally to the fable. But all depends on the real interest of the writer, and the central control. The convention is a licence, a liberation of the imagination, but for what? Commerce with a new race of clichés and puerilities? Entertainment as escapist as Westerns, mostly in the opposite direction? Strategics without logistics? There is of course a class of science fiction that does have imaginative quality, and no serious pretensions. A Lucianic practitioner and critic would create illusions to discredit illusions that matter, without any objection to illusions for fun. The machine has been the central modern illusion, the illusion that it will release the sons of Adam from the ancestral curse and take the burden of labour off their backs, showering a bonus of plenty. Since Samuel Butler's *Erewhon* in 1872, there have been several other fictional illusions created to disturb this simplistic comfort. The machine is the most ambiguous Promethean gift, inert and transforming, tool and master, Mephistophelian. For the machine is unworkable without a machine culture. Then machines beget machines: there is now the microprocessor. And the promise of *Walden II*, as ironical a title as 'Brave New World', but not so meant. Perhaps another illusion to be discredited by an unfolded image of what it implies.

In short, fictional canvass of possible futures is a form of the fable that is useful, and indeed inescapable, with its important bearing on the present. *Brave New World* and *Nineteen Eighty-Four* have been models. Their focus of attention on the middle distance, their exposure of the conditions of any definitive social stability were timely. The images created were complex enough to be adequate, simple enough to be immediate. Immediacy, of course, is not necessarily what is expected. A friend who teaches sociology in an American State university gave his first-year students *Brave New World* to read, and they found it a genuine Utopia. Asked about the attitude of the Savage, they replied, 'Maladjusted'. This happened twice with successive intakes of students. However, when it got around that this was not the official view of the satire, the pattern of response changed to conform with expectations.

(ii)

The most seriously adventurous astronaut of inner space has been William S. Burroughs. A first reading of some of his explorations might leave an impression that there is more fantasy than purpose – obsessional fantasy.[11] But an underlying purpose is there, as obsessional as some of his images. He is a committed writer, an activist, not a literary novelist nor an entertainer; his writing is operational, totally subversive and innovatory; and he is kinky and mythic and eclectic and prone to ambitious neotechnics like the alchemists, switched from chemicals to electricals. He sees the historical human environment as hostile, endlessly repeated forms of power engaged in conditioning and manipulating people who are ready to submit. Political revolution simply means more of the same. Addictive needs are induced and multiplied to exploit dependence. Both power and submission are rooted in sexual energy and striving. Escape from this cycle begins with understanding, but would go on to require the dismantling of established social structures centred in nation and family and traditional methods of reproduction and child-rearing. This removal of fixed centres and structures would be in order to eliminate sources of conflict and to liberate process, allowing human beings to be self-regulated and capable of metamorphosis. Language, the most basic structure of all, conditions human consciousness. If verbalizing cannot be abolished, at least language can be transformed as a method of communication – made simple, pictorial, immediate, universal, incapable of being stereotyped into verbal impositions and used as a principal unrecognized means of control. However, his grand strategy for a guerrilla attack on this whole historical order crumbles into tactics for partisan survival, methods of self-protection, ways of keeping one's own and creating a space under control, a model of non-subservience.

His imagination is metaphoric. He treats life as a film; the characters exist only 'on set'. His methods of composition borrow film techniques and rely on familiarity with films. 'In writing, I see it as a whole set. It's got a script, it's got pictures, and it has a sound track.' He developed a condensed, taut, highly controlled and flexible narrative style, using parody and cut-ups as well as these film conventions, packed with allusions of wide range that buy resources of expression at the cost of communication.

His obsessional images are repeated until they are distanced. There is this element of self-therapy in his work, deliverance from his own addictions. Some sort of transcendental (non-theistic) deliverance is the orientation, in despair of demythologized and deconditioned man.

How seriously should one take Burroughs, who is absolutely serious, and to what end? As seriously as one should take Swift, with the same attention due to the truth of an extreme vision or version, not varnished by common sense. Or he can be heard as a coda to the variations in this chapter on the theme of self-destructive violence.

Modern fantasy

(i)

Last, not least, there is Angela Carter (b. 1940), who represents a point of view markedly missing in this context, presenting in her fables the world as seen by a highly individual woman. Two of her books have been crowned as King Penguins (1981): *The Bloody Chamber* (1979) and *Heroes and Villains* (1969).

'A critique of our symbols is a critique of life', she remarks. This has been a specialism of Jung and his followers, and part of the vast material they have studied in this exploration has been the fairy-tale.

> The concept of the archetype . . . is derived from the repeated observation that, for instance, the myths and fairy tales of world literature contain definite motifs which crop up everywhere. We meet these same motifs in the fantasies, dreams, deliria, and delusions of individuals living today. These typical images and associations are what I call archetypal ideas. (*Civilisation in Transition*, Collected Works, vol. 10, para. 847)

Two of the most influential archetypes, regulators of behaviour, are the *animus* and the *anima*, the man within the woman, the woman within the man. The process of individuation, by which the Self achieves totality in becoming aware of itself, involves coming to terms with this inner voice of the unconscious. The influence may be negative and destructive (the woman's animus in 'Bluebeard') or positive (the animus leads the girl to fulfilment in 'Beauty and the Beast'). The promptings that come from this source have to be judged and filtered by conscious standards. To be simply identified with animus or anima is disastrous. Fairy-tales picture symbolically these failures and successes, as also other features of the process of individuation. The king has fallen ill or grown old, the royal couple are childless, the kingdom is plagued by disasters: these are obstructions encountered, or imagined and projected, or the emptiness felt in the early quest for identity and purpose and meaning. The cure is something very special, unique and hard to find. Dr Marie-Louise von Franz has studied the fairy-tale on Jungian lines in *Man and his Symbols*, on which she worked with Jung and which she edited after his death; and in *Introduction to the Study of Fairy Tales* and *Problems of the Feminine in Fairy Tales*. (See also Chapter 6, 'Exegesis', p. 240).

The assumption that fairy-tales are or manifest projections of the unconscious is more general than Jung's interpretation, and it would distinguish them decisively from the fable, which is a deliberate representation of its theme. A fairy-tale may be retold as a fable, and this is to interpret and use it as a critique of life; or traditional features of a familiar fairy-story may be used allusively in this way. Of course, a fairy-tale may also be retold otherwise, in a personal way, as La Fontaine retold his *Contes*; or to put it in modern dress, or as pastiche. In 'The Bloody Chamber' and in 'The Courtship of Mr Lyon', Angela Carter preserves the story-line transposed to a modern setting, taking pleasure in the telling, faithful to the tradition, with a faintly mocking lining to the romantic outline and a hint or two of deeper perceptions. 'The Tiger's Bride' is quite different. This is 'Beauty and the Beast' used as a fable. The loving father stakes and loses his daughter at cards to the Beast, the Tiger made up as a man. In the house and hands of the Tiger and his simian valet, she is provided with a clockwork lady's maid in her own image. The valet transmits his master's desire that she will show herself to him unclothed. In her virgin pride, she refuses. All three go out riding in the deserted winter landscape. She reflects metaphysically that they are six beings and not one soul in the official view of the world, merely beasts and a woman, one of those without the rationality denied by men 'to all those who were not exactly like themselves, in all their unreason'. The place is cleansed of man. They halt by a river, and the valet transmits his master's request that she consent to see him unclothed. Fearful and hesitating, she is impelled to consent. The sight of his male magnificence in tiger form strikes her like a wound. The Tiger and his valet go hunting, and then with the spoils they return together. She learns that the Tiger has paid her father's losses. He will honour his pledge and send her home. She sends in her place her image, the clockwork maid. She goes to the Tiger's room, and on the straw among the bones to the roar of his heavy purr he licks her skin with his rough tongue. 'And each stroke of his tongue ripped off skin after successive skin, all the skin of a life in the world, and left behind a nascent patina of shining hairs.'

The fantasy separates the historical reality of the man-made world of the father and the female puppet from the projected image of the virgin responding to sovereign maleness on a level of equality in full reciprocity, consummated in the deserted winter landscape. This is a fairy-story used as a fable, a critique of an ancient symbol that is a critique of life.

In *The Magic Toyshop* (1967), there are still the lineaments of ancient story – enslavement by an ogre, a prince in disguise, escape – but present in the fortunes of an orphaned girl of today, who with her brother and baby sister goes to unknown relatives and finds herself in circumstances very different from those to which she is accustomed in terms of comfort, cleanliness, and personal relations. Good and evil are revealed in terms of tenderness and spontaneity, Irish warmth subtended by sexuality, on the one hand; and tyranny, miserly greed, arrogance, envy, puritan strictness and ingenious mechanical fanaticism on the other. The disgusting filth and continual discomfort, which are in obtrusive contrast with remembered luxuries of freshness and comfort, form a minor counterpart, negligible in comparison with human warmth in an awkward world.

(ii)

The heroine of *Heroes and Villains* (1969) remarks towards the end: 'When I was a little girl, we played at heroes and villains but now I don't know which is which any more, nor who is who, and what can I trust if not appearances?' Profoundly, the social conditions of such social distinctions have gone. After a global catastrophe (unspecified), the main survivors form a Laputian community of Professors, with a fixation on the past, continuing their habitual performances in a white tower of steel and concrete, protection against incursions of the Barbarians who inhabit the devastated surrounding countryside, sub-human Yahoos beyond and below whom are shadowy Out People. The Barbarians raid and plunder the Professors in petty incursions; the Out People, the Barbarians. The reference to *Gulliver* is explicit, and this fable may be considered a modern successor.

Marianne, daughter of a Professor of History, witnesses through a window during one of the raids the killing of her brother by a Barbarian of his own age. She retains an image of him. Her father dies, and she goes to live with an uncle, a Soldier, with whom she has nothing in common. Stealing out of curiosity into the country outside the tower, she encounters a column of Barbarians on the move, and hides. As she watches them go by, she is astonished and distressed by their appearance of wretched poverty and misery. Again, she witnesses a raid, and sees one of the Barbarians, left for dead, revive and seek refuge in an open shed. She knows the door will be locked, and he will be found and killed. In the night, she creeps out to release him. The upshot is that he forces her to drive him away in a lorry, which is later crashed and burned out. Marianne's lot is cast with the Barbarians. The main theme is her relationship with Jewel whom she has rescued, the killer of her brother. It is irredeemably ambivalent, on both sides: each is alien and attractive; there is love and hate, tenderness and violence, needs and desires: a stupor of uncertainties. They can communicate because Jewel is half-educated by Donally, a former Professor who lives and acts as a shaman in the tribe; and who has grandiose schemes or dreams for the future of Jewel under his influence. The indescribable filth, squalor, and exposure in which the tribe live, cultivated by their neglect but mainly the result of unspeakable habits, are abundantly indicated. Remnants of the old culture survive in Donally, as in Marianne herself, but these relics are in disintegration like the uninhabited buildings in the countryside, mere memory: MEMORY IS DEATH – one of Donally's graffiti. Continuity is broken, temporal dimensions lost, in a no-man's-land of detached images, a land without landmarks, without signposts, without names, a land in which reason has no orientation, and cannot long survive without bearings. But this is anticipation, and destiny is not disclosed. Meanwhile, Marianne half-monitors the slippage, in her own mind. And all the time catastrophe brings out aspects of what lies not far beneath the surface of contemporary life.

Towards the end, Jewel says to Marianne: 'Embrace your destiny with style, that's the important thing. Pretend you're Eve at the end of the world.' 'Lilith,' said Donally, pedantically. 'Call her Lilith.'

(iii)

The epigraph on the title-page of *The Passion of New Eve* (1977) is:

'In the beginning all the world was America' – John Locke

In a later chapter of the *Second Treatise on Civil Government*, Locke remarks that America 'is still a pattern of the first ages in Asia and Europe'. That was America as the first colonists found it, Old America. The New America of New Eve is the outcome of historical progress, the world when mythology is finally superseded by technology. But that is not the New World of New Eve.

Evelyn, a young Englishman about to leave to take up a university appointment in New York, spends his last night in London in a sordid cinema, indulging his half-spent fantasy affair with Tristessa, the star who was not so much a sex symbol as the feminine principle itself. New York is a Gothic nightmare in incipient anarchy, a civilization on the verge of dissolution. There is no job, and he lurches into another sordid episode, the crude raptures and ruptures of lustful infatuation with Leilah, a lush night-club dancer, eventually left in hospital after a botched abortion.

He makes for the wide open spaces, and in the desert falls into the hands of The Women, one of the warring factions in the break-up, with their relevant symbol. In their hands he is subjected to a surgical sex-change: old Evelyn becomes new Eve. He is due to be inseminated with his own sperm in order to fulfil The Women's programme, but escapes and falls into the hands of Zero, a Nietzschean poet without words, who with his guns and knives and whips and harem of seven cringing females is Masculinity incarnate, supervirility doomed to absolute sterility and an obsessive quest for Tristessa, the image that caused it, now retired to a private hide-out. Eve is violated with due violence and joins the harem, waiting her opportunity to escape. Zero, cruising in his helicopter, discovers Tristessa's retreat, a crystal mansion where she is engaged in producing glass figures and emblems, 'like an allegory of chastity in a medieval romance'. Incarnate Masculinity encounters incarnate Feminity. Her secret is discovered: she is male. Zero insists on a ribald marriage between Eve and Tristessa. The crystal mansion is whirled to destruction by its own mechanism, and Zero and his obscene slaves with it. Eve and Tristessa make their escape in his helicopter.

Stranded in the desert, parched and without hope, they abandon themselves to one another and discover the ecstasy of sexual mutuality. And thus they are discovered by a band of puritanical Child Crusaders, who shoot Tristessa dead and carry off Eve to their camp. The next day, Eve decamps in one of their vehicles in a mad attempt to return to her dead Tristessa. Eventually, her road takes her out of the desert, that 'gigantic metaphor for sterility', in which she had found herself trapped within four insulated systems, with their futile missions, and had each time escaped. She is now back in the everyday reality of current affairs, which happen to be raging anarchy and civil war. California has wrenched itself out of the Union, and is destroying itself. Caught up in a skirmish, Eve is rescued by a troop whose leader turns out to be Leilah, really Lilith, the mythical first wife of Adam. Under her guidance, she passes through a final ordeal that serves as a ritual purging, and commits herself in a frail craft to sea, bearing a child procreated on 'the star-spangled banner' in the desert: 'Ocean, ocean, mother of mysteries, bear me to the place of birth'.

What is it all about? In a kind of post-evolutionary soup of dissolution and disillusion, of beginnings and ends, the mishmash includes not only the detritus of a self-destroying material civilization but also mental and moral flotsam and jetsam of a society dedicated to happiness but doomed by Old Adam. Fantasies and futile projects, together with echoes of ancient myths and ubiquitous symbols, are in collision with time-borne experiences. The passion and purgation of Eve are in her somehow reaching the mystery of true experience through the paradoxes and contradictions of the actual conditions and processes of existence.

Favoured images in all these pages are white or black, the black predominant. On the one side, boudoir freshness and elegance, refinements of luxury in possessions and surroundings and circumstances, or such images in the natural world. On the other, dirt here, there, and everywhere, along with disgusting habits, discomfort, dilapidation, the discarded, the neglected, the obscene. The command of language, for precision or evocation, exercises firm control; and taboo words of the vulgar tongue are used appropriately with uncommon directness and familiarity. This sorts with the fundamental part of sexuality in the narratives, female and male, with its permutations and combinations, its violations, its inbred malfeasance; but containing in its marrow the mutuality needed to make human integrity – perhaps an echo of Aristophanes' myth in the 'Symposium'.

5   The Medium

Theory

(*i*)

The particular is the medium of experience, the general the medium of thought. The ability to conceptualize is needed for understanding (what goes with what, what follows what) and thus for purpose, organization and management. In this economy, it is the function of fable to show what the general means in practice, and in this way to bring to notice a matter that demands attention, and leave it to reflection in the light of what has been shown.

To put this shortly: a fable is a story devised to show something of general import and importance not generally or not sufficiently recognized. That will do to put fable on the agenda for analysis. There are three parts to be examined: the story, the matter of general import, responsive recognition. In the Introduction, the three parts were identified as idea, image, and expression. 'Idea' and 'image' are as vague as vast; 'expression' is only half of the equation, since without responsive recognition of what is shown there is no fable. However, the integral identity of the three parts was properly noticed; for the story, as a fable, implies the recognizable general import of what it is invented to show.

The story is devised to 'show' something. To show may mean to make plain (Q.E.D.), but fable is not argument; its 'showing' is translation of the general into the particular, what is meant in prac- tice. At its simplest, this might be by an observable example: the boy who cried 'Wolf!'; the dog in the manger. These are immediately recognizable as types of behaviour that may be found in various contexts. By definition, the particular cannot be used with a general connotation or denotation, but what is concrete and particular may be used to indicate the *kind* of thing it is, and be seen to do so. Biographical portraiture is specifically of a particular individual. The delineation of 'Characters' originated by Theophrastus is of types, a form of the general. La Bruyère: 'il crache fort loin . . . Il est riche . . . il crache presque sur soi . . . Il est pauvre' (he spits right out . . . he is rich . . . he spits almost on himself . . . he is poor). Assuming that spitting in public is general in the manners of the time, the particular manner of it which is habitual (that is general) can be used

[handwritten marginal note: another reason for diff in culture]

to show memorably the kind of thing that self-confidence and the lack of it mean in practice, with the implication that affluence is a condition of self-confidence: a general observation represented by a particular observation chosen to show the kind of thing it means in practice.

In most Aesopic fables, a form of behaviour is abstracted from its normal human context and presented in a particular example that represents its class. 'The desire for more loses what one has, like the dog in Aesop': this is Democritus enunciating the fundamental ethical principle of the later Epicurean philosophy, illustrated by a throwaway reference to a classical instance. However, independently this fable does not merely represent all the instances comprehended by this generalization. The action represents impulsive behaviour as well as greed, the need for principled conduct in one's own interest: 'impulsive behaviour makes one a prey to oneself'. This is a different class of behaviour for which the same action may stand. There are two related points here, liable to be overlooked. A fable shows what it has to show, and leaves it open to reflection; it is not in the business of illustrating general propositions, although it may be used by others for that purpose. It shows the kind of thing the general means in practice, but the general is not necessarily a proposition; it may be any matter of general import and importance, and the use of promythia and epimythia with Aesopic fables has encouraged the serious mistake of consummating a fable in a proposition, reducing it to illustration. Its main function in more complex fables is exposure. *A Clockwork Orange* is a sequence of particular events initiated by teenage violence, devised to expose the notion of violence for reconsideration. *Brave New World* and *Nineteen Eighty-Four* expose for consideration the problem or policy of establishing conditions of permanent stability in a modern society, by showing the kind of thing this means in practice. *Lord of the Flies* exposes for reconsideration an assumption about the behaviour of boys taken out of adult society, by showing in a particular case the kind of thing this would mean. In each of these cases, the particular action brings to light for consideration far more than is indicated by these central concerns mentioned. A world of representations is organized by the action. It can be said that the poles of the fable's sphere are memorable illustration of the familiar and exposure of the unrecognized.

In the fables just mentioned, the particular events invented to show the meaning of the matter of general import were, or seemed to be, observable events, possibilities. In such fables as *Gulliver*, *Rasselas* or *Erewhon*, the particular action is not particular in this sense of verisimilitude, drawn from experience. It has been shown how a particular may represent a general, and be seen to do so; how can a pseudo-particular do so that has no place nor part in anyone's possible experience? One might say a world of misrepresentations is organized by the action. That would indeed be so if these representations estranged from the experienced world did not, all the same, refer to that world, and be seen to do so. They do not represent particular things of a kind that happen, for they refer to other realities of experience: the extreme seriousness of human evil, cultural relativity, the questionability of obvious quests, the paradox of beneficial invention. Representations that have no counterpart in actuality are justified by recognizable reference to experience. It is therefore indifferent whether the particular action invented to show the chosen matter of general import is factitious or merely fictitious, fabricated like a collage or a design or model, or a fabricated history. This freedom of inventive representation is an immense resource distinctive of the fable, its nuclear capability.

The Aesopic use of animals is the primal and simplest form of this freedom of representation. In 'The Fox and the Crow', the Fox is any agent of cunning (or diplomacy), the Crow any susceptible party in possession of something coveted; the flattery is grossly implausible – an *a fortiori* argument. Thus the *kind* of behaviour is *seen* (shown), memorably. *Gulliver* shows a bold imagination using what never was on land or sea to seize attention for matters in the experienced world. Impossible transformations of that world show hardly noticed things that really are or happen.

Freedom of representation is of course limited to what is recognizable. The reference to the experienced world must be clear enough, with clues if necessary. A fabulist can afford even less than a poet a merely private language. A need for more than one reading is in order, riddles rarely. Because the matter of general import is usually not a proposition it is likely to have several aspects, and the focus of interest may be open to doubt. Usually, what is exposed exceeds the intention; the spotlight becomes an illuminated patch. Even 'the dog in Aesop' exhibited at least two forms of behaviour. The writer has in mind what he wants to show. The reader may recognize it, and find other use for what it offers.

Here the role of conceptual thinking in fables has to be considered.

Although a fable, even an Aesopic fable, is not to be resumed in a
generalization, and is not merely a particular instance or an illustration, if it shows what something general means in practice, that
meaning is also formulable in abstract propositions. The fable told, it
is perhaps allowable to speak of translation of the general into the
particular, but at the time of conception it is not likely that an idea
was given an image; rather, the matter was conceived imaginatively in
a particular form, was seen that way in embryo. But both in the
making and in the reception conceptual thinking is necessary. If fable
is an aid to thinking about important matters, or a rough awakening
to them, the thinking has to be expressible, discussable, testable. A
fable, like a poem, survives discussion and is intact. It remains both a
means of thinking and an object of thought, in virtue of what it does
as a fable in combining general and particular in a way that enables the
senses to supplement cognition, and not be supplanted. Thought
generalizes the particular; a fable in its own way particularizes the
general, a matter that has been thought to have commanding importance. In this sense, a fable is a piece of concrete thinking.

There are two minor fables which show a general point applicable
to fable. In Lucian's 'The Cock', Mycillus can be presumed to know
the argument against setting one's heart on riches; then he is taught
by his cock to make comparisons, and learns of the troubled and
tangled lives of the great and prosperous. He is partly convinced in
his head, but his heart from boyhood has been filled with this hope.
This changes when he is taken to see two of his envied neighbours,
whose riches have ruined their happiness. The other fable is of the
argument between a man and a lion as to which of the two generically
is the stronger, as told by Marie de France. The man's argument is
transparently unsound. He is then shown a physical example of the
lion's superiority, reinforced later by his finding himself at the mercy
of a lion. In both cases, it is first-hand experience that clinches the
matter. Fable, as particular and general, concrete and abstract, moves
halfway towards experience; and itself induces unsettlement, an
openness to change.

There remains what I will call 'the jester factor'. The court jester
was licensed to speak his mind in the act of playing the fool – allowed
token subversion. A fable writer is not necessarily subject to the
caprice of political authority; it is the proper business of a writer to
speak his mind. But this writer takes – is allowed – the freedom to do
so in his own unexpected ways, which may be to bamboozle and

unsettle, to tease, to delay, to play all the tricks in, and not in, the book. There are the antics of Aristophanes, thinking with materialized ideas. There may also be the surge or stab of underlying passion, reminder of the regular detachment of such a writer. In short, the simple melody may be orchestrated with chromatic complications for the amplitude of its effect. The cast of mind that produces a telling fable may seem pathological – has done so. It is ever likely to be not normal when it claims intellectual respect for extremes, to be taken extremely seriously, not countered by other considerations, and discounted. Paradox is constitutional. As Hazlitt put it: 'Man is an intellectual animal, and therefore an everlasting contradiction to himself' (*Characteristics*, CLVIII). The jester factor may or may not be there; it is not in the commission nor the convention, possibly in the particular contract. Whether or not there is the 'sudden glory' of laughter or anything of the sort, there is a bruising seriousness that demands and detains attention.

Fable is paradox: representation of a particular action has general propositional properties; it has graphic and illustrative qualities, and is seen to transcend historic time and place and to represent what is. In this sense, a fable is not about something; it is itself a matter of general import and importance not generally or not sufficiently recognized.

(ii)

In support of what has been said in this description of fable here and in the Introduction, witnesses down the ages can be assembled to give evidence, most of them already noticed in place. This shows a groping understanding of what fable is and how it works. As interesting as the discernment has been the more common confusion and groping. The Aesopic fable has been the model, and also the main source of confusion. The room for groping is measured by the distance between Johnson's narrow definition in reference to Gay's *Fables* and Breitinger's nomination of *Aesop* as the paradigm for poetry in general.

The common confusion with the classical myths and with allegory and parable has been sufficiently represented in Chapter 3, and was made explicit by Addison in the miscellaneity and anomalies of his category of the 'allusive' in literature. A more perceptive discrimination had been made earlier by Bacon, in his magisterial way. He too used the term 'Allusive' to categorize this kind of 'Poesy'. The passage in the Second Book of *Advancement of Learning* is worth examination.

> The division of Poesy which is aptest in the propriety thereof . . . is into *poesy narrative, representative, and allusive.* The *Narrative* is a mere imitation of history . . . *Representative* is as a visible history; and is an image of actions as if they were present, as history is of actions in nature as they are (that is) past. *Allusive* or *Parabolic* is a *Narrative* applied only to express some special purpose or conceit. Which latter kind of parabolic wisdom was much more in use in the ancient times, as by the fables of Aesop, and the brief sentences of the Seven, and the use of hieroglyphics may appear. And the cause was, for that it was then of necessity to express any point of reason that was more sharp or subtile than the vulgar in that manner, because men in those times wanted both variety of examples and subtility of conceit: and as hieroglyphics were before letters, so parables were before arguments: and nevertheless now, and at all times, they do retain much life and vigour; because reason cannot be so sensible, nor examples so fit.

Bacon goes on to describe 'another use of Poesy Parabolical' of an opposite kind, not to demonstrate but to conceal, and proceeds to exemplify allegorical interpretations of myths and the like. Bacon here divides this form of narrative from any history or quasi-history, as attached to a special purpose, the delivery of a conception removed from popular assumptions. He divides it also from narratives to convey veiled or hidden meanings, as of an opposite kind, to demonstrate openly what is general. (The difference is unknowingly exemplified in the *Gesta Romanorum*, where the fable of the ass and his master's lap-dog is taken as an allegory of a layman's usurping the office of a priest; what is general is assumed to be particular.) He also sees this form of narrative as both a primitive form of argument and as permanently valuable in its power to do what abstract argument cannot do: deliver thought in an appropriate concrete demonstration. This thumbnail *apologie* is the most perceptive and complete until Lessing's analysis.

The intuitive conception of a fable – perhaps its ultimate distinction from allegory and parable – was recognized early, and has been repeatedly. It is the reason for Hazlitt's eulogy cited in the Introduction. Aristotle said of poetry, and again of oratory, that the greatest thing by far was to be a master of metaphor, which was something that could not be learned nor taught; it was the mark of inborn genius, an intuitive perception of the similarity in dissimilars (*Poetics*, 22, 1459a). But he seemed not to have recognized that this was true also of fable. In the *Rhetoric*, he says that examples are like proofs in oratory and are of two kinds – relation of what has happened, invention of comparisons or fables. He goes on to say that in public speaking it is difficult to find similar things that have really happened, but easier to invent fables. He says that they must be invented like comparisons, if a man is capable of seizing an analogy, and that this is easy if one studies philosophy. This seems to reduce the status of fable to merely an example that can be borrowed and adduced, or else invented for the purpose of illustration. Instead of fabricating a history offered as an example to illustrate a point, fable conceives the point in an imagined action, by which it is formed and informed. There is a difference, a deep divide, which divides also those who have recognized the difference, intuitively or analytically, and those who have not been aware of any. Plato did, manifestly in the *Phaedo* where Socrates sees and says that the Aesopic fable is a poetic composition in a thought idiom that is different from discussion, and one of which he was not master. Addison as manifestly did not when he tried to do what Socrates would not attempt (above, p. 97). Quintilian's exercises for training in rhetoric used fables for paraphrasing, abridgement, embellishment, but he did not require pupils to invent fables as they were set to write aphorisms, moral essays, and delineations of character in the manner of Theophrastus (*Instit.* 1, 9; V, 11). Philostratus, in his description of a painting of Aesop, says that he is smiling, with eyes fixed on the ground: 'The painter knows that for the composition of fables relaxation of the spirit is needed' – not an intellectually trained intelligence. G.H. Lewes, who remarks that to imagine a good experiment is as difficult as to invent a good fable, gives (in *The Inner Life of Art*) as an instance of 'the merely *recherché* illustration suggested by thought or perception of analogies purely intellectual' Byron's lines in 'The Dying Gladiator':

> And through his side the last drops ebbing slow
> From the red gash, fall heavy, one by one,
> Like the first of a thunder shower.

Rational thought, methodically controlled by procedures, cannot be expected to produce the results of a leap of imagination, a juxtaposition or a fusion almost routinely excluded by the discipline of logic. Lastly, Odo of Cheriton was one who in his practice showed awareness of the difference between the built-in similitude of a fable and the *ad hoc* illustration supplied by a parable.

To turn from intuition to discussion and analysis, Voltaire's rough sorting out (above, p. 115) is discriminatory, and goes nicely with Bacon's more diagrammatic sketch. Otherwise, it is Lucian and Lessing who deserve attention. Lucian it was who said plainly: Let us grow up and discriminate fact and fiction. Let history be purged of fiction, as far as possible. Let us cleanse our imaginations of make-believe which is half believed because we want the wonders we delight in to be at least not untrue. Let fiction not be afraid to be incredible, so that we may enjoy with complete diversion what poets and others invent to amuse us; and if in the frankly incredible there remains some deposit of what even philosophers amuse themselves with, no one need be offended: the Muses will not disapprove. This was his blithe way of saying what he had to say, but his underlying purpose was preparation for the innovation he was himself attempting. The Aesopic fable fused wit and wisdom in a primitive way. There had been imaginative development of each, by Plato in the Socratic dialogue, by Aristophanes in the antics of the stage, both communicatively human. Perhaps there could be an imaginative synthesis of the two, of wit and wisdom at a sophisticated level. It was in this indirect, but integral, way that Lucian's comic fiction was a development of Aesop; no less authentic because he was probably unaware that the innovation he was bent on did have this essential connection.

Lessing's cool clear perception of the limits of fable as well as of its genius, stripping it as an imagined action of the human dimension which made drama (and the novel), and leaving it with the didactic function that did not properly belong to poetry ('delightful teaching'), was prompted by the absurdities in which aesthetic theory was trapped by established assumptions. Cassirer cites an author of the Cartesian school on poetics: 'First of all, one should choose an instructive moral thesis suitable to the nature of the purposes one desires to fulfil; then one should think of a general event involving an action which concretely illustrates the chosen moral.' The Swiss critics looked at the matter the other way round. 'What the mere concept and the abstract doctrine cannot achieve is to be accomplished by the proper choice of metaphor and poetic imagery.' But the image is for the sake of the truth it carries. As in Sidney's *Apologie*, poetry does the work of philosophy more effectively or more popularly. And the truth is not conceived as the image, which would be the logic of the point they made. On the contrary: 'Just as a skilful physician gilds or sugarcoats his bitter pills, so must they also proceed who wish to utilize truth to the furtherance of human happiness.' It was for this reason that Breitinger declared Aesop's *Fables* to be the most perfect poetic genre because they best perform this double task. The fable had been invented as a pleasing artistic disguise to gain access to human reception of the driest and bitterest truths (Cassirer, 1951, pp. 336–7). It was this misconception both of poetry and of the Aesopic fable which Lessing perceived and corrected. The confusion could not be dispelled so long as the narrow view of poetry's commission persisted, since this consistently pointed to the fable convention as paradigm, 'because reason cannot be so sensible, nor examples so fit'.

Finally, in this summoning of witnesses, let La Fontaine have the last word not by reference to his Preface, in which he too goes back to Socrates in the *Phaedo*, and the assimilation of fable to poetry, nor to what he allows himself to say about fable in one and another of the fables. In these remarks, he may or may not hit the mark: it does not matter, and is not to the point. His *Fables* is not a magazine of stories like the *Contes*, for it is an integral work, a complex action that demonstrates what was meant by Voltaire's summing up of 'tolerance', since La Fontaine sees and feels himself and his reader and all others in the particular actions of his animal agents. Merger of a particular action in general reconciliation with defective humanity is the highest achievement of comedy.

Particular distinctions

(i)

Modern fables have to take their bearings on the terrain of modern fiction. But the ancient context has not lost all relevance. It was by differentiation from myth, legend, folk or fairy-tale, parable, allegory that fable established its identity, its nature and function. It has a generalizing power to be compared with and distinguished from that of poetry and comedy; and it has other respects in which it resembles and differs from these particular forms of invented narrative.

'Myth' is problematic. There are ten or more rival modern theories; perhaps no more than an indication that there are many aspects. Myth is not necessarily connected with ritual but anthropologists have found the connection, and it does usually have a communal character. There are powerful myths, ancient and modern, which idealize a decisive action in the life of a people: the Passover or the Long March – or Dunkirk. Myths, so long as they remain communal and efficacious, are accepted as true, substantially true. Even without historical exactitude they may remain true. Paradise Lost, the Last Supper, the Resurrection and Ascension as mere stories would lose their virtue as myths. Even the Oedipus complex or the primal parricide are interesting only in so far as they represent a belief about the way things are. Of course, the Freudian myths are not myths in the same sense as religious or communal myths; they are not binding and bonding rituals, like the Mass or the ritual killing of a snake in Mexican mythology, regularly re-enacting the meaning of powerful symbols. They were used by Freud as cognitive myths, the one invoked from Greek myth-drama as representing then as now a submerged reality of human experience, the other an invented speculation roughly in the form of an aetiological myth, but connected with the theme of the first, the two repressed wishes of the Oedipus complex. Freud adduced new data for the interpretation of ancient myths and attempted to reconstruct and construe all the relevant data to point to his conclusion: 'In the beginning was the deed'.

The character and use of myths vary widely across different cultures and in different stages of development. In Hesiod there is a mixture of personification, allegory, speculative myth, fable, literal statement, loose association, intermittent logic and narrative shrewdness (Kirk, 1970, p. 241). This confusion of types of statement must have been characteristic for a long time before Hesiod but by the time of Aeschylus, some two centuries later, myths are deliberately selected, reworked, and adapted to a new social purpose. As Kirk remarks, myths can vary from apparently pointless but gripping narratives to deliberate cultural analyses loosely tied to mythical characters. Hindu myths differ from the Greek in their assumptions and concerns; for example, the influence of dream

modes of thought and the distancing and depreciation of present
reality in the Hindu, or Greek preoccupation with family strains and
stresses and their appalling consequences. With all these different
patterns of thought and areas of concern, there are a few permanent
themes: men and gods, nature and culture, the origin of evil, the
condition of the dead. But the sheer story element comes first and
last: first, because the story may be there before it is developed by
accretions into a socially determined myth under the pressure of
events or communal needs – pre-existing material is usually there;
last, because the story may survive when the myth is extinct, a fossil
preserved in the narrative, discernible only to the palaeontologist in
his modern literary guise. The content may not be so important as the
cultural setting. This was illustrated by Laurens van der Post in a
BBC radio talk (Radio 4, 16 April 1978, 'With great pleasure'). He
spoke of a Bushman convict who had taught his father the language.
On a visit to the gaol, his father found the man downcast because he
was feeling acutely deprived of the stories of his people: the nexus
with his native world was severed. The stories told and retold had a
lasting hold on him, and by means of them he had a hold on his
world. This bond is a main function of myth, and it works by a ritual
use of story in which the content serves the function whatever its
intrinsic character: the medium is the message.

When myths are retold by an Ovid or Robert Graves for their
intrinsic charm or perhaps for their anthropological interest, they
become merely stories. Graves, writing of Greek myths, distinguished 'true myth' from twelve other types of fiction found in
Greek literature, and characterized it as a reduction to narrative
shorthand of ritual mime performed on public festivals, and often
recorded pictorially (Graves, 1955). This is to insist on its communal
character, with the implication that a 'true myth' ceases to be one as
soon as it loses its ritual counterpart. However, it is still distinct from
other forms of fiction with which it is then most liable to be confused.

It is interesting that in societies where myth is alive, it is carefully
distinguished as 'true history' from 'false histories' and other stories
with no claim to truth. The criterion is in what affects the people
directly, or the human condition itself (Eliade, 1962, pp. 18 f.). Myth
is a manner of conception and participation and manipulation. Eliade
remarks that in proclaiming Incarnation, Resurrection, Ascension,
early Christians were using categories of past mythological thinking,
but did not acknowledge myth-making; and of course this would be

true of the eschatological concepts and doctrines (pp. 204 f.).
Georges Sorel has shown how similarly modern revolutionary political myths work in enabling masses who share them to conceptualize
and participate in and manipulate the historical world; an expression
of will, total and inaccessible to criticism, a different form of thinking
from any Utopian model (Sorel, 1950).

Enough has been said to distinguish fable in character and ethos
from myth. As mentioned in the Introduction, a particular myth, as
story, may be used as a fable. The aetiological myths which have
crept into collections of fables sometimes do better as fables. The
beetle that gets its own back on the eagle for having violated sanctuary for the hare (Perry, 3), which was said to have been used by
Aesop to dissuade the Delphians from violating his sanctuary and
was used so splendidly and savagely by Erasmus against the tyranny
of kings, was supposed to have originated in explanation of why
eagles lay their eggs at the time of year when no beetles are about. In
general, myths are a first-order direct conceptualization of
phenomena, whereas fables are a second-order conceptualization, or
in a supplementary way re-formed, on a special example. The one is a
direct representation, the other a double representation reciprocally
informative and involving a detached individual awareness. Myth is
more of a metamorphosis than a metaphor, involving the whole
person, and usually a whole community. Fable is cognitive, partial,
rational, ethical, an individual addressing an individual, offering
something for contemplation and reflection, never the means of any
kind of bond or union, social or cosmic. There could hardly be a
more profound difference in ethos and form, nor, therefore, a more
absurd confusion.

Legend has customarily been linked with myth. The heroes and
saints of legend form a strong strand in the bond of folk memory and
religious tradition, sustained in religious cults by continued association with alleged miracles. Achilles in Greek literature is a legendary
hero, Heracles the supreme mythical hero. Myths and legends alike
in the end succumb to criticism and rational standards; their cultural
conditions are eroded, their efficacy impaired. Another and final
contrast with fable.[1]

(ii)

In the introduction, it was said that fable is independent and general,
parable particular and *ad hoc*. That is how Odo of Cheriton distin-

guished them in his own practice. A parable is a story used in the exposition of a conception – 'The kingdom of heaven is like . . .'. A fable is a story invented or adapted to generate a conception, or to expand, refashion, refine or reinforce a conception. A parable refers to something there, a fable to what it puts there: exposition and composition.

Among Edgar Allan Poe's *Tales of Mystery and Imagination* are two in sequence entitled 'Shadow – a Parable' and 'Silence – a Fable'. The parable is a message from the dead writer to the living reader in the form of a luridly related incident or experience in which Death is present to poison and excite the merriment of a feast, present in the corpse of one of the company, in the raging plague of which he has died, and with the intrusion of a mysterious Shadow that speaks in the familiar tones of their many departed friends. The fable is related by 'the Demon', a supernatural agent who sets the scene in a remote region, exotic and desolate, focused upon a solitary godlike figure sitting upon a rock, lost in thought. The Demon tries to disturb the figure by rousing the elements and enraging the beasts, without effect. Failing, he reduces all to stillness and silence. The figure flees. That ends the relation by the Demon. The writer who records it is impressed more than by an oracle. But he cannot join in the laughter of the Demon. Ultimate cosmic mockery is not funny to the thinker. ("'Le silence eternel de ces espaces infinis m'effraie' (The eternal silence of these infinite spaces terrifies me) – Pascal's *Pensées*, 206.)

In Henri de Saint-Simon's famous political pamphlet *Parabole par Henry Saint-Simon* (1819), he imagines what would happen to France if 'les trois mille premiers savants, artistes et artisans' (the 3,000 top savants, artists and artisans) were to die suddenly, and then if, instead, all the grandees (named by title) and top ministers and officials were to die, 30,000 individuals reputed the most important in the State. In the latter case, the nation would be grievously bereaved, although happily bereft of a grievous burden; in the former, the nation would be 'un corps sans âme' (a body without a soul), unable to compete, falling out of the company of former peers. This was a straightforward hypothetical argument, not even a narrative but dubbed 'parable' to cover the author, who all the same was at once in trouble. Although formally not a fable it could be said to be so functionally, since it was framed to illustrate a point in an ongoing argument, to expound a conception. Saint-Simon's point was that the foundation of the post-Revolutionary society was the citizen as worker, with tools or skills, not Rousseau's citizen with opinions. His 'parable' presented what he wanted to say concretely, with a backward look at the surviving *ancien régime*.

Kafka provides instructive, and tricky, examples. In *The Penguin Complete Short Stories of Franz Kafka* (1983), there are 'Two Introductory Parables' and there is 'A Little Fable' and 'On Parables'. The one called a fable is a brief Aesopic beast fable. The 'Two Introductory Parables' are taken out of context from *The Trial* and *The Great Wall of China*. In these contexts they are used as parables to represent and illustrate a situation. In both cases they are used as descriptions of something under discussion – a long, tortuous, and inconclusive discussion in *The Trial*. Kafkaesque, such parables may hold clues, but they hardly function as parables to illustrate and make things clearer; they tend to reproduce enigma within enigma, a kind of homeopathic treatment. Put to stand independently, as in the forefront of this collection, they are fables, or nonsense. Similarly with the piece that stands last, 'On Parables', as a kind of commentary on the whole collection, Kafka's justification of his art; for this *ad hoc* purpose, it is a parable. On its own, it is a fable on fables. That is, parables, like myths, taken out of context may be used as fables. Use made of the story, what it does, is the principal criterion. The words used, 'parable'/'fable', may still be entirely misleading as to that.

(iii)

Tolstoy had a special interest in folk literature, which at one time (when he was writing *What is Art?*) he rated above the novel as 'incomparably more important and more fruitful', because the simplest feelings were accessible to all, and these productions were valued by all and retained, not ephemeral amusement of the well-off. When he was concerned with the education of peasant children, he wrote fables for them. These were Aesopic fables or fables adapted from or imitating Indian fables in the beast fable tradition. But he also retold folk-tales and other stories. In the collection translated by Aylmer Maude, *Twenty-three Tales* (World's Classics, 1906), Maude divides them into seven groups, which include Popular Stories, A Fairy Tale ('Ivan the Fool'), and Folk-tales Retold. None of the folk-tales is a fable. They are directly about the kind of people by and for whom they were told, peasants or tradesmen or other commons. A king or other public personage may play a part. And so may a supernatural agent, if this derives from the beliefs of the people. They often have a humorous or a satirical vein, and an ingenious or witty ending. They are devised as entertainment.

The fairy-story employs magic and marvels as part of the entertainment, rather than as a recourse. A dominant type is the romantic tale adapted for the nursery. Prince and princess are hero and heroine, true love is instant, and runs its obstacle course to end in happiness ever after. Voltaire's *La Princesse de Babylone* is a perfect parody of the type. The courtly romances, with their enchanted places and marvellous adventures, are in the adult background. *The Arabian Nights* are also adult relations. The population includes, besides royal personages and good and bad fairies, giants and dwarfs and honest peasants and adventurous tailors and other homely folk. The brooding menace of the forest is as evident as the glitter and fortune of the palace in rightful hands. Misshapen malignancy schemes against upright bounty. In short, there are black shadows to show off the white lights. In this literature there are distinct patterns, and hidden sources in folk consciousness and folk lore. This is a main difference from fables, which are individual and explicitly reflective. 'Jack and the Beanstalk' may be interpreted in terms of some nine different theories of myth, with interesting results. The surface landscape indicates resources for a mining industry. 'Once upon a time . . .' is not all there is to it. Since Freud, the deep unconscious has been exploited for different ends. Surrealist painters have brought to light 'hidden landscapes of the mind', that must disclose themselves. Dreams and fairy-tales and myths and legends are explored for recovery of a forgotten universal language of symbols. This is dangerous territory, in a logical sense. Undoubtedly, however, there are deep forces at work in the human psyche, not under rational control, dangerous and destructive but also powerfully creative. Parallels in literatures of this kind, widely separated, indicate collective meanings. No coded messages are to be suspected, of course, but romantic fantasy and dramatic themes may be expected to draw upon and draw up such buried material. The point here is that this is not the territory of fable; its inventions have a different orientation and source, openly explicable. A fine distinction is not called for. For a comparison between the authentic product and a sophisticated modern reworking as a fable, Angela Carter's 'The Tiger's Bride' can be studied (above, p. 170).

(*iv*)

The obvious about 'allegory' has first to be heavily underlined – that it has been used freely in reference to material that has been interpreted allegorically, and properly in reference to compositions in a certain convention and tradition. 'Allegorized' material is allegory by assumption, but frequently not so in the original. What is composed as an allegory usually appears as what it is: *Le Roman de la Rose* (1230–40), *Piers the Plowman* (1362–77), *The Faerie Queene* (1590 f.), *The Pilgrim's Progress* (1678–84). All are manifest allegories, in the customary guise of a dream. Allegorical representations may of course be made in paintings or sculptures, as by G.F. Watts in some figures once well-known, and extant. Fable is narrative, and it is with allegory as a literary composition, as in the above examples, that any comparison has to be made.

First, the bogus allegories, allegories by assumption, have to be noticed, for the extraordinary partiality there has been to this way of thinking or reading. Sometimes it has been a despairing attempt to salvage what can no longer be accepted literally. In classical times the Greek myths were allegorized, and even the Iliad and Odyssey. In the Renaissance, there were very different allegorical interpretations of the myths. Theologians and others have allegorized the Bible. The 'Song of Solomon' could hardly appear in the canon naked. In the Middle Ages, the mania for allegorizing was an insatiable digging for meanings and a dependence on visual thinking. The Neo-Platonism of the Renaissance was a hotbed for a new growth of allegorizing connected mainly with alchemy. *Amadis de Gaule* was treated as such an allegory. Even the *Roman de la Rose* and its supposed source could be regarded as heavily veiled alchemical treatises. There is no limit to and no control over allegorical interpretation; as there is none in speculation. Successive interpretations of the same material, say the Greek myths, show how culturally determined such readings are. The perversity of the process is evident in the established Renaissance practice of *theologia poetica*, in which there is 'a conversion of the literal poetic image into a moral, or a natural-philosophical, or a theological truth, which is a statement in general terms' (Trinkaus, 1970, p. 688). The perversion here is not merely of natural meaning, but mainly of allegory itself.

Allegorical compositions refer to recognizable pre-existing material: the life of a Christian, the condition of England, the matter of love, a national legend. This entails a series of correspondences in the allegory, a sequence of metaphors. In *The Pilgrim's Progress*, a narrative is imposed on the scheme of salvation. Any part of the allegory has a counterpart in the material allegorized, but at points the material may intrude into the narrative as a disruption, and at points the exigencies of the narrative may take over. The relation between the story convention adopted and the material, and in general the interplay between narrative and material, are special to the particular allegory and give it a character of its own: so that to call a composition an allegory says less than may be supposed.[2]

Langland's use of the fable 'Belling the Cat' in the Prologue to the text of 1337 calls for special mention. He brings it in to expand it into a quite different fable for his own purpose. The point of the original fable is ignored, or left to offset the new point made by the intervention of the wise mouse – the slow sure destruction of the commonwealth on which all depend by the habitual activities of rats and mice, unless kept in check by the light depredations of the court cat, soon to be replaced by the kitten. Fable-wise, the new turn represents a general principle, consonant with Langland's conservative philosophy. As a dream within a dream, it merges into the allegory, with references to contemporary persons and a particular situation. It is at the margins of fable and allegory. Odo and Bozon and others had used this fable against those who murmur about the behaviour of those in authority, but fail to speak out; that is, using its general applicability, not adapting it to a particular application.

'Allegory' derives from the terminology of Greek rhetoric, and means primarily a series of metaphors; and when several continuous metaphors flow, a parallel intelligible language of another kind is formed, as Cicero noted (*De Oratore*, xxvii, 94). By contrast with this sequence of metaphors, fable is a metaphorical action. It is in this different use of metaphor for a different purpose that the distinction is to be seen. Allegory uses metaphors to express or to celebrate some conception or other matter. Fable is invented to form or inform a conception in the image of an action. It might be thought that a masque does or may do just that, being both allegorical and general. A masque, like an American musical, was highly adaptive in invented entertainment and could and did float conceptions, not merely represent abstractions. A masque was not a narrative. Even more to the point, a theme is not knowledge.

Spenser composed fables and an allegory which has been described

as 'an immense undramatic masque', and he indicates some understanding of the difference in theory as well as in practice. The
differences between *The Faerie Queene* and *Mother Hubberds Tale*
are obvious in style, in tone of voice and in content, but the underlying difference is between a personal vision of imperial destiny and a
general representation of the corruption of regimes: the expression
and celebration of a visionary theme and the focus of attention upon a
conception by a construction of its concrete meaning.

Allegorical compositions enjoyed respect still into the eighteenth
century, and brief examples were acceptable copy in the new polite
journals; in effect occasionally as pleasing as figure-skating, too often
as boring as obsolete catalogues. A more substantial piece, Thom-
son's *The Castle of Indolence* (1748), frankly in the manner and on
the model of *The Faerie Queene* and the tribute of one poet to his
master, was perhaps the dying echo of a species of composition.
However, in this declared allegory there reverberates the theme of his
major and earlier work, *The Seasons*. The 'direct and close description' which is the excellence of this work would put it by Addison's
rule in the category that excluded allusive species. Yet it would not be
straining things, vicious allegorizing, to reinforce the importance of
The Seasons by reading it as an allegory of the natural theology that
inspired the scientific movement for a century and a half. The seasons
as they change are 'but the varied God'.

> The informing Author in His works appears

It had been with relief that men had found themselves able to turn
from bloody contentions in reading the Word of God to collabora-
tive investigation in reading the Works of God, a discovered
Revelation. This is the theme that is celebrated throughout *The
Seasons*. In this sense it is the last of the great allegories. In this way,
as a continuous celebration, it is in no sense a fable.

Modern fiction

(i)

In making distinctions, there remains a question of the fable among
the protean forms of modern fiction. To go back to the eighteenth-
century *conte philosophique* for a starting point, was it simply

absorbed in and superseded by the development of the novel? Certainly, fable disappears with that development in nineteenth-century fiction. The problem of fiction was to gain credibility, to create illusion. To feign literal truth, as history, memoirs, letters, was a transparent device that had to be left behind as writers gained skill in direct and close description of interiors, clothes and manners, individual characters, social institutions, class relations, the appearance and the temporal structure of social existence. Descriptive ease and, not least, management of the plot without recourse to gross improbability established an art of narrative fiction with an acceptable convention having the dignity of literature enjoyed by poetry and drama.

It has been assumed that with Rousseau and later writers the novel became fully capable of handling the ideas of the *conte philosophique* in the context of a story of 'real life'. The devices of imaginary voyages and the like were no longer necessary, as obsolete as the faked letters and memoirs in the early novel. Thus Vivienne Mylne, after reviewing the reasons for the different concerns of the *conte philosophique* and the serious novel, concludes:

> In the end, however, it was the *roman* which triumphed and took over the functions of the *conte philosophique*. During the nineteenth century one no longer finds French writers utilizing a satiric approach and a deliberately unrealistic fictional world as a means of expressing their views on serious topics. (England provided at least one honourable example in the tradition of the *conte philosophique*, Butler's *Erewhon*.) And while twentieth-century writers of fiction have invented or rediscovered various forms of fantasy or anti-realism for the handling of serious themes, one no longer thinks of classifying these works in a separate category, since the *roman* is now accepted as a suitable genre for discussing any of the major issues in human life and thought. (*The Eighteenth-Century French Novel*, 1965, p. 188)

In a later passage, the author recognizes that such a story as *Candide*, by its abstraction from real life, creates its own form of illusion through suspense and tension and resolutions in terms of the movement of ideas, in which the reader is led to new standpoints (p. 269). This concession is a half-recognition of what fable is about, completely missed in the above passage, which finds room in the modern novel for 'views on serious topics' and discussion of 'the major issues in human life and thought'; which is not what fable is about. The sophisticated modern stage has not put the puppet theatre out of business.

André Gide's narrative fiction illustrates particularly well the surviving usefulness of fable, and its relations with the traditional novel and present tendencies in fiction. He called three of his earlier works *soties*, a word used in the fourteenth and fifteenth centuries in France for a theatre piece in which the characters behaved as if they were mad, a method useful for political satire: in general, wisdom is presented in the guise of folly. Gide's *soties* – *Paludes* (1895), *Prométhé mal enchaîné* (1899) and *Les Caves du Vatican* (1914) – are *contes philosophiques*. But it is particularly true of Gide that any of his works should be sited and cited in the context of his *œuvre*. After the *soties* are his *récits* (which present follies in the guise of wisdom), and after these *Les Faux Monnayeurs* (1926), in question as a novel, which puts the art of the novel in question–perhaps a *faux roman*. All his works (save *Les Nourritures* (1921, 1935), he said) were ironic and critical. They contain or project parts of himself from which he has distanced himself. In the *soties* he is playing concretely with abstract ideas, re-living the emotions and ideals to which he was at some time half ready to commit himself; as in the *récits*, buds of his personality developed only in fiction. The *soties* disturb, lead on and mislead the reader, so that he is thrown back on himself, made to think for himself. This leaving a great deal to the reader and expecting a great deal of the reader is a main device of Gide's fiction. His avoidance of commitment, his horror of choice, coupled with his moral serious-ness, defines his didactic role as awakener, enlarger, disturber: to open windows, to multiply perspectives, to correct or to contradict himself, to insist on the multivalence of fiction to match real possi-bilities. The *soties* belong to the world of Lucian's fiction and Voltaire's; and Gide's careful distinctions defined by his *'sotie'* and *'récit'* and his management of the complex attempt at a contemporary novel parallel at a more advanced level Lucian's distinctions and experiments with fiction.

(*ii*)

E.M. Forster (in the Clark Lectures, 1927) made a useful working analysis of the novel in advance of more recent developments, *Aspects of the Novel*. The story is basic, and is about what happens next. 'It is the lowest and simplest of literary organisms. Yet it is the highest common factor to all the very complicated organisms known as novels' (p. 43). The story that can merely keep the reader wanting to know what happens next makes the pot-boiler – and the 'Waverley' novels, says Forster. The plot is another matter. The story may be improvised as one goes along. A plot is plotted to the end. In the fable a plot is more basic than the story, for it is the action that counts, and interest can be maintained by other means than by suspense or exciting curiosity. In the novel, the plot is likely to be subordinated to or bound up with other aspects of the story: human character, the aesthetic (pattern), or what Forster calls 'fantasy' and 'prophecy', instancing *Tristram Shandy* for the first and *Moby Dick*, among others, for the second. These two aspects, however named, might seem to cover the fable. Yet not so in Forster's classification and examples. The transcendence or overtones or distinctive intentions of *Moby Dick* or *Wuthering Heights* or *Women in Love* or *The Brothers Karamazov*, the beguiling traceries, whimsies, pauses and returns of *Tristram Shandy*, the inconsequences of *Zuleika Dobson*, are not marks of the fable. Like the fable, they seem to say more than they say, but what goes beyond explicit telling in the case of the fable is not a reverberation nor an explosion nor an epiphany nor entry into a private chamber nor poetic transfiguration, nor anything idiosyncratic nor personal, although it may be stained with passion; it brings about a supervention of understanding, and is not a conquest of expression.

The subject of a novel may be in the abstract banal or melo-dramatic, and the author may make six volumes out of 'une petite fille qui ne veut pas coucher avec son maître, à moins qu'il ne l'épouse' (a young girl who does not want to lie with her master unless he marry her) (Voltaire's version of *Pamela*),[3] or write the story of a servant girl (*Esther Waters*). The unpromising subject is then made interesting, in whatever way, not by an infusion of red blood from real life but by a literary enrichment that comes from skill in evoking for a limited purpose images, associations, resonances from the reservoir of experience, with which to create trustworthy appearances. The subject of a fable may in the abstract seem interesting, and the author may form it into a content that is unfamiliar and brings a response different from that usually sought in fiction. The novel uses the material of common experience to construct its images, or constructs them with constant reference to a common world. The fable sits loose to this world in the images it constructs, but the reference is implicitly there. The serious novel unavoidably communicates a point of view, but the quality of the image is paramount: it is a property. The fable was called above a conceptual artefact. It furnishes a text to be used rather than enjoyed, thought about more often than reread.

(iii)

To appreciate the importance (or the unimportance) of the distinction which it is attempted here to formalize, it will be necessary to go a little further into contemporary discussion of the novel.

After the establishment of the novel as an acceptable 'illusion', a work of art, the whole elaborate machinery, Forster's 'complex organism' has come under suspicion, so that its credibility, achieved as art, is undermined.[4] There is something bogus about the pretences, however condoned by readers. After all, a novelist's real subject all the time is himself, his real material is his own experience: what is wanted of him is 'authenticity', not verisimilitude. Again, the language and the literature impose themselves on what is there: narrative forms partly preform, and cannot mirror, what they represent. The traditional novel sets out to reflect the common illusions of daily life and to sustain the illusion of its own convention, with is special impositions. Genuine realism would be in an anti-novel that set out to destroy all this and jolt the reader awake.

A delightful example is Raymond Queneau's *Pierrot Mon Ami* (1942), a little masterpiece because it communicates so much pleasure in providing its little food for thought that the Muses would not altogether spurn. The story is a lightly sketched burlesque set realistically in the lower show-biz world of funfairs and circuses and menageries. There is deft characterization under a surface rippled by rituals of several descriptions, obscene, bizarre, quotidian. Planned inconsequence is threaded on consequent passages, entraining the casual and the causal, with casualties; all developed with incomplete exposition but unflagging amusement. After an abrupt and absurd conclusion expected of a popular romance, there is an Epilogue to tie in all the loose ends, until the last two pages, which introduce an incongruously formal re-encounter that explodes a volley of questions which would reopen the whole story. Appropriately, in the last sentence Pierrot 'se mit à rire'.

Burlesque of the novel? Or just a teasing fantasy? There is perhaps a clue in the Epilogue. Pierrot, getting up with the intention of going to the opening of the new Zoo, becomes unusually reflective.

Une sorte de courant l'avait déporté loin de ces rencontres hasardeuses où la vie ne voulait pas l'attacher. C'était un des épisodes de sa vie les plus ronds, les plus complets, les plus autonomes, et quand il y pensait avec toute l'attention voulue (ce qui lui arrivait d'ailleurs rarement), il voyait bien comment tous les éléments qui le constituaient auraient pu se lier en un aventure qui se serait dévelopée sur le plan du mystère pour résoudre ensuite comme un probleme d'algèbre où il y a autant d'équations que d'inconnues, et comment il n'en avait pas été ainsi – il voyait le roman que cela aurait pu faire, un roman policier avec un crime, un coupable et un detective, et les engrènements voulus entre les différentes asperités de la demonstration, et il voyait le roman que cela avait fait, un roman si dépouillé, d'artifice qu'il n'était point possible de savoir s'il y avait une énigme a résoudre ou s'il n'y en avait pas, un roman où tout aurait pu s'enchaîner suivant des plans de police, et, en fait, parfaitement dégarni de tous les plaisirs que provoque le spectacle, une activité de cet ordre. (pp. 211–212) (Some kind of current had carried him far from these casual encounters where he was not held fast to life. It was one of the episodes of his life that was the most rounded, the most complete, the most self-contained, and when he gave his mind to it with all the needed attention (which moreover happened to him rarely), he saw clearly how all the elements which made it up could have been bound together in an occurrence which would proceed like a mystery to be cleared up later, like a problem in algebra where there are as many equations as unknown quantities, and how it had not been like that, – he saw the novel that it could have made, a detective story with a crime, a guilty party and a detective, and the required reconciliation between the different discrepancies of the proof, and he saw the story that it had made, a novel so devoid of artifice that it was not at all possible to know if there was a puzzle to resolve or if there was not one, a novel in which everything could be linked in the course of the police investigation, and, indeed, utterly without any of the entertainment of fiction, an activity of that nature.)

Life is *at best* 'une activité de cet ordre'; that is, in Oscar Wilde's words, 'it is always the unreadable that occurs'. So that here all the makings of a readable tale have been turned into a broken marriage between fiction and the facts of life, to put in question any possibility of a faithful marriage between such incompatibles. The title, with its reassuring suggestion of the familiar and the confidential, mocks the presentation of realistic fiction. Neither 'Pierrot' nor 'mon ami' is real in the sense in which such titles pretend to be real.

The tradition, then, has reached a point of disintegration. The river no longer flows on, broadening from precedent to precedent with its intake of tributaries. It has reached the delta. As Picasso said, there is no more painting; there are no more novels. Of course, this is rhetoric, not criticism; but the models are dispersed, and standards of judgement are affected irreversibly. The novelist has to find the form that will mould the content he has in mind. The resulting fiction, or mixture, may be called a novel to differentiate an obvious product of imagination from reportage, journalism, documentary writing. What is real is the artefact, not a reality artificially reproduced. So the text is not closed by the intention of the author and the faithfulness of the reproduction. It remains open to the reader, not foreclosed by a plot that could always have been otherwise; its meanings are always 'en jeu': 'dans le texte, seul parle le lecteur' (Barthes). This is an extreme statement, to emphasize that the meanings and patterns are created by a writer and his readers, not discovered in the world.

The new caution is straightforwardly exemplified by John Fowles, a professional French scholar, in his novel *The French Lieutenant's Woman* (1969). He proceeds in the ample reassuring manner of Victorian novelists (the scene is laid in the 1860s) until chapter thirteen, where he begins to take the reader into his confidence unaffectedly, to expose the false assumptions of the convention and his refusal to be party to them. Conventionally, a novelist fixes the outcome, and is judged by his skill in doing so without being seen to do so and by what the outcome shows of his own attitudes and beliefs. John Fowles contrives to offer alternative versions of his story at two turning points. One is the likely course as plotted by a Victorian novelist, at the first of the turning points, in contrast with his preferred alternative course which he makes the narrative take, and which shatters the whole Victorian world of the early part of the story. The second pair of alternatives conclude the story, with a softer or harder option, and the author's preference for the latter. The strategy works as a critique of the hypocrisies of the Victorian

novel as well as of Victorian society, and is carried through effectively. '*The French Lieutenant's Woman* is clearly a landmark in
contemporary fiction', wrote David Caute (*The Illusion*, 1971, p.
253). But what Fowles says to his readers raises other questions about
authenticity in fiction, considered below (p. 244).

(*iv*)

Marx's call on philosophers to concern themselves with changing the
world instead of merely with understanding it has been followed by
similar calls by artists and writers on their fellow-craftsmen in a
number of movements to intervene in the world by their art, to bring
about changes, to be subversive, revolutionary, violent, even using
their art to deny their art. This was a role always played to some
extent by some writers and artists, and to a great extent by a few. In
contemporary fiction in France, Henri Peyre sees a fulfilment of
Matthew Arnold's view of the function of poetry:

> The French novel is thus, more than ever before, a novel of
> moralists more than of storytellers, of seekers of wisdom more
> than of creators of characters. It aims at increasing the reader's
> understanding of life, at sharpening his lucidity and his sincerity.
> (*French Novelists of Today*, 1955; Galaxy, 1967, p. 11)

Novels of this description will incline to and include the fable. Have
they absorbed the function of the *conte philosophique*, so that
Vivienne Mylne's contention should be accepted without quibble?

A main point here is that there are appreciable differences in the
ways in which these novelists conceive and carry out their philosophical job. Some are described as creators of myths (Malraux,
Bernanos), some as allegorists (Giraudoux); and there are the
ideologists – Surrealists, Existentialists, Symbolists, Marxists. In
general, such writers are engaged in grand imaginative attempts to
encompass experience, to reorder, suffuse, transmute, dissolve.
They are total even when anarchic. Fable stands off against them all
by its limits. It implies an open-eyed refusal to attempt Arnold's
ambition, to see life steadily and see it whole. This can be pictured in
the focus of a spotlight or the bounds of a floodlit patch. A writer of a
fable is not applying to something a committed attitude or approach
to all things. He/she is trying to inform the conception of something.
He is not expressing by example his view of all things; just trying to

construct a just view of something. There is reason here for distinction between the author of a fable and the author of 'metaphysical'
fiction.

In his noteworthy attempt to grapple with the problems of a
politically committed writer of fiction, David Caute insists on an
explicit break with illusion. He will have no sympathetic involve-
ment of the reader, 'as if' in real life with real characters, for that
sends him back into his world untouched: he has been reading only a
story. He even faults Orwell in *Nineteen Eighty-Four* for striving
'with all the weapons of the illusionist novel to persuade us to live
within it, within this literary world, this book of printed pages,
without critical detachment' (The Illusion, p. 260). He seems to fear
that just because of the hellish horror of the social vision, this gives a
let-out: it can be taken as simply a horror tale. The reader who is as
stupid as that cannot be helped. The Winston–Julia part of the story
is integral to the intent, in no way dispensable, nor a concession to
the convention. If the love theme had been given a romantic twist,
against the grain of the narrative, that would have been a fault, but so
evidently destructive of the intention that it is out of the question.
Orwell was fully aware of the problems in combining a naturalistic
novel with a fantasy of the future, but he was in no danger of giving
away too much to the expectations of the ordinary novel-reader. He
is at no point deflected from his control of the material for the
purpose in mind. To make a dogma of this exposure of fiction as
illusion is to fall into superstition and set up new forms of pretence, as
well as to diminish the resources and spoil the prospects of serious
fiction. The most spell-binding novel can throw up outstanding
images that remain, to accuse, warn, shame, or in whatever way
awaken and aid responsible reflection. The author can do what he
wants to do, without concessions and without self-conscious intru-
sions to dispel illusion. He can use the devices of naturalistic fiction,
or not, to go about his business of creating the vision of life he wants
to bring into the world.

(v)

Joseph Heller's *Good as Gold* (1979) is not a fable, nor formally like
one. It is not a realistic novel either, however like one. It is written at
two levels of the preposterous – rather more than fairly, and utterly –
with bouts of plain fooling or teasing; and the author brings himself
in casually as a casual author, with a theme he toys with like a college

essay: he was supposed to write about the Jewish experience in America, and is not sure he can or wants to. At the right moment he stabs to the bone or brings to light an underlying tract of lived-with anguish or bleakness, or brings home the uneasing grip of circumstances, or passes by the running sores of urban rot, or parades the contradictions that baffle and bedevil proclaimed public policies and unquestionable national ideals. There is not a credible figure in the book, and the social context is chaotic. At one point the author drifts into notes for another doubtful book, which will write off Henry Kissinger. In short, it is a distorting mirror that is held up to the social scene; but the bold lines and crazy shapes tell their story of American reality today and of a Jewish family in its midst more effectively than could be accomplished with the finished surfaces of a subtly nuanced novel of contemporary life in Jewish New York. It is as terrifying as a fable, because like a fable it is extreme, unredeemed by the reality of appearance, proclaiming a rough truth not ground by contact with its rivals. It shows modern fiction doing idiosyncratically the work of fable, but outside its limits, within the ambience of the novel. The force of a fable is in its single-minded concentration.

(*vi*)

What is the upshot of this phase of epistemological criticism of the art of fiction, as it affects the fable? Verisimilitude remains an option, but for 'authenticity' a stricter accountability is required, with the recognition that it is the author who imposes a form upon his chosen subject to mould its content, that he cannot escape the subjectivity of his work through the impersonality of the form or any claim that he has merely captured what is objectively there, taken 'a slice of life'. The convention is thereby relaxed, the contract is open to renegotiation. A writer can try to come to an understanding with his readers in his own way. A reader may be induced to accept the universe as a piece of cake if he can be induced to be interested enough in what the author will do with that proposition. This relaxing of the rules, and the more subtle understanding of the art of fiction and its diversities, have distributed generally the freedom which the fabulist used to obtain for himself by certain devices that eased him out of the established convention. The fabulist benefits, since he can do without such crude devices. Boundaries are blurred, but the fable does not therefore lose its identity and its territory. It does certain things, and does not do other things. Genre may become more important,

not a pedantic irrelevance, in the confusing diversity of modern
fiction. Consideration of that point is postponed to the next chapter.
Meanwhile, description of the traditional fable is completed in terms
of the devices and the language used.

And it should not be overlooked that outside this preoccupation
with serious fiction and critical evaluation of its functions and possibilities, there is the vitality of popular fiction which bounds on
without inhibitions; although most of it may be escapist, some of it
influences the imagination of many. It can create myth, and be subversive or binding.

Devices

(i)

The relation of a fable may be assumed to employ the usual techniques and devices used in telling a story, the 'rhetoric of composition'. Retrospectively, all the actions and events, including the
most trivial, can be tabulated in chronological order. Prospectively,
the 'telling' consists mainly in choosing the person and 'voice' of the
narrator, the starting point of the narration, the timing and manner
of bringing in required information (exposition; causal or other
relations between events), selection of episodes or phases of the
action for 'showing' rather than telling, with a larger allotment of
space taken up with dialogue or dramatization – and so on. In relating
a fable, devices of the mimetic novel to give verisimilitude will be
used occasionally, if at all. There is no large block of time and space to
be filled with an accumulation of descriptive detail and to provide
scope for the development of character. Devices specific to the fable
have been for the general purpose of excusing the narrator from
having to satisfy such expectations of the reader, allowing him to set
up another point of view and frame of reference. These devices have
been mechanical, stylistic, philosophical, arbitrary: use of animals as
dramatis personae, voyages or visits to bring in other ways and
views, deformation of normal conditions, obliqueness and ambiguity, arbitrary fantasy. The kind of device hardly matters, for
they all serve the general purpose of isolating an image for consideration, an aid in the construction of a concrete image that is an
abstraction.

The basic primitive device is that used in most of the Aesopic fables, in which the agents of the action are animals. There was the myth that animals at one time shared the language of men, and community and identification with animals are close in husbandry and hunting. But this is not the likeliest source of their representative use. Claude Lévi-Strauss has tried to show that, in Totemism, animals may have been more significant culturally in helping men to conceptualize than in their sense of physical dependence on them or community with them (*Totemism*, 1973). Species of animals and birds had recognizable identities and differences for which they had been given specific names, and this provided a ready-made scheme of classification for human group identities and differences which it was socially important to recognize and to maintain. Similarly, thinking about human behaviour in the abstract is assisted by attributing it in examples to animals, both because they seem to embody specific traits as pure types and because they abstract behaviours from human contexts. The tiger represented innate qualities of the evil man 'just as the milk of the cow is naturally sweet' (*Hitopadesa* I). Philemon tried to systematize the abstraction: each genus has but one character; lions stalwart, rabbits cowardly, foxes audacious dissemblers; 30,000 foxes would all have one nature, but men have as many different characters as bodies. If this was nonsense, and if the typecasting was as inconsistent as prevalent, that did not affect the usefulness of the device as a semi-abstract way of thinking about human behaviour and experience, with some detachment. The animals of Aesop are not animals in nature. They are conventional, fictional characters with stereotyped reputations. It is as such, neither as animals nor as humans, that they serve their purpose in putting examples of human behaviour before the mind's eye in ways that add their own meaning.[5]

It was remarked in the first chapter that Indian fables show a livelier sympathy and identification with the animals' characters, instead of using them as puppets for the enactment of behaviours; and it was suggested that the doctrine of metempsychosis, which puts all beings on the same level in a shared unity, is likely to have influenced this difference. Similarly, there is a difference today in attitudes to animals and their use in fiction, probably influenced by the modern doctrine of biological evolution of species, which also underlines affinity. Kafka remarked to Janouch apropos David Garnett's *Lady into Fox* (above, p. 132): 'It's a matter of the age. We both copied from that. Animals are closer to us than human beings.

That's where our prison bars lie. We find relations with animals easier than with men.' Again, animals as a simplification as in Aesop, but 'as a matter of the age', useful for the projection of typical anxieties ('The Burrow', 'Confessions of a Dog'). Thurber exploits the convention as a resource and as a licence. His animals play recognizable characters in satirical sketches. Or they frolic around in his own fashion for his pleasure. They can be or do anything for convenience or for wit or for wishes. Orwell's animals play the parts for which they are cast as to the manner born – a strange thought. The animal device is far from being a primitive simplicity or a nursery toy or an amusing idea. From early times, as in Aristophanes' *The Birds*, it has served to shift the point of view and open up new aspects, shown graphically and memorably. Modern writers have found it a resource for diverse purposes. Germaine Bree and Margaret Guiton, in *An Age of Fiction: The French Novel from Gide to Camus* (1957), refer to new treatment of certain inherited themes:

> One is recurrent and rather frightening animal symbolism: the violent insect activity we find in some of Queneau's novels and in the jungle world of Malraux's *La Voie royale*; the animal menageries of Bernanos; Camus's plague-ridden rats, dying in hordes. It would seem that Ayme, in reducing the entire human species to a particularly ferocious category of the animal kingdom, had carried the symbol as far as it would go. But Pierre Gascar, one of the best of the younger novelists, has used it in an entirely different way. *Les Bêtes* is a book of short stories in each of which the animals escape from man's control with disastrous results. The revolt of the animals, somehow connected with an abscure carnal part of ourselves, no doubt expresses a deep-lying anxiety. (p. 236)

It is a vision of a world which never ceases to kill in order to live. Symbols are not fables, but these are signs of the modern interest in animal behaviour and its relevance to reflection on human behaviour, which has led to the new science of ethology as well as to unscientific popular views about human nature.[6] Queneau, who includes entomology in his polymath studies, remarks that 'beetles outdistance by a long shot the *Cent vingt jours de Sodome* by the Marquis de Sade. The habits of these little beasts are repellent; horrible, unspeakably vile', On the other hand, the life of the grasshopper contains 'the germs of countless meditations'. Ethology, enlarging the view of identity and difference through detailed perceptions, helps to make reflection on human behaviour systematically more general; whereas animals as symbols or as agents in actions related in fables dramatize particular reflections on human behaviour or particular forms of human behaviour; the latter a mode of reflection, the former an act of expression.

Very differently, another contemporay French novelist, Giraudoux, using allegory in the belief that reality is available only when abstracted by some device from its context in space and time (as in poetry), finds in La Fontaine his great master of allegory, one who had discovered in animals a third race between the inconsequent inhabitants of this planet and the ever-present but lifeless figures of Greek mythology, having the actuality of human beings without their inconsequence and the poetry of the mythical figures without their loss of vitality. This fanciful view of the matter is nevertheless part of the evidence that there are modern writers of fiction who have rediscovered animals as a resource, an aid to expression or to reflection.

(ii)

Extraction of behaviour from the human context by the use of animal agents has been one main method of abstraction practised in the fable. Variation of the context is another. The voyage has been the classical means of accomplishing this: the voyage, the ship-wreck, the island, and there is isolation in a new context. Lucian opened up almost all the possibilities in 'The True History'. From that launch into illimitable space to the plunge over the embankment into a deserted concrete island immediately below the motorway covers over a thousand years and scores of fictional voyages of the kind, taking as landmarks one from each of the previous chapters: after *The True History*, *The Tempest*, *Gulliver*, *Lord of the Flies*. There are other devices of insulation: Camus's *La Peste* (1947) or David Rousset's *L'Univers concentrationnaire* (1946). Kafka's K is cut off and isolated without leaving the system, precisely by the labyrinthine methods of postponement and referral which is the system.

In some of these examples it is a community or company that is taken out of its normal context and isolated. The behaviour then exhibited is that of different individuals in the same exceptional circumstances, affecting all relationships. We learn about real boys (*Lord of the Flies*). We see the compulsions of a colonial regime (*The*

Tempest) or of a fascist regime (*Mario*), seen in little in a special context; just as on their own, in changed conditions, Robert Maitland learns about himself and Robinson about the human condition. The extraordinary setting is matched by an extraordinary psychological set in the co-operative reader. The dislocation puts him less critically in the hands of his author, off his accustomed ground. This special power over the reader runs greater risk of losing him, but is the cue for new thought.

The voyage or other prelude to insulation has been only one common way of varying the normal context of behaviour. In the eighteenth century, the oriental tale was another. The Happy Valley is quite as extraordinary as the Enchanted Isle or Lilliput. A more natural way of bringing about the variation is by visiting other societies around the world or by bringing a stranger to look at our familiar institutions through alien eyes. Voltaire loved to do both.

(*iii*)

Extraction of patterns of behaviour from the human context; variations of the context: more drastic is variation of the normal conditions of human existence, not merely of the circumstances. The simplest case is variation in scale, as in *Gulliver* or *Micromegas*. More complex and significant is tampering with the time dimension, elimination of the past, as in *Brave New World* or *Nineteen-Eighty-Four*, or of the future, as in *Huis Clos*. This deformation of the conditions of human existence can be seen at two levels: as an illumination of those conditions, an insight into the necessity of temporality; or as an actual danger, an extrapolation of present trends. Either way, fables in this category have made the strongest impact and have the profoundest implications. Perhaps a refined science fiction will be of this kind.

(*iv*)

Perhaps slightly corresponding to suspense in the plot of a story is the manoeuvre of indirection, to baffle, tease, and eventually key up attention, a device concentrated on play with the reader, but disposing the material for the end in view. *Absent Without Leave*, *Slaughterhouse 5*, *Good as Gold* have been notable examples of this indirection as a capital device, but in tone of voice and style it has been time and again a whip in the driver's hand to flick across the ears. In the examples named above – especially the first two, and pre-eminently the first – the allusiveness of the devious progress is seen to refer to what has engendered smouldering passion, cumulative in intensity and punctuated by spits and flares. Intensive expressiveness dependent upon indirection and suppression is another, and opposite, side of fable virtuousity.

A staple device in this play with the reader is irony, serving to entrench the intellectual detachment of both parties. Formally, irony is contrary to metaphor in that it depends on incongruity, not resemblance; but it is the metaphoric action itself that is ironic in so many of Lucian's pieces, as also in *Candide*. Lucian and Voltaire were masters of irony, and use it with telling effect in the delivery as well as in the structure of their fables. The Socratic irony is not to be forgotten in the attraction of the dialogues for Lucian. It is associated with inconclusiveness, the unsettlement which may be the principal purpose of a fable.

(v)

A Clockwork Orange might seem to be an example of the 'well-researched' novel, one that could be documented as a representation of the mores, behaviour and lingo of a specimen sample of rough and tough teenagers in New York. However, the story is wholly and solely the story of your so-plausible narrator, and it is he who is not so plausible after all. Everyone and everything appear as he sees them, and he is totally self-isolated and inhumanly consistent, an automated vivid agent, an invention as ludicrously monstrous as a clockwork orange. This is, in a highly sophisticated form, as much a removal from normal contexts and conditions as in fiction that brings this about by any of the devices just considered. I have not seen Stanley Kubrick's film of the book, but I have examined his book of the film (Lorrimer, 1972), and it seems to me to misread the book all the way as a naturalistic novel. That is like not noticing irony. As a naturalistic novel, it would be vulnerable, if not absurd. As a fable, it is true to life in quite another way (that could not be documented), and is among the finest of our time.

(vi)

All these devices have been ways of bringing about reduction, abstraction, detachment, disengagement from the appearances and relations of the familiar world in respect of the material, and therewith of the reader's response. There is interference with the contexts, relations, sequences, and conditions of human existence as experienced. Such reduction leaves the sustaining interest in danger. Fiction is not metaphysics, 'a ballet of bloodless categories'. A fable ventures into paradox, as Lucian recognized, in combining elements in danger of mutual rejection, appealing to the appetite for comedy as though it had a head for philosophy. A fable is devoid of all the interests that fill people's lives, and are reflected in fiction; but is not void of interest. There may be images charged with meaning, or a strange perspective on the appearance of the world, or slight shifts hardly noticed, or a dislocation of conditions, or a suspension of necessity: an imagined reordering, controlled by relevance. A fable is an heuristic fantasy, to quicken understanding. There is little or nothing with which a reader may become sympathetically involved; everything is there to facilitate an active mental response. The narrative devices are narrowly ambitious.

Language

(i)

Titian's painting of Actaeon surprising Diana with her nymphs bathing is naturalistic, sensuous, complete. His sequel 'Death of Actaeon' is drained of this visual richness; the hounds leap up to destroy him like flames, the avenging huntress is anonymous. The two paintings speak different languages, the one mimetic, the other abstract. The one depicts a scene, the other a fate. The one is as much an illustration as the other, but the language is adapted to the theme. There is a smaller difference between the language of general fiction and that of fable.

The most general early division in literary language was between a 'high' and a 'low' style, the epic or the courtly and the easy and familiar. The language of tragedy or of romance must be the 'wrong' language for a fable, an absurdity; unless adopted, as it was, in parody both to make the narrative amusing, acceptable, and to do its work of 'distancing'. The fable, then, belongs decisively to the low level of style and diction, at home with 'Satires and Epistles' in poetry. This admitted a variety of differences in 'voice', personal tone, both in the whole telling and within it. Voltaire's unspeakable detestation for human abominations is discernible in a change of tone when the words used are perfectly neutral. In general, the tone maintained in *Candide* is a rapid, blithe, disenchanted detachment. La Fontaine undertakes to retell the fables with all the charm he can lend them, which does not prevent his showing his scorn when roused. Swift speaks in the matter-of-fact reporting tones of Gulliver, and reserves his own voice as a resource for irony. The tone of voice of Alex is special and specialized, consistently keyed in character, with a set vocabulary and his own limited set of variations. Böll's teasing tone is combined with a conjuror's manipulation of his ploys of indirection. In all, the tone of voice is suited to the narrative intention at the outset and as it goes along, as in any narrative. Use of irony and oblique expression of strong emotion – but not tender emotion – are marked characteristics. Since a fable is like a searchlight focused on a target, not the visual field of broad daylight accommodating everything, the tone of voice tends to be collected rather than expansive, with time for playfulness as it strides along but not with room enough for Rabelaisian ease.

(ii)

Two main, quite disparate, reasons for resort to fables are: one tactical, a need for concealment, the other 'philosophical', development of thought. The only thing in common is their having something serious to communicate in fictional form. Phaedrus stressed the use of fable to evade official punishment, a device for anyone in a dependent position; and he mentioned his own case. The need is paramount in totalitarian states today. In Poland, it is said that readiness to read between the lines is so constant that an explicit statement, in the appropriate context, is likely to be assumed to mean the contrary. In Czechoslovakia, revival of a seventeenth-century play may be the best available means of getting today's message through. Something other than the contemporary scene is presented, and a comparison implied.

However, in considering the fable as a permanent form of fiction it is the 'philosophical' reason that is important; and this, again, means offering for comparison something other than the present and familiar state of things. Micyllus says: 'Do you not see how you have already taught me to make comparisons, friend cock?' (above, p. 30). In *Tiom*, Lucian takes a proper regard for and use of wealth as a well-conducted marriage with Riches, which bears fruit in several thoughtful implications. Metaphors born of reflection become pregnant with new thoughts. Metaphor elaborated in the action of a fable may create an image of behaviour that, when compared with the usual conception of that kind of behaviour, brings out what was not noticed or thought about. The story of the ass that imitated the behaviour of his master's lap-dog can put in question received ideas about place, 'my station and its duties'. The image for comparison might be of another state of affairs elsewhere, or indicated in the future by extrapolation, or brought about by accident. The image produced by the invented action is offered for comparison with the conception produced by familiar particular examples in actuality, with the intention to add or refine meaning.

Metaphor as an implied comparison has two main uses, one logical and didactic as a category of example (Aristotle), the other stylistic. Stylistically, it adds force to the expression of a conception: 'Old age is a general multilation' (Democritus). Didactically, it adds thought to the conception: The Old Man and Death (La Fontaine I, xv & xvi); What the Old Woman Said to the Wine Jar (*Phaedrus* III, I) – she eagerly sniffed up the odour in the empty jar; 'Ah, sweet ghost, how good you must have been, when even your remains are so excellent.'

(iii)

'A dog was crossing over a river with a piece of meat in her mouth.' The language of narrative in a past tense is used alike in report, in story-telling, and in a fable. A fable is not seriously about anything that has happened nor about a quasi-historical action. Essentially, it is about what can be thought of without time or place, for instance a type of behaviour. The image presented is not offered as a possible instance of this behaviour; it 'pictures' its identity, what makes it what it is. The narrative may, as narratives must, assert that a certain action took place, but what is asserted thereby is that certain behaviour exists in the form in which universals exist, that it has certain characteristics, and is prevalent or possible in particular instances. This is 'un ouvrage qui dit plus qu'il ne semble dire', more than and other than it seems to say. If there is this highly important difference in the assertions implied in these three forms of narrative, and none in the form of the language used, how are they distinguished? It lies with the author to make clear whether his narrative is intended to be allusive or quasi-historical, whether or not by excluding the possibility of the latter.

(*iv*)

The Aesopic fables have been retold untold times, and have at different times been used in schools of rhetoric and elsewhere for exercises in telling, in using different language to communicate the same content. There was, so to speak, a folk melody, with no composer's score for arrangement, orchestration, performance, until a classical text was produced by Phaedrus or La Fontaine or Neckam. Retelling is the more attractive the more scope it offers for variation, for nuances, for supplementation, for modelling. The Aesopic fables offered some but not much, which was probably why La Fontaine had some preference for his *Contes*. The language should say all that needs to be said; promythium and epimythium should be redundant, or impertinent. This runs the risk of obscurity when the aim is concision.

The language of fable, concise in Aesop, is economic in general; almost diagrammatic by comparison with the expansive, the copious language of full rhetorical resources: 'The Death of Actaeon'. This restricted language has its own resources; it is not primitive. Without recourse to copiousness and the plenitude of expression, which would smother its voice, fable speaks by ambiguity, deviousness, silence, suppression, understatement, by putting the reader off, by multiplicity of languages in the tersest forms. Samuel Beckett demonstrates this in a short piece, *The Lost Ones* (1966). He makes use of some seven distinct types of language: the language descriptive of a self-contained physical system, the language of aesthetics, the language used to give the rules of a game and instructions for play, the language used to indicate what follows if a notion holds (if . . ., then), the language of categories, behavioural descriptions, gruesome human images: all these are used in a description of unspecified inward experiences, of searching, of seeking rest, respite, of beginning to desist, of abandonment, of renewal, of extreme discomfort, of frustration. The piece is not a narrative; it is a selection of general features and conditions of experience, in order to show them as without repose and having no exit. It is relevant because it exhibits the possibilities of using incongruous languages to speak indirectly for a positive effect. Fable has its linguistic resources, not equal to those of poetry because it is finite.

Development

(i)

Early fables belonged to an oral culture. There is a natural bond
between Aesopic fables and proverbs. Quintilian pointed to the
kinship with proverbs, and said there was a class of proverbs which
may be regarded as abridged fables and understood allegorically:
'The burden is not mine to carry, the ox is carrying panniers'. Perry
identifies this class of proverbs as one which is 'identical with
Aesopic fable, in respect to both its function as metaphor and its
underlying structure as narrative of an event in the past' (Perry, xx);
and he says that this class is peculiar to Western Asia and Greece,
compared with other kinds of proverb. He particularly excludes
from the Aesopic type precepts in the imperative mood and general-
ities stated explicitly in the present tense. Thus Lucian's 'Out of the
smoke into the fire I ran' would qualify, but the Indian 'Tempests
uproot trees, not grasses' would not, although there is a classical fable
which says just that. Similarly, 'Donkeys prefer chaff to gold'
(Heraclitus) or 'Every creature is driven to pasture with a blow'
(Heraclitus). In a few cases a proverb may be identical in form with
Aesopic fable, as narrative and as metaphor, Perry's strict requirement; but in vastly many cases a proverb in the imperative or more
often as an explicit general statement will form what might be the
promythium or epimythium of a fable: 'Men who shun death pursue
it' (Democritus); or many of the popular sayings which share the
context with fully fledged fables in Indian wisdom literature: 'If a dog
were made king, would he not gnaw his shoe?' Or, 'To him who is
shod the earth is as carpeted with leather'. Both forms are capable of
metaphorical and memorable pictures of some kinds of truth, and
both are rooted in the soil of common experience. (Aesop himself
was reputed to have made a collection of proverbs.) But the fable is
not a development of the proverb, or if and when it is so regarded,
what makes the development possible is the difference in form,
which is the reason for Perry's insistence. This has to be the starting
point, clearly and firmly apprehended, if the fable is distinctive and
its development traceable. For:

> Around a nucleus of proverbs and fables that picture a truth
> metaphorically, with the gnomic idea clearly outstanding, a large
> number of only partially and externally similar narratives, both

short and long, have accumulated, by a kind of snowballing process, in the Greek and Latin fable-books, with the result that many fables, loosely so called, make their appeal to the reader primarily as something clever or amusing in itself, while the gnomic ideas or morals that they convey, if any, are not easily discernible. (Perry, xxviii)

Perry goes on to give examples from 106 Sumerian fables and parables of Aesopic type which have been identified by use of his definition.

Aphoristic sayings of Heraclitus and Democritus – and they could be multiplied – were included among proverbs cited above to suggest that there was an early link between philosophic thinking and this type of fiction. Democritus himself refers to Aesop: 'The desire for more loses what one has, like the dog in Aesop' (Kathleen Freeman, *Ancilla to the Pre-Socratic Philosophers*, 1948, p. 112). He was a great traveller, and familiar with the literature of Western Asia. But the preoccupations and patterns of thought of the Pre-Socratics were far different in the main from those of a shrewd and witty observer. They were headed in different directions: the images of fiction, abstract systematic reflection. At the same time, the development of fable was bound up with ways of bringing them together. And early philosophers showed decided appreciation of fables. It was Demetrius who made the collection which became the established source.

(ii)

Cultural innovations are generally brought about when several independent developments come together. The Aesopic fable had its own development from oral sources through the schools of rhetoric until it attained classical form in the compositions of Phaedrus and Babrius. The two developments which fascinated Lucian were the Old Comedy and Plato's happy deflection of philosophic discourse into the Socratic dialogues. The Old Comedy was itself a mixture, a satiric, political, literary, fantastic, allegorical, witty, farcical, ribald, operatic miscellany. Aristophanes used this malleable medley freely to model his concrete thinking for delivery. In *The Birds*, a go-getting, empire-building, executive-type Athenian seeks his fortune elsewhere in the kingdom of the Birds, where he assumes and extends authority, and projects the building of a new city, accomplished in no time behind his back by the natural enthusiasm of the industrious, ingenious, diversely talented birds; and all the time there is scope alongside the action for lateral allusion and comment and amusing by-play. The licence and fertility of fantasy allowed an author to invent an action packed with meaning of general relevance.

In the Socratic dialogues, Plato began an exploration of conceptual thinking by raising for the first time the question 'What is bravery?' with men for whom bravery was not a question. He broached for examination, prompted and guided by Socrates, the notion of a concept, mainly in raising the central question, What is justice?

It was said above that the Aesopic fable fused wit and wisdom in a primitive way, and that Lucian by combining Aristophanic comedy and Socratic dialogue did this at a sophisticated level (p. 182). That covered up what the conjunction fundamentally was; not merely wit and wisdom, but concrete representation of ideas integrated with conceptual thinking, at the time of their independent development. Lucian's own mental constitution and habit of mind inclined him to be more at home with images than ideas, and fertile in their production. At the same time, he was particularly interested in philosophical ideas as developed in the doctrines of the schools, interested with a sceptic or eclectic attitude of detachment. Image thinking is supposed to be more or less primitive undeveloped thinking, such as was general in the Middle Ages. However, it remains a necessary tool of developed thought (including physical science), which is never for long free of dependence on metaphor, as on language. Fable is born of the interdependence of conceptual and image thinking; at its simplest in the Aesopic story, in more complex forms in Lucian's comic fiction. In this last, there came together the two independent developments with Lucian's own cast of mind and rhetorical profession. Both types of fable were then available for and capable of further development, to this day.

Inevitably, links with allegory and myth, as with satire and comedy, involved confusion, at its most prevalent and preposterous in the eighteenth century. Lessing had the sharpest eye for the fundamentals, and in particular distinguished between the action in a fable, with two dimensions, and the action of a novel, which had the dimension also of inwardness, a secondary action.[7]

Unfavourable cultural conditions

(*i*)

'Distracted by its new philosophies, its new political ideas, its new inventions, its immense industrial development, it was in no mood to listen to the East, still less to seek patiently to listen to its thought.' This remark on the nineteenth century by Professor Gibb (*The Legacy of Islam*, p. 205) may not be relevant to fable in that period, but it is indication of a climate of thought not encouraging detachment. In the particular field of fiction, writers who were not out merely to amuse or please their readers, and who were not themselves primarily romantics, aspired to a more authentic realism. The development of scientific methods and scientific attitudes had applications to fiction. Man and society were objects of scientific study, and serious authors of realistic fiction could not ignore the results of such study. The convention allowed the omniscient and omnipotent author absolute rule. He knew the thoughts and feelings of all his creatures and ordained their destinies, even if he was expected to contrive not to show his hand. But this divine power was a frivolous absurdity to writers who claimed to be writing about life as they found it as faithfully as they could, and who laboured to bring to their descriptions and inventions a new truth to life.

In the first pages of the seventeenth chapter of *Adam Bede*, George Eliot addresses her readers ironically to make clear to them that her ideal as a novelist is not the idealized fiction they may have been used to, but the everyday realism of the Dutch painters; she aspires to give a faithful account of men and things as they have mirrored themselves in her mind. The mirror is defective, and it is a very hard thing to say the exact truth, even about your own immediate feelings; but she feels bound to try as if she were in the witness-box narrating her experience on oath. One sees that this austere ideal of faithfulness is supported by a moral faith and a moral ideal: faith in the basic decency and reliability of human feelings; belief that such feelings have the power to transfigure and redeem the ordinary uninspiring reality, that there is some soul of goodness to be observingly distilled. This is one high level of aspiring realistic fiction: the seriousness and faithfulness of sincerity.

There is an even higher altitude: an internal verisimilitude to match faithful description of the observable. This aspires to apply the author's acquired knowledge to show why the characters are what they are and do as they do, not merely in terms of the story, but mainly in terms of heredity and environment; and not in declaratory form, but currently giving a character the limited knowledge and limited judgements that could reasonably be expected at any point in the narrative, and using this in its necessary development. Writers of serious fiction of this kind would pay more attention to considerations of psychology and sociology in the delineation of their characters than to the expectations of their readers.

If one thinks of systematic seriousness on chosen grounds in the art of major novelists of the century, English, French, Russian, a reservation seems justified in regard to Dickens, in spite of his copious documentation of the industrial scene and his own reforming interest and purpose. For all his detailed coverage of the sordid and the squalid and the scandalous, he is stubbornly reticent about anything he suspects might upset the susceptibilities of his middle-class readers. He never, for example, exposes the hypocrisies of family life. He goes for high morality and refined sentiments where they are unlikely to be found. His verisimilitude, the detailed descriptions for which Kafka profoundly admired him, is not matched by internal verisimilitude. He remained, as he remains, a popular novelist.

(*ii*)

Turning from fiction to ideas and the issues which occupied public attention, one might be struck by the polarities which seem to structure discussion. Some of these are reflected in well-known titles: *North and South, Culture and Anarchy, Past and Present, The Man versus the State.* One is embedded in Ruskin's reassessment of political economy, 'There is no wealth but life', which engendered profound hostility and rejection at a high tide of industrial expansion, until it matured as a seminal influence in the nascent British Labour Party, and in the life of Gandhi.

After the Augustan age of the eighteenth century – which, as the name indicates, was a time when the cultivated thought that European culture had attained a level comparable with Roman civilization at its best – the following century was a time of unprecedented change (the population of England doubled in the first half), forced by the rapid development of science and practical mechanics. This was in almost equal measure exhilarating and threatening, the climate of Samuel Smiles and of Darwin and Malthus. Science, especially the Darwinian theory, threatened the foundations of religious faith.

Industry promised progress, but at the expense of tradition and stability. Civilization had to face the peril and uncertainty of the coming democracy. Tocqueville had made a realistic assessment of the great American experiment (the first part published in 1831); and Mill feared that equalitarian pressures and democratic control would encroach on and override the claims of personal liberty (*On Liberty*, 1859). Herbert Spencer believed passionately that the true beliefs of liberalism were being betrayed and witch-hunted, since 'The great political superstition of the present is the divine right of parliaments' (*The Man versus the State*, 1884). The growth of collectivism was later studied by A.V. Dicey: *Law and Public Opinion in England*, 1905. In Germany the State had laid the foundation of social services, which Matthew Arnold believed was the way to save civilization from an ignorant and anarchic individualist democracy (*Culture and Anarchy*, 1869). The century had begun with Malthus (*Essay on Population*, 1798), and his warning about the ratio of mouths to hands remained an increasing worry, with the unprecedented expansion. Marx was waiting in ambush down the road (*Kapital*, vol. 1, 1867). Finally, it was the great period of European nationalism, which intensified competition and the expansion of imperialism; and at the same time offered Cobden's vision of international commerce and free trade that assured lasting peace by the ties of interdependent interests.

A background to these major issues and controversies were certain iron laws newly discerned: in physics, the Second Law of Thermodynamics, which presaged the heat-death of the universe; the theory of the biological evolution of species, which made the struggle for survival the law of organic life; the economic law of diminishing returns, the finite character of resources; not least, determinism, the universality of causal law, which put in question the basic assumption about the human person. The message of such laws was more grim than encouraging.

(iii)

Divided by such polarities and oppressed by such constraints, thoughtful people were likely to find detachment as untenable as compromise. There was a tendency to take sides against the enemy seen to stand for all that was most feared. There were the quarterlies in which the debates raged. There were the leaders and their followers, names that still ring loud today: Gladstone and Disraeli;

Huxley and Spencer; Mill and Arnold; Ruskin and Carlyle; Cobden and Bright; Newman and Maurice; Bagehot and Morley; Cobbett and Bradlaugh: party leaders, tribunes of the people, publicists, prophets, intellectuals. Such leaders of thought and opinion spoke out directly and forcefully. Matthew Arnold steeped his polemic in persiflage in *Culture and Anarchy*, but it was personal, demonstrating rather than renouncing his control of the show. The obliqueness, the use of fantasy, the turning things upside down, the characteristic manipulations of the fable were out of place and out of mind on this scene.

Carlyle, certainly no less a preacher than any of them, comes nearest to the indirectness of the fable in *Sartor Resartus* (1834), which is part mystification, part teasing, part despair; the action of a painter who throws a sponge steeped in many colours at the canvas, as he hints – not out of the question, given time. It is not a narrative, but written with the imagination of a writer capable of a powerful fable if he could have spared his continuous intervention, presenting a construction instead of having his say and having his say. An original work in form and content, it is Carlyle's idiosyncratic invention for the deployment of his ideas in a context of diversion; and in coming as close as it does to a possible fable, it is perhaps an indication that fable was not a readily acceptable form of fiction in the period.

As the eighteenth century characteristically borrowed the oriental tale, both for diversion and to speak reason in the form of a work 'qui dit plus qu'il ne semble dire', the characteristic recourse in the nineteenth century was to the Middle Ages, a recovered and romanticized Middle Ages, a faint analogy with the revival of learning in Europe in the fifteenth century. This recourse was partly to revive and sanctify traditional values and ideals, lost or threatened, partly for romantic entertainment; in either case offering a counter-attraction to, rather than detachment from, the contemporary scene. Tennyson or William Morris, or many another, took their idealized Middle Ages far more seriously than Voltaire or Johnson their oriental tale. The Past in this form spoke to the Present, had its own message or was given one to bear, and was not merely a device for 'distancing' the present for a detached view. *News from Nowhere* creates an image of one golden day in the 1970s which reflects the fourteenth century in which William Morris sees, or affects to see, the fellowship and the enjoyment of craftsmanship of ideal socialism.

(*iv*)

A century so crowded with changes and contradictions is likely to betray anyone into generalizations that are rash if not silly. And there are at least three distinct periods, more marked than usual, in three successive generations. However, in recalling landmarks of publication, preoccupations and dominant issues and controversies, underlying assumptions, the tone of public debate, the ambitions of realistic fiction and the high seriousness of temper that prevailed in all endeavour, enough has been brought together to suggest that the climate was indeed unfavourable to fiction in the form of fable.

All the same, there were two famous exceptions in which the vitality of the fable reasserted itself, in the Aesopic tradition and in the longer narrative tradition of *Gulliver*: Grandville's *Vie privée et publique des Animaux* (1842) and Samuel Butler's *Erewhon* (1872). Perhaps, after all, there is nothing to be accounted for; there is always an element of fortuity in cultural conditions, and the appearance or non-appearance of such a rogue plant as the fable may not call for remark. However that may be, the positivity of the spirit of the age was alien to the critical independence of an age of analysis which had favoured the fable. G.H. Lewes has the following footnote in his discussion of the influence of the Idea of the age on its poetry: 'It will have been apparent that we have used the word "Idea" in its European philosophical sense, as the synthetical expression of each great element of the spirit of the age. Thus analysis was the dominant Idea of the eighteenth century, humanity (liberty, progression) of the nineteenth . . .' ('The Inner Life of Art').

(*v*)

Gerard was the proper name of Grandville, an accomplished and imaginative designer, not a writer, who illustrated La Fontaine, Florian, and *Gulliver*, but his lasting reputation was achieved by his illustrations of a special collection of contemporary tales. The revised and augmented edition of 1867 has on the title page: *Vie privée et publique des Animaux*. Vignettes par Grandville, publiée Sous la Direction de P.J. Stahl (Pierre-Jules Hertzer). The editor has fourteen collaborators, talented writers of the day, who include Balzac, George Sand and Alfred de Musset. The 29 animal narratives, averaging more than 5000 words each, are set in a frame story that begins with a constituent assembly of all animals to deliberate and advise on measures to be taken to better their lot and shake off the human yoke.

They meet on the anniversary of the death of La Fontaine, to whose memory they pay their respects, and the debate concludes with a decision to write their own illustrated popular history and to apply to Grandville, an honorary animal, to illustrate it. This is a revolution in a land and a century of revolutions and rumours of revolution; and at the end, under the heading Dernier Chapitre, we read, 'Où l'on voit que chez les Bêtes comme chez les Hommes les révolutions se suivent et se ressemblent' ('In which we see that among Beasts as among Men revolutions follow one another and are alike'). Meanwhile, occasion has been taken to depict with irony or hilarity 'scenes de mœur'. A Parisian sparrow investigates on behalf of his fellows systems of government among the ants, the bees, and the wolves (George Sand). *La Vie privée* includes 'Peines de cœur d'une Chatte anglaise' by Balzac, a loving portrayal of puritanical English hypocrisy by the author of *La physiologie de mariage*, in the story of a well-brought-up cat married to a milord, and her delayed but inevitable fall to the Gallic allurement of the nonchalant M. Brisquet. Here is the racy vitality of the Aesopic fable on a range of themes, from the fatality and absurdity of love or the futilities and imbecilities of the pursuit of happiness in private life, to the ridicule of academicians and politicians in public life, and including ironic revaluations of the stereotyped characters of the Aesopic genre. Grandville made the volume, and it is simply for his work that there has been an English republication, *Public and Private Life of Animals*, illustrated by J.J. Grandville (1977). But if it would be *Hamlet* without the Prince of Denmark to publish the texts without Grandville, it would be as pointless to reprint Grandville as to stage the Prince without the other players. The texts are what the vignettes are all about, to coin a phrase, as they say. They enlarge the scale of La Fontaine's *comédie humaine*, with new sources of mockery in the doctrines of 1789 ingeniously applied to the animal world, in the light of post-revolutionary events and politics.

(*vi*)

Samuel Butler was an odd man out, of strong independent opinions. He has given an account of the incremental, almost accidental, way in which *Erewhon* came to be written and published. Its unexpected prompt success, unhelped by the failure of his other books, was explained by a friend as the charm of 'the sound of a new voice, and of an unknown voice'. In this unknown voice it would not have been difficult to catch an echo of the once-familiar *Gulliver* in the manner of the narrative. The satire works at two levels. There is the break-up of the cake of custom by the switch in the treatment of crime and of sickness, by the two currencies, by the educational system, by the ways of thinking of births and the family. These displacements give occasion for sharp observations on ways and whys, and ironical portraits of types. At the other level, relying on the main premise of the thinking of the age – the universality of causal law – there is a focus on the main'feature of the age, the machine, not merely as a symbol but mainly as the agent for the making of the future and the remaking of man: either as an indefinite extension and multiplication of bodily powers, the promise of supreme mastery; or as the competitive rival, outstripping human capacities, determining every step, completing a downward spiral to permanent servitude and degradation. All is related in the course of an adventurous romance with an abrupt, gratuitous, and farcical ending.

Machines are metaphorically the new race that will improve on and supplant man, for men breed and perfect machines, and subordinate all interests to that end. The further the process goes, the more engaged they are, far past the point of no return. The machines serve only on condition of being served, and they become ever more capable and more demanding under the pressure of constant competition. The voice is the voice of Swift or of Mandeville, but the dilemma is the typically paradoxical problem of the twentieth century. The fantasy is only in focusing the gaze on the knot before the stranglehold is felt.

(vii)

In Shaw and Wells there is a new race of fiction writers, and the fable begins to come into its own again. Shaw turned one of the most fatuous old fables into a useful contemporary play in *Androcles and the Lion*, which he allowed to be as farcical as the fable but used skilfully enough to bring under scrutiny universal patterns of behaviour, representing martyrs and persecutors of all times, and which, overtaken by events, had justification in 'the terrible topicality given it by the war'. His own most serious aspiration, he said, was to be an iconographer, image-maker, for the living religion of the time, his version of Creative Evolution – an authorship far more likely to raise new sublimities on old foundations of myth or legend than to play with fables. Fortunately, the heat and burden of the forenoon was borne by native wit producing his broadsides on current questions. His radical mind, delighting in his skill in dynamiting embedded assumptions and stock attitudes, accomplished by other means the analytical work of fable in fiction, the shake-up of ideas.

6 The Message

What fables do

(i)
In a brief piece on George Eliot, Marcel Proust concludes:

> Une des conclusions qu'on peut tirer de ces oeuvres (et qui n'est
> pas indiqué), c'est que le mal que nous faisons *est* le mal (nous
> faisons le mal à nous et aux autres). Et qu'au contraire le mal qui
> nous arrive est souvent la condition d'un plus grand bien que Dieu
> voulait nous faire.
> (*Contre Sainte-Beuve*, 1954, p. 419)

> (One of the conclusions which one can draw from these works
> (and which is not pointed out), is that the evil we do *is* what evil is
> (we do evil to ourselves and others). And on the contrary the evil
> that happens to us is often the condition of a greater good which
> God would do us.)

Assuming that the novels may be resumed in this way, may be said to
mean this, how does the work of these novels differ from the work of
a fable?

In one main respect, this corpus of novels and a fable do not differ:
they are not resumed in any statement; what they say is co-extensive
with what they show. The reading of George Eliot may leave Proust
with the conclusion he states, and that is relevant. George Eliot is not
teaching that; nor is that the 'moral' of her work. There remains a lot
more to be said, by others and by Proust himself. When all is said, the
novels remain as though nothing had been said. It is the same with a
fable. The image it forms is irreplaceable: it can be thought about; it
cannot be replaced by a thought. Its message can never be, Think
this; always, Think about this.

The difference from a novel is not in this main respect, nor merely
in comparative brevity and restriction to a two-dimensional action.
Rather, it is not 'a faithful account of men and things' (George Eliot),
but is about conceptual matters and how something is to be thought
of. Moreover, a fable is usually focused on a single matter of a general
character, and is not about things in general. Although its whole

business is to be concrete, it is so in a more or less abstract way, and in order to show the kind of thing some conceptual matter is in practice.

Imagine a ritual murder of a prisoner by fellow-prisoners serving life sentences in a brutally conducted criminal gaol. The affair has exacted long preparation demanding ingenuity and resource, and is bizarre and obscene in detail. The victim may consent. The incident may have happened, and be documented in direct and close description, so that all the observable facts are brought together. Psychopathology and anthropological data might be brought to bear on the event to try to explain it. Or such an event might be invented as a fable, to show the fatal tendency inherent in degradation: to suffer degradation becomes self-degradation apt to inflict degradation. This is not generally recognized. An extreme and bizarre case could be used to show what it means. The extreme, if it can be seen to bring out what is inherent, exposes what the more normal half-conceals or leaves unsuspected. A fable takes or invents representative material offered to reflection. It is a fruit of insight, not itself a form of reflection.

This fable would show the consummation of degradation in a way that showed the irrelevance of any protest that 'real life is not like that' or of taking it as simply a tale of the macabre. The story would be seen to be *of a kind* designed to represent a matter for serious thought. How that would be done is the business of the particular fable.

(ii)

If a fable has a structural meaning which it yields to reflection, what is the evidence for its validity, why should it be taken seriously? Also, how does it come about? The first question is better discussed below under 'Criticism'. The other may be less serious. We are closely preoccupied with the verification of hypotheses, and not bothered about their provenance. The fiction of the Muses has gone the way of the myths, after being tiresome too long.

Nevertheless, there is a certain interest in the matter. A writer of fiction may have an idea for a story which would be an idea of what would happen, the kind of people involved, the setting, the upshot; at least some of these items. Having the idea and thinking well enough of it, the writer would proceed according to his habits of authorship to process it by the rhetoric of composition and therewith to modify, model, expand, eliminate, and shape what it is he wants to give a local habitation and a name. In this process he continuously breeds what could not have been in the original conception, and what gives the story the imaginative content, not intended, on which readers will draw in their own measure and to their own purposes. It is by this fecundity that fiction writers are themselves measured.

This natural fecundity is the danger for the writer of a fable (as William Golding found). He is more closely bound by his original conception when it is fully formed, and must rigorously exclude and eliminate the temptations that crop up, the material that would make a novel. What starts him off, the germ that does need development, may be ridiculously trivial – the sight of a small boy leading a cart-horse. Where there is an established convention, as in the Aesopic fable or the Indian similitude, the telling invention comes with the conception. The folly of a prince in sacrificing on suspicion a faithful servant is intensified to insanity when that servant manifests in his very presence the massive patience in dedicated service of an ox, or the unique fineness of an ascetic jackal. In an Aesopic fable, it may be that a cheap-jack gospeller is measured by his effect on a young bat lured from home by his adolescent fantasies. (Notice that the measure is a reticent register of ultimate revulsion, rather than an exposure of behaviour to reflection.) The action is the whole of the invention, and it is an action invented to show something that is, and is not usually seen, or not fully seen. The action has to be constructed to do this, and that construction is in the telling, bound faithfully to the conception.

In this respect fable may seem, and has seemed, closer to poetic composition than to the fabricated histories of the story-teller. As each poem is said to have its own poetics, so has each fable its own ground of justification. What the resemblance really amounts to, and what help the comparison may be in understanding fable, is worth consideration.

Poetry and fable

(*i*)

Poetry communicates pleasure and profit to those who respond to it, without being miscalled 'delightful teaching'. The profit may be wholly personal or, in certain forms of poetry, communal. Fable is heuristic, rather than positively didactic; and its meaning is general but not communal. This is an underlying contrast that may be presupposed. Reverting to the primitive definition of fable, 'a fictitious story picturing a truth', is poetry ever really about truth? This has been rigorously denied (I.A. Richards): it is emotive utterance, not informative statement; evoking and organizing feelings and attitudes, not extending nor consolidating knowledge. In De Quincey's dichotomy, it belongs to the Literature of Power, not the Literature of Knowledge. In this division, fable is in the opposite class.

This categorical categorial difference, justified or not, is too abstract for a useful comparison between poetry and fable. Assuming a bottom-line difference of this kind, I want to make the comparison in five particular respects: image and idea, generality, metaphor, indirection, language.

(*ii*)

Poetry may itself be roughly divided as about things or about ideas, as painting may be representational or abstract. The two are inherently not fully separable, but one or the other may be the focus of interest. Fable is equally enmeshed in both, focused on something concrete that represents something abstract. One urbanely unbuttoned form of the poetry of ideas has been the reflective verse of Satires and Epistles, as practised by Horace and Pope and others; in search of truth, Horace insists, allowing that such verse is not properly poetry, as generally understood. Occasionally he borrows a fable by reference, an already poeticized truth, although a commonplace one. And he retells without retailing the tale of the two mice, so that it remains among the best of versions. In general, an Aesopic fable was readily assimilated to this context, but it was not the kind of composition that did or could generate a fable. The discursive flexibility of the form was against it – the digressions, the freedom to leave the thought for a whim and to return, the spontaneity and improvisation of an essay, with the unfailing accompaniment of pleasing rhythm and rhyme. By contrast, a collection of fables is a collection of images within rigid frames; a series of slides, not a film. The slide picture, with its singularity and immobility which halts and focuses the gaze, is clinical; the subjective play of the mind is free.

A modern form of reflective verse was Robert Bridges' *The Testament of Beauty* (1929), this time written in a precious style and seeming to disdain association with fables, 'in humorous compact with philosophy' (IV, 582–94). Images are freely used, either to aid the expression of ideas or as examples in illustration, not entering into their constitution. Indeed, that can be done only when the whole is conceived for that purpose and dedicated to it. The images are invented and deployed here in service of the expression of ideas. Thus 'social Ethick'

> is but in true semblance, alike for praise or blame,
> a friendly domestication of man's old wolf-foe,
> the adaptable subservient gentlemanly dog,
> beneath a groom'd coat and collar in his passion unchanged
> (IV, 266–9

The metaphor here is an attempt to show the limits of the conception in the illustration; but the conception is taken as generally understood, and the metaphor is used as a personal observation on it – although claimed as a pictured truth.

Mother Hubberds Tale is an original fable in verse, but not a poetic fable. The particular image, with its conceptual implication, might have been less pleasurably, but effectively, formed in a prose narrative. A poetic fable would have to rely solely on poetic resources to produce the image with its implication. Something rare. Consider this poem by Edwin Muir, *The Combat*.

> It was not meant for human eyes,
> That combat on the shabby patch
> Of clods and trampled turf that lies
> Somewhere beneath the sodden skies
> For eye of toad or adder to catch.
>
> And having seen it I accuse
> The crested animal in his pride,
> Arrayed in all the royal hues
> Which hide the claws he well can use
> To tear the heart out of the side.
>
> Body of leopard, eagle's head
> And whetted beak, and lion's mane,
> And frost-grey hedge of feathers spread
> Behind – he seemed of all things bred.
> I shall not see his like again.

As for his enemy, there came in
A soft round beast as brown as clay;
All rent and patched his wretched skin;
A battered bag he might have been,
Some old used thing to throw away.

Yet he awaited face to face
The furious beast and the swift attack.
Soon over and done. That was no place
Or time for chivalry or for grace.
The fury had him on his back.

And two small paws like hands flew out
To right and left as the trees stood by.
One would have said beyond a doubt
This was the very end of the bout,
But that the creature would not die.

For ere the death-stroke he was gone,
Writhed, whirled, huddled into his den,
Safe somehow there. The fight was done,
And he had lost who had all but won.
But oh his deadly fury then.

A while the place lay blank, forlorn,
Drowsing as in relief from pain.
The cricket chirped, the grating thorn
Stirred, and a little sound was born.
The champions took their posts again.

And all began. The stealthy paw
Slashed out and in. Could nothing save
These rags and tatters from the claw?
Nothing. And yet I never saw
A beast so helpless and so brave.

And now, while the trees stand watching, still
The unequal battle rages there.
The killing beast that cannot kill
Swells and swells in his fury till
You'd almost think it was despair.

(*Collected Poems, 1921–1958*)

The first line removes the action from common experience: it is unique. The image of the combat is created poetically by allusive resonances, descriptive notes and overtones, impressionistic responses, symbolic presences; and is finally taken out of time and space by being left to ritual re-enactment. Such a uniquely particular image with a general implication could be formed in this compass only with the concentration of poetic resources and licence. The image of the action is as far removed as possible from a bout of arms, from chivalry in the background, and therefore from a general conception of 'combat'. It does its work as an extreme and wholly invented example which injects a new perception into the conception, only to be uncovered in an extreme and impossible case. This is indeed a poetic fable, not a poeticized fable.

R.C. Blackmur has said of Muir's poetry:

> This poetry is a kind of thinking in verse, which is a very different thing from versifying thought, for the verse is in the vital mode rather than the mere mode of the thought and is thus the substance of what we remember as well as the memorable form. It is a thinking in verse – as thinking in algebra or in farming or in love – which so far as it reaches form is poetry alive with the action of the mind, and which when it does not reach form has the dullness of the active mind failing.   ('Between the Tiger's Paws', p. 33)
> Later: 'so much of the poetry is nearly not words at all, but the action of the mind itself taking thought . . . (p. 42).

Blackmur's overall view of Muir's poetry – he is quoting Croce on Virgil – is 'a human feeling of bitter memories, of shuddering horror, of melancholy, of home-sickness, of tenderness, of a kind of childish pietas', an acceptance of it all resumed in a double focus, labelled Incarnation and Resurrection. This is poetry far beyond the scope of fable, which is limited in reference to a particular conception, as in The Combat – to a class of experiences.

(iii)

There are several types of generality in poetry, different from the conceptual representation which is the business of fable. One main form of generality is discerned in underlying patterns of shared experience repeatedly renewed, the generality of ritual re-enactment, with its expressive, bonding, renewing, redeeming function. The many attempts to specify archetypal patterns in poetry, or abstract meanings associated with a world-view repeatedly renewed, link up with cultural analysis of social structures bound up with myth and ritual. The universality of biological human needs and typical situations and relations rooted in them in a social context is inevitably reflected in patterns and images repeated in stories. Thus 'The Ancient Mariner' can be interpreted both as a personal projection and as a redemption story. This type of generality in poetry is essentially communal and practical, however far from its roots it is found. It is affective and conative, and does no cognitive work. If any world-view is implied, it is a communal one. The meaning of a fable is not to be construed on this model.

Another form of poetic generality is in polarization of absolutes abstracted from reality, pre-eminently good and evil; as in *Othello* a noble nature is infected by one corrupt. The unreal or distorted separation and projection of tendencies universal only within the individual makes them manageable – not cognitively, one function of abstraction, but, again, affectively and conatively in imagination, facilitating ideal identification and redemption.

One dominant type of the poetry of ideas is exemplified in Lucretius or Dante or Milton, who celebrate in expression an organized body of ideas received, or taken as enjoying unchallenged general truth. Similarly the Greek poets, including the poets of the great tragedies, used the myths repeatedly as examples or arguments of the way things were and had to be. In all these works, detailed and close description takes over from time to time; imaginatively real, sometimes incidental, not always relevant. Spenser's allegorical *The Faerie Queene* is also of this kind, and not continuously and closely allegorical, translating ideas into images.

In being a kind of prophesy or projected ideal, a personal synthesis of communal elements, Spenser's poem is another kind of poetic generality. Walt Whitman's 'Passage to India', drawing on the myths of history and summoning generations of heroic pioneers, prophesies the universal follow-through to all voyaging and exploration and discovery and achievement, consummated in the reckless 'farther, farther' of the poet's awakened and liberated soul. Whitman is nothing if not universal throughout, in this strain. His 'Song of the Redwood-Tree' is the voice of a dying giant, rising to a prophetic Whitmanic roar, saying farewell to the uncultivated land of the ages, announcing an abdication in favour of the arriving superior race, blessing these heirs to an immemorial past. Such projected ideals are general in their claim, but conceptually fragile if not facile. No less poetic – if less characteristic, and entirely personal – is the natural symbolic image of a tree which prompts Whitman's reflective awareness of his incapacity for self-sufficiency: 'I saw in Louisiana a Live-Oak Growing'.

Generality is inherent in such great traditional themes as the legend of Prometheus or of Faust, a generality reflected in the many versions there have been, and probably will be. Goethe brooded and worked on his *Faust* during some fifty years of his creative life, putting into it whatever was relevant in his imaginative stores and his surrender to impressions, bringing to view what he himself described as a rich, varied, and highly diversified life. It was intended to remain incommensurable, inviting repeated study. Care had been taken only that single masses in the work should be clear and significant; there was no single pervading idea; it was to be miscellaneous, indefinite, unfinished, defying description. Santayana has described it, at length, in one of his most characteristic, discerning and splendid essays (*Three Philosophical Poets*, 1910), as a many-sided manifestation and justification of the essential romantic aspiration and experience. As such, it is comprehensive and diffuse; a Gothic architecture, for it does have a theme. Santayana discerns in the poem – as in Goethe's own life – a latent philosophy, a vital tenor, which informs them both and is inexplicitly expressed most adequately in this way. Indirection, but not that of a fable.

Thomas Mann has shown how adaptable the material and presentation may be. His remarkable last novel, *Doctor Faustus*, is not a poem but might be described as a literary fugue, an allusive variation on the theme, hinting a bitter parody of the legend in the form of a fictitious biography of a German composer of genius by his lifelong totally devoted friend. The modern crisis in art, the alienation of the hero, the ambivalence of the narrator, the levels of German culture and of German political aspiration and adventure are interwoven themes with the subject, all tragic voices that move to a resolution in the hero's triumphant last work, 'The Lamentation of Dr Faustus' – a consummation in pure lamentation, a triumph of lamentation itself.

Prometheus, an even more time-worked theme, is ostensibly the hero who benefits mankind and suffers, like Heracles; to be exalted and honoured. But, like other material, the story can be adapted and presented as a fable, say in the hands of Gide. The material is the first word, not the last. Ficino and other Humanists interpreted the myth to express the paradox of humanity, sense-bound and rational.

There are other forms of poetic generality, some in the province of the comic or even the burlesque; and it is no surprise that these may come closer to fable. Shelley's 'Peter Bell the Third', written to delight and instruct, and Byron's 'The Vision of Judgment', a more finished performance, are skits, but with serious intent, indirectly a passionate reaffirmation of the poetic ideal, the poet as free spirit. Not exactly fables, but with some of the marks. Molière's *L'Avare* is a prose comedy, not formally in the poetic genre. That apart, it shows avarice as a form of addiction, with the compulsive corruption that involves; so that one is looking at a victim rather than a vice. In so far as this is so, the piece introduces in concrete form a conceptual innovation, which is what a fable does: it has a message.

The other forms of poetic generality that have been looked at have no message. They are established and familiar beliefs, to be poetically elaborated or celebrated, and thereby reinforced; poetic expression of what is communal. Or, as projected ideals, they are personal and likely to be ephemeral.

(iii)

Metaphors may be used stylistically for expression or logically in contribution to the connotation of a conception: expressively or constructively, a distinction which roughly corresponds to their use in poetry and fable. As a device of poetic expression the metaphor may be pressed, as if to make it total or literal: lovers experience an 'exchange of hearts'. Expressive use of metaphor need not go that far, but hyperbole is a poetic habit. The metaphors are used as occasioned figures of speech, unless in series as in allegory. The narrated action of a fable is itself the constructive metaphor.

Poetry, working by analogies and metaphors to express and evoke feelings and attitudes, moves away from direct description or statement and is inevitably involved in what would be paradox if taken literally. Being forced by his manner of working into this indirection which may verge on paradox, the poet may exploit the necessity, not merely by incidental hyperbole but in the design of his composition. Consider the use of images and ideas, metaphor and indirection, in two poems and two fables all founded on the sea: the Old English

'The Seafarer', Baudelaire's 'L'Homme et la Mer'; Babrius's fable 'The Sea' (71), and a tale by the Capek brothers, 'The Living Flame'.

The Old English poem (there is a modern version by Ezra Pound) is natural and direct as a whole. The Seafarer tells in graphic images of the extreme hardships and privations endured in the icy northern seas, indirectly accentuated by the failure of land-dwellers in their enjoyment of comfort to understand what the Seafarer goes through, thus adding the alienation of an exile to his lot. But the spell is compulsive, the wanderlust which tears him from the temptations ashore. The Seafarer goes on reflectively to see his life in context with the lot of others on earth, even the great and fortunate. In the end (omitted by Pound) his choice of life is justified as a preparation for the destiny of a Christian. But in the body of the poem it is a personal bond with the sea. The images are occasionally metaphorical, as when the cries and sounds of the sea birds serve for his games, laughter and drink, but mainly they are images of what is around. Ideas take over in the latter part, with images of bodily decline and the passing of delights and achievements.

Baudelaire's poem of four stanzas assumes in the first line a natural bond between the sea and a free human spirit and poses the sea as a mirror in which to see or on which to project his own inwardness, a matching disturbance and bitter depth; and he can immerse himself physically in it; it is the image of his being. This idea, in a general not personal form, is expressed in images of consonance. Then, in the last stanza, the indirection of metaphor turns to open paradox; they are age-long enemies, both (again identified) insatiably bloody, ever-lasting fighters, implacable brothers.

In Babrius's fable a farmer, seeing an overloaded ship dipping below the waves, exclaims that the sea is a pitiless element, an enemy to man. The sea replies that it is turbulent only when exposed to the winds, and not responsible for the harm it is made to do. In itself, it is gentler than the stable land.

The Capeks' tale is of a land-bound city man who jumps impulsively into a boat taking a drunken sailor to his ship, about to cast off. The harsh experience of seafaring does not discourage him. The rest of his life is spent at sea, as roughly as can be imagined. Old and dying, he is taken from the street into a hospital, and agrees to confess and receive the last sacrament. The priest, a dignitary, puts the usual questions and gets unusual answers – only stories of his wanderings, nothing about his sins. Totally frustrated, the priest curses him and leaves. He can go to hell as he went to sea.

The first two behave as poems, the second two as fables. 'The Seafarer' is mainly direct but uses indirection and metaphor, and blends images with reflective ideas, all in the simplest manner to express a chosen way of life in the world as it was known, a complete condensed story in three-dimensional outline. Baudelaire's poem is conceived as a metaphor, and this is sustained in a way that is not a conceit, a passing idea; for it expresses a psychic bond that is no mere image, comparable with the natural bond which held the Seafarer to the sea. The psychic bond is implicitly personal, explicitly general. Neither poem is a fable. Baudelaire's single metaphor might be said to be used constructively in an affective sense, rather than express-ively. In matching man and the sea, it invests the physical sea with a total meaning that remains a possession. This is to make a symbol, rather than to use one.

Babrius's fable, in the simplest Aesopic manner, invents an event which is an abstract image that exposes a common pattern of human behaviour, in this case a typical kind of mistaken judgement. The Capek brothers make their short and simple story say more than it seems to say by the implication of the juxtaposition with which it ends. An accepted frame of reference relied on to classify and make judgements simply does not apply; communication completely fails.[1]

Poetry shows her many expressive faces, painted perhaps but all animated, most deceiving when most passionate and compelling, like a lover's oath. Fable puts on a mask, comic perhaps but always there to call attention from illusions of reality to a feigned reality. Where poetry proclaims hyperbole, fable hints a distraction, or makes a gross digression to say a little. One may go all round the Wrekin to step next door, in order not to say by the way that neighbourhood is not nearness. It takes the long way round to get there because reticence is the sincerest language of truth, and silence is not the habit of language. There is more than a hint of this in an early amusing poem of Auden, 'The Truest Poetry is the most Feigning'. The last stanza:

> For given Man, by birth, by education,
> Imago Dei who forgot his station,
> The self-made creature who himself unmakes,
> The only creature ever made who fakes,

With no more nature in his loving smile
Than in his theories of a natural style,
What but tall tales, the luck of verbal playing,
Can trick his lying nature into saying
That love, or truth in any serious sense,
Like orthodoxy, is a reticence.

The truest poetry is the most feigning, for the truth of poetry is the instant truth of expressed passion, not the constant truth for which thought strives, the instant truth that the lover swears when he deceives his mistress and himself. Expressive immediacy, lyrical fundamentalism, is out of sight when poetry is divided as about ideas or about things. Also there is pure fantasy, about neither. Ezra Pound has a twelve-line poem, 'The Tree'. Imagined identity with a tree in the wood is a password into the archaic realm of sylvan presences whose truth is known and enjoyed for the first time, 'That was rank folly to my head before'. Similarly Wordsworth, versed though he was in the consolation of natural images, the nurse of his being, imagined escape from the world in glimpses that would leave him less forlorn:

Have sight of Proteus rising from the sea,
Or hear old Triton blow his wreathed horn.

'Ever let the Fancy roam!' Fable too is fantasy, but teleological, which is not poetic.

However, if love and truth are both 'a reticence', that could be a bond in the language used. Something to be expressed, not something expressed; something to be said, not something said; something implied. There does seem a hint of kinship. Something to be expressed is of course not yet poetry, and may never be so. This is a reminder of the relativity of reticence; it is in a context, it is occasioned; it is a resource. If it is silence, it is an expressive silence. Detachment is implied, and something withheld. This may be temperament, habit, decorum – or teasing. To say that it is in a map, not a landscape, would be absurd. Both may be sketches, but that is not to the point. It is a behavioural characteristic, not a character of an object. It may be characteristic of a class, say Greek poets. In that case, it is a withholding of something not considered appropriate or, perhaps more likely, not considered at all – say, self-expression. As actually a form of communication, reticence withholds expected expression, anticipated in response; say, when the situation compels grief. The silence, or the inadequate expression, is more telling than words, partly because the reader or listener is left to come more than half-way to meet the need. Similarly, the indirect representation of a fable leaves the reader to complete in mind what is intended. Even Addison picked on this dependence on the reader as the secret of fable (above, p. 100). It is the reason why Aesopic fables must be shorn of intrusive promythia or epimythia.

The indirection of fable is structural, in the formation of a concrete image of what is abstract. Expressive reticence in poetry is incidental, used to express intense feeling. In this, and perhaps also in the other, there is some distrust of language and a desire to escape the doom that overtakes words. Blackmur, quoted above on Edwin Muir (p. 229), said: 'so much of the poetry is nearly not words at all, but the action of the mind itself taking thought'. Distrust seems like despair in Whitman's 'A Song of the Rolling Earth', for which an earlier title was 'Carol of Words' and of which the first stanza is:

A song of the rolling earth, and of words according,
Were you thinking that those were words, those upright lines?
those curves, angles, dots?
No, those are not words, the substantial words are in the ground
and sea,
They are in the air, they are in you.

The *reductio ad absurdum* of 'substantial words' is in Swift's burlesque account of the Academy of Lagado in the third of Gulliver's voyages. The remedy is otherwise.

Aldous Huxley, in a masterly intervention in the 'Two Cultures' controversy raised by Lord Snow, underlined the point that both in their different ways try to use language to transcend language (*Literature and Science*, 1963). Describing the structural devices by which this is achieved in literature, he mentioned the 'calculated, one-track objectivity of *Candide*, from which private experience is deliberately and, so to say, flagrantly omitted for the express purpose of emphasizing the criminal stupidity, the absurd as well as hideous wickedness of human behaviour'. He contrasted that with the 'systematic shifting of attention from one order of experience to another,' a modern literary device which is 'built into the structure of almost every good novel' – and which he had exemplified in *Point Counter Point*, in the title itself and in the interplay of the resolute ways of life of the three important characters.

Metaphor is at the heart of the literary attempt to use language to transcend language. By naming one thing and meaning another, in a limited way language surpasses its function and keeps the mind open to what is intended. This is carried a step further when the metaphor is purposely incongruous. This is merely an abuse of language unless the incongruity sharply brings to attention what is perceived in the object, in effect by its perversity does dramatically the work of a true metaphor. In *Renart*, the animals are metaphorically feudal lords and ladies and clergy, and this focuses attention on certain kinds of behaviour attributed to them. Then the incongruity of the resemblance is brought out, and brings attention back to the full human reality from which types of behaviour have been abstracted. The originals are looked at again, more realistically; certain assumptions have been unsettled. The shifts and renewals of attention effected by this play of language keep the mind on the ball.

Modern movements in painting have been preoccupied with this question of how to renew attention to appearances too familiar to be noticed. Displacements, distortions, strange juxtapositions are intended to startle attention, so that the real object is looked at again with opened eyes, with curiosity. Such movements are fugitive, not least because at bottom an artist wants his images to receive attention for their own sake, rather than for an idea. In 'René Magritte', an *Omnibus* film biography by David Wheatley (BBC1, 15 February 1979), the painter speaks of his trying to enhance the sense of what a thing is by making it look as it does not. He demonstrates how one might draw a glass of water, and finishes with a half-filled glass balanced on top of an opened umbrella – incongruity in a represented reversal of expected roles. This does not come off: there merely remains a rather pleasing image, pleasing by the way it is drawn. Painting is back in business, and the customer pays no attention to the implied sales chat – or the next glass of water.

Language is properly what it does, and is duly transcended in having successfully done what was intended. In science, this is eventually formulation of a general rule concerned with what goes with what or what follows what. Meanwhile, for this purpose, language is reduced to notation, a single reference for each sign, elimination of possible ambiguity. This is the polar opposite of the poetic ideal, to enrich expressive power with multiplied meanings; Shakesperian copiousness, a language phenomenon. Even poetic genius, however, is liable to paint the lily or to be intoxicated with rhetoric, and become maudlin (*Richard II*). Sound without sense is another matter, proper enough in its proper place. The poetic vocation remains, with language itself, to use mint language for poetic purposes. The liability is that language becomes estranged, alienated and private: a different death.

In a fable, the language used is transcended if it represents an action which shows a general matter it was invented to expose. A main liability here is in loitering or deflection, a lapse into mere or sheer story-telling or satirical excursions. Language is a form of communication; its transcendence is sealed in the response. Response to a fable is closer to the response to science than to poetry, mainly for its practical effects. But indirect expression of passion may attend a fable narrative. It may indeed be its entire purpose.

(*v*)

This comparison with poetry has underlined several points of difference which may help to elucidate the character and place of fable in literature. Not least, comparison has brought out the limited and special character and place of fable. It is not a kind of poetry, even if in verse; identity, as perhaps in the case of Muir's poem, is highly exceptional; it has an exclusive and utilitarian purpose. The use of metaphor is the central difference – expressive in poetry, conceptually constructive in the other; incidental in poetry, the entire action which a fable invents. This implies detachment and distancing on the part of the fabulist; by no means a requirement of the poet as poet. Poetic generality is given, to be re-enacted or celebrated. Fable is the achievement of a significant generality shown in concrete form. In this sense, poetry has no message; fable has nothing else. The medium is the message of a message.

Exegesis

(*i*)

A fable has unmistakable meaning, or else it fails absurdly. Mime also, one might say, must communicate instantly. Unfortunately, mime needs a spectator and fable a reader. There are risks inseparable from the transaction. When what you say means 'plus qu'il ne semble', or when you say one thing and mean another, the risk is obvious. Irony is a *façon de parler* that might seem designed for disaster as plain speaking. Indirection, concealment, teasing are indeed put in to put off, even if it be a way to catch attention. If what is to be understood is only implied, it has to be unfolded in being taken in. In short, there is an element of delay built into the fable as communication, with the liability of loss on the way. If what the fable would say could be said directly, it should be. Thus, although a fable is not a riddle, both the amusement and the message are served by taxing the reader's wits. Collaboration is called for, and relied on.

A variety of material has been studied recently on the assumption that important meanings are encoded within it, not manifest. Included are myths, fairy-tales, folk-poetry, nursery rhymes; traditional material of this kind, some of which is strange to common sense. Myths and even Aesopic fables were allegorized in past periods and cultural contexts, but the present approach is more sophisticated in theory and method, in its attempt to be objective where direct test is not practicable. Is the Aesopic fable properly subject to this kind of scrutiny? The fables are listed in Stith Thompson's *Motif-Index of Folk-Literature* (2nd edn. 1955), and the references are given by Perry (p. 421). Although they have been consistently separated as distinct in kind from this other traditional material, there is a case for looking at this again in the light of modern findings and methods.

(ii)

This can be looked at in three connections: in a comparison with folk-poetry studied in this way; in a consideration of archetypes and thematic cultural patterns; in the general context of symbols and cultural conditioning and control.

In 'decoding' folk-poetry the assumption is made that the poems, particularly folk-songs, have a communal basis and meaning and function as an influence in the social control of behaviour. The 'rules' for generating new texts are in the precedents and have been assimilated with the tradition. They are formative and normative; and the poems are not simply expressive. (Compare the 'rules' for the use of a restricted speech code.) Interpretation, finding clues in repeated elements and sequences, uncovers shared unstated assumptions which underlie social reaffirmations in the particular poem. So long as the tradition survives, this inner content persistently and consistently derives from an age-old way of thinking.

This might seem to contradict what was said above – that in contrast with fable poetry has no message; since the main business of this traditional poetry is to pass on a message, on the assumption made. But in this case the message itself is traditional, renewed, not new. The genesis and purpose of an Aesopic fable are different in a way that removed it from the assumption of this approach. A fable of this kind is an abstract representation of a pattern of behaviour or the like familiar in observable instances. It is immediately recognizable and applicable, and is explicit and practical in this sense. Babrius's fable 'The Sea', mentioned above, shows simply, swiftly and sharply the mistaken or inadequate grounds of common judgements, regardless of earth sciences relevant to meteorological complexities, as 'The Ant and the Grasshopper' shows the kind of thing improvident present enjoyment is, regardless of the behaviour of real ants and grasshoppers. The representation shows far more of the abstract behaviour than a general proposition could state. That and its memorability are the beginning and the end. There is no communal continuity nor function. The message is a general one, Think about this; not a communal one, This is the behaviour that is blessed.

Based on Jung's theory of the symbol-creating function in the unconscious psyche, common inherited patterns of emotional and mental behaviour (and Coleridge speaks of 'asking' for a symbolic language in nature for something within him that already and for ever exists), Marie-Louise von Franz has examined fairy-tales for their archetypal foundations, acknowledging that this is a background activity and not the only factor in their literary understanding. In this case, what is discerned does not derive from an ancestral world-view or dominant cultural pattern but deciphers 'the message of some seemingly purposive, evolutionary tendency of the unconscious'. Although the assumption is that these formative patterns in the psyche must apply to every human activity, it is puzzling to know what the surplus is in the seemingly straightforward performance of an Aesopic fable.

Similar material, nursery rhymes, have been treated in a quite different way by Norman Iles. He calls the first of his two volumes of reconstructions *The Nursery Rhymes Restored to their Adult Originals*. This makes them out as bowdlerized versions of more explicitly sexual rhymes: the decoding is guided and informed by another basic interest communal in a different sense, helped out by hints, speculation, and some data.

Examining imaginative thought and speech in poetry for archetypal themes and image sequences that recur, Maud Bodkin speaks of the function of poetry to communicate through the sensuous resources of language the experience of an emotional but suprapersonal life leading to increased awareness and fuller expression and control of our own lives 'in their secret and momentous obedience to universal rhythms'. (*Archetypal Patterns in Poetry*, 1934, p. 89). On the relation between poetry and philosophy, between 'concrete intuitions and abstractions', she says that poets and imaginative writers of fiction objectify in imaginative form experiences potentially common but exceptionally deep and vivid, revealing a certain tension and ideal reconciliation of opposite forces in actual life (pp. 327–30). The effect of poetry – due to the way in which the interplay of different factors, sensuous and intellectual, removes customary inhibitions of the mind – is to release deep responses. These remarks bring into sharp contrast the reading of poetry and fable. Aesopic fables objectify in imaginative form common experiences, vivid in the images representing them, but hardly inner experiences involving tension and resolution. And in general, the interplay of factors introduced to throw the mind off balance and suspend inhibitions is devised to engage attention for what is to be shown, not to release buried elements within the reader's psyche.

There remains the general background of cultural conditioning through social structures and their related codes of communication. Bernstein's work on the evidence of data in schools distinguished home-bound restricted speech and frames of reference which encode the pattern of social relations of family and class, mediate and reinforce it, and the elaborated linguistic code developed in response to the demands of a complex industrialized society for general use and as an independent tool of thought. These findings have been generalized by Mary Douglas in studies that explore the relations between social structures and symbolic systems, which are the means of thought and the regulators of experience. Communication, the means by which thought is conducted and social control exerted, is largely determined by language forms, rituals, myths, symbols of all kinds, themselves dependent on social structures and relations. In this nexus are the material processes of conception that produce socially related symbols that influence perceptions and choices. Seen historically and reflectively, this is a manifestation of the tension of the polarity between self and society, from merger of the individual to separation and alienation. Mary Douglas's own interest is to contribute through understanding to a liberating awareness that is a condition of informed personal choice, at best combining a maintained critical independence with participation in social experience.

This line of analysis may have some bearing on the fable. One might see in the origin of the form, as Phaedrus did, the slave situation: many Aesopic fables speak out under this cover against oppressive authority; the lion embodies unscrupulous power. Also, at a primitive stage of culture humans have a two-dimensional appearance, seen only in their social roles, which facilitates the abstraction by which the agents of an action are indifferently animal or human. Both these social conditions might be seen as the start to what becomes one of the strong characteristics of fable, its critical detachment. With the authoritarian social structure of Sparta, and its dominant ideals, rituals and disciplines, the fable could hardly have the place it came to have in the schools of rhetoric or in general education and in linguistic discipline. In India, too, it was in education, under the patronage of princes for their families, that fables were taken from the wisdom literature to be valued and developed. There were inherent qualities in fable, both in the Aesopic and the Indian versions, by which it transcended state and cultural conditions and frontiers and circulated freely, with a permanence that contrasts with forms that are products of time and place and do not survive the advance of knowledge, like the Bestiaries.

The interest of the analysis then shifts to ways in which fables of both kinds were adopted, adapted and used, which bear the mark of the societies and cultures of time and place. The Persian version of 'Kalilah and Dimnah' cannot stomach the unpunished rascality of Kalilah in the Indian original. *Renart* reflects the aristocratic assumptions and prejudices that belong to its provenance; and later is made an instrument of personal and opposed ideas and ideals. Above all the religious cultures, Zoroastrian, Islamic, Christian and Hebrew, put their stamp on the fables they adopt and adapt in no uncertain terms.

Fable is itself a restricted speech code and at the same time enjoys freedom of inventive representation, for both are technical and purposive, not socially determined. Fables may frequently be concerned with some aspect of the relations between self and society, but cognitively, not ritualistically nor in any other such concrete communal way. In sum, these approaches seem inappropriate to the content, purpose and history of fable, except for marginal comment. It may be satisfactory to note that Mary Douglas's analysis and the historic role of fable meet in *Brave New World* and *Nineteen-Eighty-Four*, where the condition of socio-ideological control is shown to be abolition of the conditions and sources of personal experience. Individuals are returned to their social roles or subordinated to imposed rituals.

A word might be added on an attempted application of this kind of approach to *Gulliver* by Professor Donoghue in a radio talk, 'The Brainwashing of Lemuel Gulliver' (Radio 3, 15 June 1979). He argued that Swift gave his narrator no independent character at all: he made him merely reflect and report faithfully what he observed as a true-born prosaic Englishman, leaving the reader to join in with his own reflective judgements. Among the Lilliputians, the Brobdingnagians, the Houyhnhnms – as among the English before his voyages began and in due course after he finally returned – Gulliver is said to reflect and adopt the opinions of those among whom he finds himself, including their opinions of himself. He is relative to those he is among, a cultural artefact. Swift, it is suggested, puts up the idea that man has no nature, only behaviour culturally determined.

Professor Donoghue here himself reflects current theories of fiction and current theories in cultural anthropology. It is in the nature of a fable to provoke the reader to think for himself about the images with which he is presented, and such thinking is bound to be contemporary. But is Professor Donoghue justified in taking out one dimension of the text to demonstrate 'the great power of habit and prejudice'? The thesis destroys Gulliver as agent of a process of enlightenment that learns to recognize cultural relativity, but is not limited to that, and not focused upon it.

The metaphorical action of a fable shows far more than could be compassed in a propositional statement. It is and remains without an official meaning, and without unoffical message from the depths. Its meanings are open to reflection, in a sense in which the meaning of a proposition is not.

(*iii*)

To hand over a fable to hermeneutics could be only to parody the science. Epicurus held that nothing is as it is in order that we may use it, but whatever there is has its uses, which can be discovered and improved upon. Even in the arts, where there is without question an organizing mind at work, the Epicurean line is now preferred. The artist does not have exclusive rights. He produces a public object which is then independent of him and his intentions. Those whom it interests bring to their response their own experience, their own associations, their own feelings, needs and questions, which enter into the determination of what is its relevance to them, which cannot be taken account of in the intentions of the maker. The richer the work, the public object, the more diverse the possibilities of its understanding – as was noted above in the mention of Goethe's *Faust*. Since the fable is constitutionally poor, a more or less drastic reduction, its possibilities are correspondingly reduced; there is more sense in looking for an 'official' meaning, an intention, a message.

Before going further, let me remark on one extravagance in the modern admission of multiple meanings, with stress on the reader's part. For instance, when John Fowles, after the first dozen chapters of *The French Lieutenant's Woman*, takes the reader into his confidence and contrasts the convention of the novel with the real autonomy of the characters and the openness of the action, so that author and readers are on the same footing, he is bound to be disingenuous – in refusing to be party to the convention. For the author cannot evade his responsibility, nor even share it. There are three possibilities. (1) The author manipulates his characters as puppets to his own ends. (2) The characters have a degree of autonomy which the author respects. (3) The author offers alternative outcomes to his story. (2) is spurious: what kind of autonomy is this? How can it mean other than (a) consistency or (b) unplanned developments which suggest themselves as the author broods on the character he has imagined? In neither case is there any independence, and there could not be any. A writer of fiction fabricates in the workshop of his craft what he has formed in his imagination, whether merely to please the reader, as he hopes, or to communicate in this form some part of his own experience. If the author offers alternatives (3), he is inviting his reader into his workshop to see the work before it is finished; if he refuses to finish it, leaves the alternatives open, that is neither more or less than any other abandonment. In short, the author engages to manipulate, does manipulate, and can-not but manipulate his characters and events, whether to entertain or for a more personal and creative purpose. An author remains always with sole authority for what is produced, not for interpretations put upon it or uses made of it. The openness of the author of *The French Lieutenant's Woman* is serious and refreshing, and a way of educat-ing the reader, but would be insufferable as a way of writing fiction – as a hoax may be excellent to dine out on but not so good as a career.

In most popular fiction the writer's intention is neither here nor there. Intention may be of interest and in question when more than entertainment seems implied. The 'intention' of an artist is always the work itself, not any independent purpose. The work is likely to develop and change as it proceeds, whether or not the artist himself does or can give an intelligible account of this. That is not part of his responsibility. The question about intention may be removed from speculation or biographical probing by concentration on the work.

In the case of a fable, there may be three forms of uncertainty: about the image that has been created, about what it refers to, about what follows (what? what for? so what?). The first is the most serious form of uncertainty, since if there is no definite public object there is nothing to begin with; but the image in question may not be imme-diately discernible, may have to be uncovered, may require the readers activity – deliberately. The second question gives infinite scope to allegorizing and speculation, sometimes legitimate, often not. J.R.R. Tolkein would not allow that his elaborate *Lord of the Rings* was an allegory (it has been likened to *The Faerie Queene*) because allegory is dominated by the author, and he wanted to give his readers complete freedom. (That has not prevented the founding of an exegetical industry on his works.) The third uncertainty is removed with the other two, or is irremovable, but there may be alternatives. These kinds of possible uncertainty about a fable are inherent in the genre, but it is the business of the genre to settle them.

(iv)

'Genre' has nothing to do with correct labelling unless it has first to do with understanding, with expectations, with how to read, with the contract between author and reader. The genre is a conception shared by writer and reader within which the particular intention can

be developed, because the conception facilitates partial anticipation,
as language structures do. Genre need not be in question unless and
until there are doubts or contradictory judgements, as the grammar
of a language is not examined so long as the meaning is clear. The
American film 'Holocaust', which ran on television in four parts for
nearly seven hours, attempted to depict Nazi extermination of the
Jews, and others, by showing events and scenes in two parallel
families over ten years, the Jewish family of a Polish doctor in Berlin
and the family of a young lawyer making a career in the SS. The film,
watched by millions of viewers, excited a mixed and confused
response. Some television critics reviled it as 'soap opera' which
cheapened an unspeakable crime and insulted its victims.

Granted that it was right to remind the world a generation later of
what was done, there were three obvious ways in which to go about
it: a 'fictionalized drama', as this film was termed; a documentary; a
highly selective representation, like the German film 'Ein Tag'. Each
method uses a different vocabulary, and has in mind a different
public: each is in effect a different genre. The genre chosen aimed at a
comprehensive coverage that would have the widest appeal. The
critics who labelled it 'soap opera' would not recognize or accept the
vocabulary used, the genre. It was not in the least 'soap opera', and
could have been so called only in derision by critics who could not
tolerate a fictional element that was not restricted to pure reconstruc-
tion (as of a trial faithful to the transcript) or who could take only a
concentrated work of art, like 'Ein Tag'. The film was of course open
to criticism, but only on lines which showed understanding of its
vocabulary and respect for its purpose.

A great part of the puzzlement in reception of Kafka's *The Trial*
and *The Castle* probably came initially from not knowing how to
take them because of their not having an assignable genre. They were
not obviously satire or burlesque, and were obviously not crime or
mystery stories. One can reasonably ask why no recognizable convention is used, and what is intended. In the last resort the answer is
in the public object produced, which in the first place tells us to
abandon unfulfilled conventional expectations as a condition of
learning to see what is there. One can hypothesize; there are alternative possibilities; there is the possibility of a hoax. In the end, if I fail
to find satisfactory answers to the three questions, the story fails or I
fail. A fable is not a sealed book, and a sibylline mode of discourse is
utterly alien to it, but the enigmatic is its property. Jean Hytier,

writing of Gide's *'soties'*, described them as enigmatic satires:

> Their very mysteriousness has a specific purpose. A work must make us work; it must not leave us where we were when we began it, it must instruct us, 'broach' us, as Gide says, and in order to do this is not the best way to disturb us? ... A mysterious book grows even deeper on re-reading; it develops its implication and it is not impossible that the author's thought may then be followed – correctly, according to its course – even beyond his own awareness. (*André Gide* pp. 68–9)

Gide himself said:

> Before explaining my book to others, I expect others to explain it to me. To attempt to explain it first is immediately to limit its meaning; for, if we know what we wanted to say, we do not know if we were saying only that. – One always says more than THAT. – And what particularly interests me is what I have put in without knowing it ...

There it can be left. The part of the reader is not to do the work of the author, or relieve him of any part of his responsibility, but to meet him halfway and to complete the work for himself (and perhaps for others) as only he can.

A further word on 'genre', for it is a category which is liable to degenerate into a cliché or a formula, or it is a pedantic labelling, not always a needed clue to understanding. An example of the first is given by Brian Aldiss, writing of science fiction:

> When Gernsback started his magazines in the late twenties, he invented sf as a genre, a category. No chance of the 'once-for-once-only' approach here! By their very nature, the pulps appeared regularly, with a regular amount of space to fill. So modern sf was established, wherein a lot of underpaid authors rather frantically cribbed or sparked ideas off each other ... But the great distinction to be made between the two streams in their heyday is that whereas the 'once-for-once-only' stream was, by its nature, a critical literature, even in the case of its most noted practitioner, H.G. Wells, the pulp stream quickly turned to

power-fantasy and escapism. (*Hell's Cartographers*, p.195)

In one borrowed sentence Kingsley Amis unknowingly indicates the parallel and the difference between science fiction and fable: The short story is 'a structure which seems perfect to articulate and enact a single speculative conceit which (arguably) is the task for which sf is most suited' (ed. *The Golden Age of Science Fiction*, 1981, Introduction, p. 23).

'The Emperor's New Clothes' is as simple and great a piece of irony as was ever written, and has proved as adaptable to use in literary criticism as in a party political broadcast. Only the story as originally told has the virtue which gives it this value. Whether it is labelled fairy-tale or fable would have no interest, for there is no question how to take it and its inclusion in a collection of fairy-tales happens to be its provenance. To make a question of its genre would be mere pedantry. But pedantry thrives, like all parasites, on something that has vitality.

Mistaking the genre is confusing to the reader, mixing the genres is risky for the author, as Orwell recognized when he wrote *Nineteen-Eighty-Four*. Transposing techniques from other arts has become a common device, as when W.S. Burroughs mixes collage, image montage, scenario prose, and straight narrative. Such mixtures hardly confuse, and may be effective. Böll made play with them to good purpose in *Absent Without Leave*. Crossing boundaries for some borrowing is modern practice. A merger of territories would be impracticable or absurd. Territorial integrity remains secure, for fable as for other genres. But if there are present in a text indications on how to read it, that is enough.

(iv)

A message; no official message, no esoteric message, an uncertain message, an enigmatic message, what the reader tells him/herself; how unsatisfactory. Not really, because we are shown something every time. Some of the topics of the Aesopic fables were listed in chapter 1 (p. 9), and similarly there can be a sample of what the longer fables have been designed to show: the inescapable face of capitalism; the fatality of technological progress; the pervasive pressures of violence; the depths of complicity; the loathsome sight of human evil that infects the race; destruction of the conditions of human being; the conditions of escape from the conditions of social existence; the many ways of being human; the fact that the cosmos, dreadful as it is, cannot be bettered by human intervention; the absurdity of dreams of Utopia, and the nightmare of their enactment; the waste of life in high-minded quests; the flimsy foundation of familiar institutions in custom and consent; the thin crust of civilization; the delirium of escape into irresponsibility; the starred course of sexual love; the tainted mutuality of colonial relations; the innocence of the young and the guilt of adults as sister images; wilful and woeful reductions of human communication; transformation by accidental detachment from attachments.

It could be packaged differently, but this is the merchandise of the fable trade.

Criticism

(i)

'The Fable as Literature': of what quality? There has been incidental criticism of particular fables throughout this study. In this last section, attention is directed to the distinctive aesthetic, ethical, and epistemological aspects of the fable.

The division of metaphors into logical and stylistic according to their use (p. 210) put fables in the class of logical metaphor, serving argument not expression. Whatever has structure or performance (as argument has) has aesthetic possibilities. The fable is not 'a well-made story', but it may be well or ill made in an aesthetic sense. The metaphor is a single integral action that holds all there is. Destruction of the asethetic and intellectual unity of *Gulliver* by separation of the books destroys the fable. Fable is a focused concentrated form, and when it is seen to be so in a particular way there is aesthetic pleasure.

Constant use of fables in linguistic exercises, and concentration on the retelling of familiar stories, developed refinement in economy of expression, fewer words to say more, sharper words to penetrate further. The elegance or force was achieved in poetic forms, and belongs to poetic expression.

The distinction between a logical and a stylistic use of metaphor can be followed by a distinction between congruous and incongruous metaphors. Taking fables of all kinds in general, one finds a riot of incongruities, sometimes of the greatest extravagance; but not merely for fun. Incongruity is used in the fables in two ways: in comic episodes; in the structure. Renart's obsequies (and resurrection), casting into the lower city from the Acropolis for avaracious pseudo-philosophers, extinguishing the palace fire in Lilliput, are episodes made ludicrous by incongruity. The fable itself is often formed out of some kind of incongruity: the use of animals in Aesop to portray human behaviour; the dubbing of chosen beasts of field and forest with proper names to play prince, peers, and prelates of realm and church; the conversation between Mycillus and his cock; the auction of philosophies; incongruity of scale in *Gulliver*; incongruity of inner and outer in *Candide*; the incongruity of an Oxford don as God with an amiable fool and ex-hero-worshipper as his adjutant, of a man in a Jaguar translated to a life below the road, of a revolution in a farmyard, of a Savage who has brought himself up on Shakespeare and tries to adjust himself to the brave new world he sees for the first time, of an insect as son and brother, of children trying to carry on as adults, or filling the ranks of a modern army, of razor-slashing to Beethoven's sublimest music, of a bat outraged by an Inspirationalist, of a vulgar charlatan lording it over his mental and moral superiors by personal ascendancy. The list is long, and might be longer. Add to episodic and structural incongruities the regular use of another form, parody.

Incongruity arrests attention and defeats usual expectations; therefore opens the mind, prepares it for something new – a tactical defeat of the logical mind, not the definitive strategic defeat sought by the 'koan' method in Buddhist discipline. At the same time it is a form of the comic, which sustains interest and gives release. In addition, it can be used as a form of comment. Incongruity is to the aesthetic as dissonance to harmony, the same language. The incongruity is resolved in the achievement of the fable; it causes surprise which leads to discovery. The incongruous metaphor is the distinctive aesthetic aspect of the fable.

(ii)

For centuries it was not questioned that poetry was justified by teaching morality. When that was seen to reduce art to a means that served another purpose, it was set up for its own sake as a world apart. Aesthetics and ethics, still baffling in themselves after more than two thousand years of subtle discussion, are in their relations more so. Fortunately, both art and conduct have subsisted all this time in good health on a plain diet of common sense, leaving philosophers to entertain questions that refuse to go away. Anyhow, fables, like all fiction, have, directly or indirectly, to deal with a world of which morality is an essential part. How they deal with that part is the question, bearing in mind that fables are mainly engaged in forming images of human behaviour.

Fables do not teach morality in any direct didactic sense. As was noted above (p. 8), the Aesopic fables are more descriptive than prescriptive and the morals added as promythium or epimythium were useful for indexing, rather than integral to the text. But these fables, like proverbs, were invented for a practical purpose in the form of memorable epitomes of life's common experiences. La Fontaine offers them as a mirror for self-examination; and uses them for the expression of some of his own moral judgements and passions. In longer fables, devices are used to unsettle established views and judgements, or to expose unnoticed aspects of behaviour, or to show the familiar in a new light. This unsettlement of established morality for the enlargement of awareness tends to distinguish fable from satire, which expresses anger, indignation, disgust, contempt, ridicule in an attack on what is familiar. Satire is incidental to the narrative in fables, seldom its purpose. Fable inhabits the ambiguous borderland of the aesthetic and the ethical in Kierkegaard's sense in *Either/Or*, interested in displaying what is there, leaving the issues open in a Socratic manner. There are two parties in play, author and reader. The author is most likely to have made an ethical judgement and a personal commitment, or a deliberate refusal of commitment, and that is why he writes the fable, to face the reader with what he has faced – or he makes up the fable in the process of forming his own mind. Kierkegaard himself made complicated use of an indirect method of authorship, as did Gide of one less complicated. The reader has to be left to make his own choice, or not, after the author has done his best to engage him.

A moral criticism of fables as a class of fiction might be that they tend to engender cynicism, since they exhibit mainly behaviour that is clearly foolish or evil, and strengthen an assumption that this is the kind of behaviour most characteristically human. It is said of readers of science fiction that they read a great deal of it, and some of them read nothing else. Fables are not a genre in that sense. There are unlikely forms of addiction, but this would be the unlikeliest. Anyhow, supply forbids it.

(*iii*)

The epistemological aspect of the fable is probably the most interesting at the present time. From the beginning, the fable 'pictured a truth'; and the Aesopic fable was more descriptive than prescriptive, picking out for attention a kind of behaviour. As literary behaviour, the fable does not go about lawful occasions in a regular manner; it forsakes all business to stage a demonstration. As a demonstration is not a policy but a cry, so the truth pictured by a fable is a statement that jolts, not a statement that settles; the game is flushed, not shot down. When all is said, the fable leaves all to do. Its epistemological function forces it out of the literature of fiction. In this, it anticipated modern attempts to break away from or break into traditional 'realistic' fiction, as bogus or sedative. It turns up alongside these experiments in intransitive writing, which treat the work of fiction as an artefact, a self-contained verbal structure, patently artificial, but with symbolic references. However, the fable is not itself experimental; it has its own long tradition, and is secure in its limited capability.

If it still 'pictures a truth' in its own way, what is the status of such a 'truth'? At first, the Aesopic fable was at the ground level of experience like proverbs and maxims, derived from and appealing to popular knowledge of how things are. But it has been repeatedly insisted in this study that a fable does not state anything; it shows. All the same, what is shown is shown because of its implications, which are more or less statable. Something is indicated by what is shown that is intended to be conclusive, if not exhaustive; what is shown is of general import and importance. The largest category of these 'truths' would seem to be the kind of thing not generally noticed which when brought to attention is seen to be evident. 'Evident' here is a question-begging word. Fables are, like science, concerned with connections, with what goes with what and what follows what, but at a general level not amenable to reduced and refined statement testable by quantifiable evidence; nor are their 'truths' merely loose empirical generalizations. They are concerned with connections and conditions. Not with the link between dependence on cigarettes and liability to lung cancer; rather, with seeing the mutual dependence of slave and master, and recognizing its corrupting liability. Not with high and low pressure systems as conditions of fine and wet weather; rather, with freedom of information and the possibility of comparison as conditions of human thought. There are 'truths' of this kind which when brought to notice are seen as evident, with recognition of the importance of their bearings. They are both undeniable and arguable; to deny them is to quibble, but to admit them is the first word only. The truth about the 'truth' of fables is not merely that it is something shown not something said, but mainly that it is demonstration of a second order, showing what has been left out or what has not been thought of or what has been mistakenly thought, or turning us round to look in another direction. It does not compete in truth claims. It fastens on what is generally in mind, and is radically corrective.

(iv)

A literature that began ages ago about such matters as Foxes and Birds and Outer Space, and continues today about such matters as Penguins and Boffins and Inner Space, is and remains a provincial kind of literature, one might say, outside the sphere of polite letters. But courts have had their jesters of obscure origin, and there have been a few courtiers with the talent to improve on that kind of wit and turn an art of the fugitive into the art of the memorable. The truth pictured in this similitude, the theme of this study, betokens the power of the image, the classless power of literature.

In 'Modern Instances' the fables were more compelling than playful, and this latter side of their vocation seems in danger of failing in an age of so much alarm and despondency, when it would be most appreciated. The vocation itself can continue, or recur, only if conditions are favourable. The Hebrew prophets, major and minor, waxed and waned. In an uncertain future for all enterprise, two things remain permanently certain so long as there is human survival. The pulse of life on earth is renewal, even re-enactment; all finishes end in beginnings. Above all, the spring of originality does not run dry. People continue to flock in numbers and caw opinions or huddle in silliness, but mass behaviour masks and mocks individual faces, personal selves, inarticulate probably, inexpressive never. So that Philemon can have the last word after all, for he was more right than wrong in saying that 30,000 foxes would have all one nature, but men have as many different characters as bodies.

Notes

Introduction

1 *Babrius and Phaedrus*, tr. Ben Edwin Perry (Loeb Classical Library, 1965).

2 Take 'The Wolf and the Lamb'. The image is of helpless innocence as doomed victim of undeterrable inescapable power which closes in, as in one of Poe's tale. But that is not the moment of truth in this horror story. Rather, the action exposes the need of the agent to justify the unjustifiable. This may be taken as just a graphic illustration of a familiar truth, an arresting reminder. Or it might be taken as an insight into what goes on inside the indulgence in unjust practices. Aesop's fables and the truths they picture are long and early familiar. Some have corners of the truths they picture still unexposed.

3 *Babrius and Phaedrus*, xxiii.

1 The fable in literature

1 Arthur Waley seems unaware that 'squatting' of sparrows in nests built by swallows is common. Gilbert White wrote of the swifts: 'I have suspected (since their nests are exactly the same) that they sometimes usurp upon the house-sparrows, and expel them, as sparrows do the house and sand-martins' (*Natural History of Selborne*. Letter XXI). Compare also in Grimms' Tales, 'A Sparrow and his Four Sons'.

2 Ben Edwin Perry's *Aesopica* (vol.i, Greek and Latin Texts, 1952) aims at an exhaustive study of the Aesopic fable and its cognates. In his Loeb edition of *Babrius and Phaedrus* (1965), he furnishes an Appendix which lists with summaries and sources all the fables of which he published the texts in *Aesopica*, 725 in number, making 'An Analytical Survey of Greek and Latin Fables in the Aesopic Tradition'. The number assigned to each fable in this list corresponds with the number in *Aesopica*. Because of the comprehensiveness and convenience of this Appendix, I refer to a fable by the number in his list, unless it is a specific version.

3 Because of subsequent recensions, this collection is known as Recension I. The literary history of these recensions is complicated, and not necessary information for the general purpose of

identifying 'Aesop' in the European inheritance. Perry reprints
the text of Recession I (244 fables) in *Aesopica* (pp. 321–416).

4   Joseph Jacobs, an earlier student of Aesop (*History of the
    Aesopic Fable*, 1889), had argued cautiously that some dozen
    fables did pass into the Greek stream from an Indian source,
    including 'The Wolf and the Crane', 'The Ass in the Lion's
    Skin', 'The Wolf and the Lamb', 'The Fox and the Crow', 'The
    Bald Man and the Fly', and 'The Goose that Lays the Golden
    Eggs'. His argument is that all but three or four of the thirty
    fables which occur in the Talmud and Midrashic literature can be
    paralleled either in Indian or in Greek fables, or in both. Where
    there is a parallel in both, the Talmudic version invariably
    follows the Indian wherever it differs from the Greek. He argues
    that it is hardly possible that the Greek fables could have been
    translated into Hebrew and changed by the Rabbis and taken to
    India: the reverse must have happened, especially as the *Jatakas*
    are earlier than the first collection of Aesopic fables by Deme-
    trius.

5   I.G.N. Keith-Falconer: *Bidpai's Fables* (1885); and L. Her-
    vieux: *Les Fabulistes Latins*, vol. 5 (1894).

6   In the course of the main stories and their dependent fables,
    there are 624 numbered maxims in verse. The sententiousness of
    the maxims is enlivened by the fables, but they frequently have
    their own pungency and dramatic point: '17 No anointing or
    religious rites are performed by the beasts for the lion: the
    sovereignty naturally belongs to him who has gained the king-
    dom by his power.'

    In *Bidpai*, the maxims are absorbed into the conversation, not
    separated out in numbered verses. Perhaps this separation
    reflects the work of commentators in successive redactions, less
    concerned with dramatic propriety than with didactic effici-
    ency. The Arabic versions are considered closer to the Indian
    original than are the Sanskrit texts of today.

7   English titles are used here, as in the Greek-English Loeb
    edition, vols i–viii, instead of the usual Latin titles. References
    are to the Loeb edition. Lucian's sources are dealt with exhaust-
    ively by Bompaire; his legatees are usefully considered by E.G.
    Allison in *Lucian, Satirist and Artist*, pp. 130–87.

8   There is a fable of La Fontaine in which a happy cobbler whose
    merry singing has attracted attention is given money by a rich
    neighbour; this so ruins his peace of mind that he is constrained
    to give it back in order to regain contentment (VIII, 2). La
    Fontaine seems to have taken the story from Bonaventure

Desperière, a sixteenth-century imitator of Lucian who wrote *Cymbalum Mundi*, after *The True History*.
9 Addision builds on passages from Lucian's Menippean dialogues with Zeus in his *Spectator* paper, 'Ancient Fables on Prayer' (120).

2 *Renart to Volpone*

1 Isidore, Saint, Bishop of Seville, *Etymologiae*: rec. W.M. Lindsay (Oxford Classical Texts, 2 vols, 1910).
2 M.R. James, 'The Bestiary', *History*, xvi, April 1931, 61.
3 *An Old English Miscellany*, ed. R. Morris, p. 201. (Early English Text Society, 1872). There is a translation from a Latin Bestiary of the 12th century, copiously illustrated, by T.H. White: *The Books of Beasts* (1954).
4 G.R. Owst: *Literature and Pulpit in Medieval England* (1933), p. 240.
5 It is perhaps worthy of remark here that Thomas Bewick's famous and popular *A General History of Quadrupeds*, published in 1790, is not short on the legendary and the preposterous, especially in accounts of animals known by repute, not acquaintance. The author of the text was his partner and former master, Ralph Beilby.
6 For the basic facts about the transmission of Greek and Latin literature, see *Scribes and Scholars* (1968) by L.D. Reynolds and N.G. Wilson.
7 Half of this *Romulus Anglicanus* is indirectly derived from the original Romulus. The remainder includes several episodes that are in the *Roman de Renart*, for example, the encounter of cat and fox, with their respective tricks for self-preservation; and *De Vulpe et Ursa* (LX), adeptly told about the rape of a she-bear by a fox, a precedent for Renart's violation of Hersens, wife of Isengrim.
8 For classification of *exempla*: M.J. Th. Welter, *L'Exemplum dans la littérature religieuse et didactique du moyen âge*, (1927), chap. ii; *Middle English sermons*, ed. W.O. Ross (Early English Text society, 1940), lx; G.R. Owst, *Literature and Pulpit in Medieval England, passim*, esp. pp. 110 ff.
9 A guide is indispensable. There is none more thorough than the one followed here: *Le Roman de Renart dans la littérature française et dans les littératures étrangères au Moyen Age*, John Flinn (Paris, 1963).
10 A prose version, *Die Hystorie van Reynaert de Vos*, was made,

which was the basis of Caxton's translation into English, printed
in 1481. There were more than a dozen different versions in
German, of which one was the model for Goethe's *Reinecke
Fuchs* in 1794. There were translations into other European
languages, including French; for the original belonged to a
remote medieval literature.

11 Perry lists 48 'Fables Excerpted from the Writings of Odo of
Cheriton' (Nos 588–635), which include some of the parables;
for example, 'The Rustic Invited to Dinner' (629), a model
parable that illustrates the difference.

12 *The 'Adages' of Erasmus, A study with translations*, Margaret
Mann Phillips (1964).

13 David Hume exposed the fallacy of utopian thinking in his essay
'Idea of a Perfect Commonwealth', and remedied it with a
practicable plan modelled on a reformed constitution that
existed and worked.

14 Angus Fletcher, *The Prophetic Moment: An Essay on Spenser*
(1971); Alastair Fowler, *Spenser and the Numbers of Time*
(1964); Frances Yates, *Astraea. The Imperial Theme in the
Sixteenth Century* (1975); 'Elizabethan Neoplatonism reconsidered: Spenser and Francesco Giorgi' (1977).

15 *Shakespeare our Contemporary*, tr. Boleslaw Taborski (1965).
In his Introduction to the Arden edition, Frank Kermode says:
'*The Tempest*, like its descendant *Comus*, is deeply concerned
with difficult ideas and with the philosophical genres of masque
and pastoral. Anyone who refuses to care about these things will
not begin to understand why the play is as it is, and so it is
described as a weary pantomine, or an obscure autobiography.'
This states the all-or-nothing alternative posed by the play:
either the very feeblest and tiredest of the plays, or deeper than it
seems and costing some pains to penetrate to its meanings. The
second course leaves room for diverse readings, and Professor
Kermode has most admirably provided the groundwork for any
reader's construction of his understanding of the play.

3 Olympians at play

1 He gives lists of the fables in Sir Roger's collection which have
been omitted or altered, with his reasons. Thus 58 are rejected as
redundant or as without a useful general application, 208 as
conceits or facetiae, not true apologues. There are 97 'to which
we have presumed to give entirely either new morals or new
reflections, as we thought the design of the fables more naturally

required, in order to direct them to general use; or to avoid party
or political reflections'; 34 'we have taken the liberty to alter, or
enforce, that we might accommodate them to more useful
morals and reflections'. Only five fables are taken from
L'Estrange's second volume, which both Croxall and Richardson regarded as of small value, and a concession to the impor-
tunity of booksellers upon success of the first.

2   'Vision of Mirza' (*Spectator* 159), 'The history of Almamoulin,
the son of Nouradin' (*Rambler*, 11 May 1751), 'The history of
Abouzaid, the son of Morad' (*Rambler*, 11 December 1752). Of
more interest is 'Oman's Plan of Life' (*Idler*, 22 March 1760), so
characteristically different from Voltaire's *Memnon*, on life's
major little ironies. Of all Johnson's exotic pieces, however,
none of the apologues matches in the tale and in the telling
'Anningait and Ajut; a Greenland history', whatever his purpose may have been (*Rambler*, 28, 31 December 1751).

3   Murray's *New English Dictionary* (1901), which is on historical
principles, includes 'fable' among 'familiar words of everyday
speech', and devotes to it nearly two columns. Three senses are
attributed to it: a fictitious narrative, the plot of a dramatic (or
epic) composition, a fable. The last is given the most prominent
modern sense, and defined as a short story devised to convey
some useful lesson, especially using non-human characters, an
apologue. The second meaning, a plot, takes care of itself without ambiguity, leaving to discrimination the apologue (a fable of
Aesopic type) and the tale or fictitious narrative. George Crabb
(*English Synonyms*) grew up at the end of the eighteenth century. He pairs 'fable' and 'tale', and distinguishes them by
equating 'fable' with its Aesopic type, as allegorical, with
imaginary agents, and a single action, written for instruction;
whereas 'tales' are written principally for amusement, both
agents and action are drawn from the passing scenes of life, and
there are many incidents or a complex action 'which excite an
interest for an individual' – that is, there is a hero. He quotes a
couplet of Waller to illustrate the use of 'tale':

Of Jason, Theseus, and such worthies old,
Light seem the tales antiquity has told.

True, 'fables' would not scan, so that it is not entirely evident
that Waller is making the distinction in not calling the Greek
myths 'fables' as Dryden does, and as was common. Indeed,
Murray's Dictionary cites Dryden's 'Epistle to Sir George

Etherege' in reference to the Greek myths; 'But spite of all these Fable-Makers'. It is reasonable to suggest that when the myths were allegorized, they were thought of as fables; otherwise, they were 'light' tales, repeated for entertainment when no longer believed.

4   There is a critical review of aesthetic theory in the period in the last chapter of Ernst Cassirer's *The Philosophy of the Enlightenment* (1951).

5   For the Scriblerians, of course, *Travels into Several Remote Nations of the World by Lemuel Gulliver* was a 'merry book' (Arbuthnot), for it was conceived among thèm and in many parts had their stamp upon it. Pope classed it among Swift's Ludicrous works (*The Dunciad* I, 20), and saluted it in four facetious pieces. But the merry note is too removed in time for any echo to be heard, 'merry' in the sense of Sir Thomas More and the Lucianic tradition.

Swift seems to have begun with the idea of a contribution to the *Memoirs of Martin Scriblerus*, in which Martin sets out on his travels in the same year and the same manner as Gulliver, and 'he was carr'd by a prosperous Storm to a Discovery of the Remains of the ancient Pygmaean Empire'. The ideas here and in the Scriblerian piece by Pope, Arbuthnot, and Parnell, *Concerning the Origin of Sciences*, make free use of the monographs of the physician Edward Tyson, particularly the *Ourang-Outang*, 1699. (Useful notes and references on the beginning of *Gulliver*, and antecedents in the history of ideas, are given by Patrick Bridgwater in his inaugural lecture, 'The Learned Ape', as Professor of German in the University of Durham, 1978.) Although basic features of all parts of *Gulliver* are clearly anticipated in these Scriblerian pieces in the design to ridicule 'all the false tastes in learning', the book is as much Swift's peculiar work as *The Dunciad* is Pope's. Published when he was 59, it had matured over the years of his plenitude, and in it he confronted with a full and judicial mind the world from which he had partly withdrawn.

6   A critical review of them in the context of the history of ideas is given in R.S. Crane's 'The Houyhnhnms, the Yahoos, and the History of Ideas', in *Reason and the Imagination*, ed. J.A. Mazzeo (1962).

4   *Modern instances*

1   James Thurber: *Further Fables for Our Time*, illustrated by the Author (1956).
2   Some of the early influences on Kafka's interest in the use of animals in fiction are traced by Professor Bridgwater in connection with Kafka's *Ein Bericht für eine Akademie*, in his inaugural lecture mentioned above, pp. 18–24.
3   *Conversations with Kafka*, tr. Goronwy Rees (2nd edn, 1971).
4   'Even if I had the power, I would not wish to interfere in Soviet domestic affairs; I would not condemn Stalin and his associates merely for their barbaric and undemocratic methods. It is quite possible that, even with the best intentions, they could not have acted otherwise under the conditions prevailing there'. (Preface to the Ukrainian edition, *CEJL*, III, 404).
5   'Dire: je suis pour le socialisme, mais pas pour le socialisme soviétique; je suis uniquement pour un socialisme conformé à ma representation – dire cela, même sous les formes "héroïques", "sublimes", ou "poétiques", équivaudrait à l'attitude d'une mère qui dirait: la flamme de l'amour maternel me consume, je suis l'amour maternel fait femme, mais je me réfuse à aimer mon enfant, parce qu'il a les oreilles décollées'. (*Existentialisme ou Marxisme?* tr. E. Kelemen, 1948, p. 245) (To say: I am for socialism, but not for Soviet socialism; I am only for a socialism that conforms with my idea of it – to say that, even when the ideal is 'heroic' 'sublime', or 'poetic', would be as good as the attitude of a mother who should say: I am consumed by the flame of maternal love, I am the embodiment of maternal love, but I refuse to love my child because his ears stand out.)
6   *Orwell*, Fontana Modern Masters, ed. Frank Kermode (1971). On Orwell's 'unresolved conflicts', see also Victor Gollancz's Foreword to the Left Book Club edition of *The Road to Wigan Pier* (1937).
7   I have dealt with the place in the history of ideas of *Brave New World* and *Nineteen Eighty-Four* in *Political Discipline in a Free Society* (1961), pp. 115–30.
8   cited by Virginia Tiger in her valuable study *William Golding: The dark fields of discovery* (1974), p. 38.
9   J.G. Ballard: *Concrete Island* (1974).
10 Michael Frayn: *Sweet Dreams* (1973).
11 *The Naked Lunch* (1959), *The Wild Boys* (1972), *Exterminator!* (1973). A reliable guide to the *oeuvre* is Eric Mottram's *William S. Burroughs: The Algebra of Need* (1977).

5 *The Medium*

1   Kafka (in the Third Octavo Notebook) has a neat parody of legend, perhaps of the aetiological myth; anyhow, airing the irony of explanation:

> There are four legends about Prometheus. According to the first, because he had betrayed the gods to men he was chained to a rock in the Caucasus and the gods sent eagles that devoured his liver, which always grew again.
>
> According to the second, Prometheus in his agony, as the beaks hacked into him, pressed deeper and deeper into the rock until he became one with it.
>
> According to the third, in the course of thousands of years his treachery was forgotten, the gods forgot, the eagles forgot, he himself forgot.
>
> According to the fourth, everyone grew weary of what had become meaningless. The gods grew weary, the eagles grew weary, the wound closed wearily.
> What remained was the inexplicable range of mountains. – Legend tries to explain the inexplicable. Since it arises out of a foundation of truth, it must end in the realm of the inexplicable.

2   The interplay between story and material is well brought out by Roger Sharrock in his lecture 'Life and Story in *The Pilgrim's Progress*' (Friends of Dr Williams's Library, 1978).

3   Diderot, perhaps less conventional than Voltaire, saw it differently, in his 'Éloge de Richardson'.

4   For a clear statement of the critical discredit of the traditional novel, nothing need be better than Nathalie Sarraute's *L'Ère du Soupçon* (1956) (*Age of Suspicion*, tr. Maria Jolas, 1963).

5   J.H. Fabre spends the first chapter of his *Social Life in the Insect World* (1911) showing the absurdity of the fable of the Cigale and the Ant, and speculating on how the mistake might have come about. As any countryman might know in parts frequented by the cigale, as in Greece, the insect dies with the summer, and could not eat grain – enough to kill the fable. And as the modern entomologist knows, it is the ant that sponges on and harasses the cigale. Fabre expected accurate observation as the basis of animal fables, and praised La Fontaine for his precision of detail, which is absurd on both counts. It is like

expecting a metaphor to be literally true. There must be enough general belief to give meaning to the image, just as there must be descriptive force in a metaphor. A fable is not in the category of 'parables from Nature'; it is a way of dissociating a pattern of behaviour from human contexts to see it abstractly but concretely, not a way of teaching by examples from nature. We may doubt whether foxes eat grapes, but the fable sticks. We do not need to be told that wolves do not speak to lambs, and are unlikely to be found drinking in their company: the condensed image stamps in the idea of power undefiable and undeterrable and unjustifiable – although it is nothing of the kind.

6   As an example of ethology: *A Discussion on Ritualization of Behaviour in Animals and Man*, organized by Sir Julian Huxley, FRS. Philosophical Transactions of the Royal Society, Series B, No. 772, vol. 251, pp. 247–526, 29 December 1966.

7   Take the fable 'The Middle-aged Man and his Two Mistresses' (*Babrius*, 22; *Phaedrus* II, 2; *La Fontaine* I, 17). Several novels entirely different might be written on the theme *Mulier est hominis confusio* ('Womman is mannes Ioye and al his blis', as Chaucer's Chauntecleer obligingly translates it for Dame Pertelote), each following the line of action in the fable, with a different order of subtlety and insight in modelling the inwardness of the secondary action. Of course, there is no final reason for taking this as the sole theme of the fable.

6   *The Message*

1   There is a second story by the Capek brothers in the same collection, 'The Voyage', also a fable, designed also to show some of the conditions of communication (*Selected Czech Tales*, 1925).

There is a piece by de Sade, *Dialogue entre un prêtre et un moribond* (1926), which has only the banality of expected argument between a priest and an unbeliever, which shows to advantage the reticence of simple juxtaposition no argument can bridge. (It may be remarked that the kind of shocking truths which de Sade as moralist, like de Mandeville, wanted to communicate might have been best conveyed by fables, but de Sade was preoccupied with self-justification or with his solitary fantasies, not detached.)

References and sources

1 The fable in literature

Allison, F.G., *Lucian, Satirist and Artist* (London, n.d.)

Anderson, Graham, *Studies in Lucian's Comic Fiction* (Leyden, 1976)

Auerbach, E., *Mimesis: The representation of reality in Western literature* (Berne, 1946; New York, 1957; 1971)

Baldwin, Barry, *Studies in Lucian* (Toronto, 1973)

Blount, Margaret, *Animal Land* (1974)

Bompaire, J. *Lucian Écrivain* (Paris, 1958)

Briggs, Katherine M., *A Dictionary of British Folk-tales* (1970)

Chambers, R.W., *Thomas More* (1935)

Chambry, E. *Aesopi Fabulae* (Paris, 1925–6)

Courlander, H. and Eshugbayi, E.A., *Ijapa the Tortoise and other Nigerian Tales* (1973)

Duff, J. Wight, 'In the Silver Age' in *A Literary History of Rome*, ed. A.M. Duff (1960); *Roman Satire* (1937) (for Menippian satire)

Edgerton, F., *Pancatantra Reconstructed* (New Haven, 1924)

Francis, H.T. and Thomas, E.J. (trs.) *Jataka Tales* (1916)

Grube, G.M.A., *The Greek and Roman Critics* (1965)

Hale-Wortham, B. (tr.) *Hitopadesa, or The Book of Good Counsel* (1906)

Handford, S.A., *Fables of Aesop* (Penguin, 1954)

Hausrath, A., *Corpus Fabularum Aesopicarum* (Leipzig, 1956–9)

Hervieux, L., *Les fabulistes Latins d'Auguste à la fin du Moyen Age*, 6 vols, (Paris, 1883–94)

Jacobs, Joseph, *History of the Aesopic Fable*, 2 vols, (1889)

Keith-Falconer, I.G.N., *Bidpai's Fables* (1885)

Kirk, G.S., *The Songs of Homer* (1962)

Lambert, W.G., *Babylonian Wisdom Literature* (1960)

Lever, Katherine, *The Art of Greek Comedy* (1956)

Lucian, Works, (trs.) A.M. Harmon, K. Kilburn, M.D. Macleod, 8 vols, Loeb Classical Library, (1913–67)

Perry, B.E., *Aesopica*, vol. 1 (Illinois, 1952); (tr.), *Babrius and Phaedrus* (Loeb Classical Library, 1965)

Quintilian, *Institutio oratoria*, (tr.) H.E. Butler, 4 vols, Loeb Classical Library, (1921–2)

Sullivan, J.P., *The 'Satyricon' of Petronius: A literary study* (1968)

Tournier, Michel, *Vendredi, ou les Limbes du Pacifique* (1967) (tr.) Norman Denny; *Friday or The Other Island* (1969)

Waley, Arthur (tr.), *Ballads and Stories from Tun-huang* (1960)
Winternitz, Moriz, 'Jataka' in Hastings's *Encyclopedia of Religion and Ethics*, vol. 7

Chapter 2 Renart to Volpone

Bacon, Francis, *Works*, ed. R. Ellis and James Spedding, 7 vols, (1857–9)
Bilenko, Anatole, *Ukrainian Folk Tales* (Kiev, 1974)
Burns, C. Delisle, *The First Europe: a study of the establishment of medieval Christendom, AD 400–800* (1947)
Caxton, William, *The History of Reynard the Fox*, tr. from Dutch, ed. N.F. Blake (1970)
Fabliaux Anthologies: Reid, T.B.W. (1958); Johnston, R.C. and Owen, D.D.R. (1957); Bédier, Joseph, *Les Fabliaux: Études de littérature populaire et d'histoire littéraire du Moyen Age* (Paris 1893; 5th edn, 1925)
Fletcher, Angus, *The Prophetic Moment: An essay on Spenser* (1971)
Fowler, Alastair, *Spenser and the Numbers of Time* (1964)
Flinn, John, *Le Roman de Renart dans la littérature française et dans les littératures étrangères au Moyen Age* (Paris, 1963)
Huizinga, J., *The Waning of the Middle Ages*, tr. F. Hopman (1924)
Isidore, Saint, *Etymologiae*, rec. W.M. Lindsay, 2 vols, (1910)
James, M.R., 'The Bestiary', *History*, xvi (April 1931) 61.
Jusserand, J.J., *A Literary History of the English People to the Renaissance* (1895)
Kean, P.M., *Chaucer and the Making of English Poetry*, vol. 2, *The Art of Narrative* (1972)
Ker, W.P., *English Literature: Medieval*, Home University Library (London, n.d.)
Kermode, Frank, (ed.) *The Tempest*, Arden edn (1954)
Keidel, G.C., *A Manual of Aesopic Fable Literature* (Baltimore, 1896)
Kieckhefer, Richard, *European Witch Trials* (1976)
Knowles, David, *The Evolution of Medieval Thought* (1962)
Kott, Jan, 'Prospero's Staff', *Shakespeare our Contemporary,* tr. Boleslaw Taborski (1965)
Lenaghan, R.T., *Caxton's Aesop*, ed. with Introduction and Notes (1967)
Lenmi, Charles W., *The Classical Deities in Bacon* (1933)
Lever, J.W., 'Shakespeare's Narrative Poems', *New Companion to Shakespeare Studies*, ed. K. Muir and S. Schoenbaum (1971)

Lydgate, John, *Minor Poems*, ed. H.N. MacCracken, 2 vols, Early English Text Society, Original series, 192; Extra series, 107.

Marie de France, *Fables*, sel. and ed. A. Ewert and R.C. Johnston (1942)

Migne, J.-P. (ed.) *Patrologiae cursus completus accurante*, series Latina No 117 (Paris, 1844–1904). Ignatius the Deacon's rendering in twelve-syllable tetrastichs of Aesop's fables (early 9th century)

Morris, R. (ed.), *An Old English Miscellany*, 49, Early English Text Society (1872)

Owst, G.R., *Literature and Pulpit in Medieval England* (1933)

Phillips, Margaret Mann, *The 'Adages' of Erasmus: A study with translations* (1964)

Reynolds, L.D. and Wilson, N.G., *Scribes and Scholars: A guide to the transmission of Greek and Latin literature* (1968)

Righter, Anne, Introduction to New Penguin edition of *The Tempest* (1968)

Rolle, Richard, 'The Nature of the Bee', *Fourteenth-Century Verse and Prose*, ed. K. Sisam (1921)

Ross, W.O., *Middle English Sermons*, Early English Text Society (1940)

Sidney, Sir Philip, *Apologie for Poetrie* (1595); ed. E. Arber (1905)

Waddell, Helen, (tr.), *Beasts and Saints* (1934)

Welter, M.J. Th., *L'exemplum dans la littérature religieuse et didactique du Moyen Age* (Paris, 1927)

White, T.H., *The Book of Beasts*, translated from a twelfth-century Latin Bestiary (1954)

Yates, Frances, *Astraea: The imperial theme in the sixteenth century* (1975)

Renaissance thinkers

This list is background reading for the sections 'Reformers and poets', 'The mask' and 'Cultural conditions', with particular reference to the argument and claims of Dr Frances Yates.

Agrippa, Henry Cornelius, *His Fourth Book of Occult Philosophy*, tr. Robert Turner (1665). (Facsimile reprint by Askin Publications, Chiswick, 1978) *Source Works of Medieval and Renaissance Magic*, vol. 4

Cassirer, Ernst, Kristeller, P.O., Randall, J.H. Jnr (eds.) *The Renaissance Philosophy of Man:* Selections (with introductions), translated from Petrarch, Valla, Ficino, Pico, Pomponazzi, Vives (Chicago, 1948)

Christianopolis: An ideal state of the seventeenth century, translated from the Latin of Johann Valentin Andreae, with an Historical Introduction, by Felix Emil Held (1916)

French, Peter J., *John Dee: The world of an Elizabethan magus* (1972)

Kristeller, P.O., *Eight Philosophers of the Italian Renaissance* (1965)

Plotinus, *Enneads*, tr. Stephen Mackenna, 5 vols, Library of Philosophical Translations (1917–30)

Purver, Margery, *The Royal Society: Concept and creation* (1967)

Trinkaus, Charles, *'In our Image and Likeness'*, 2 vols. (1970)

Walker, D.P., *Spiritual and Demonic Magic from Ficino to Campanella* (1958)

Yates, Frances, *Giordano Bruno and the Hermetic Tradition* (1964); *The Rosicrucian Enlightenment* (1972); *Shakespeare's Last Plays: A new approach* (1975); 'Elizabethan Neoplatonism Reconsidered' (lecture) (1977); *The Occult Philosophy in the Elizabethan Age* (1979)

3 Olympians at play

Aesop: Croxall, Samuel, *Aesop's Fables* (1722); L'Estrange, Sir Roger, *The Fables of Aesop and other eminent Mythologists, with Moral Reflections* (1692); Locke, John, *Some Thoughts concerning Education* (1693); Ogilby, John, Verse translation (1668); Richardson, Samuel, *Aesop's Fables* (1740; New York, 1975)

Barber, W.H., *Leibniz in France: From Arnauld to Voltaire* (1955)

Bate, Walter Jackson, *The Achievement of Samuel Johnson* (1955)

Bridgwater, Patrick, 'The Learned Ape'. Inaugural lecture, University of Durham (1978)

Bredvold, Louis I., *The Intellectual Milieu of John Dryden: Studies in some aspects of seventeenth-century thought* (Michigan, 1934; 1956)

Cassirer, Ernst, *The Philosophy of the Enlightenment*, trs. F.C.A. Koelln and James P. Pettigrove (Princeton, 1951)

Crane, R.S., 'The Houyhnhnms, the Yahoos, and the History of Ideas', in *Reason and the Imagination: Studies in the history of ideas, 1600–1800* (1962)

Donoghue, Denis (ed.), *Swift Revisited*, Thomas Davis Lectures (1968)

Dryden, John, *Essays*, sel. and ed. W.P. Ker, 2 vols, (1900); *Works*, ed. with Life by Sir Walter Scott, 18 vols, (1808); revised by George Saintsbury, 14 vols, (1883–9)

Gay, John, *Fables*, First series (1727); Second series (1738)

Gibb, H.A.R., 'Literature' in *The Legacy of Islam*, eds. Sir Thomas Arnold and Alfred Guillaume (1931)

Goethe, J.W., *Poetry and Truth: From my own life*, revised translation by Minna Steele Smith (1913)

Halperin, John (ed.), *The Theory of the Novel* (1974)

Hazard, Paul, *La crise de la conscience européenne 1680–1715* (Paris, 1935)

Hodgart, Matthew, *Satire* (1969)

Johnson, Samuel, *Works*, 9 vols, (1825); *Lives of the English Poets*, ed. G. Birkbeck Hill, 3 vols, (1905)

Kerby-Miller, C. (ed.), *The Memoirs of Martin Scriblerus* (New Haven, 1950)

Lessing, G.E., *Abhandlungen über die Fabel* (1759); *Laocoon* (1766); *Life and Works*, Helen Zimmern (1878)

Mandeville, Bernard, *The Fable of the Bees, or Private Vices, Public Benefits*, ed. with Introduction by Douglas German (1934)

More, Sir Thomas, *Utopia*, Latin and English texts, with Roper's Life and some letters, ed. George Sampson, Bohn's Standard Library (1910)

Prior, Matthew, *Poems on Several Occasions*, ed. A.R. Waller (1905); *Dialogues of the Dead, and other works in prose and verse*, ed. A.R. Waller (1907)

Riesman, D., *The Lonely Crowd* (New Haven, 1950)

Rogers, Pat, *The Augustan Vision* (1974)

Sainte-Beuve, Charles-Augustin, 'What is a classic?', *Causeries du lundi*, III (1850)

Spence, Joseph, *Anecdotes, Observations, and Characters of Books and Men*, A selection, ed. with an Introduction by John Underhill, Walter Scott Library (n.d.)

Taine, Hippolyte, *Essai sur les Fables de La Fontaine* (Paris, 1853; rev. edn. 1860)

Voltaire, *Candide*, édition critique par André Morize (Paris, 1931)

Wiley, Margaret L., *The Subtle Knot: Creative scepticism in seventeenth-century England* (1952)

Willey, Basil, *The Eighteenth Century Background* (1940)

Williams, Kathleen (ed.), *Backgrounds to Eighteenth-Century Literature* (Scranton, 1971)

4   *Modern instances*

Aldiss, Brian W. and Harrison, Henry (eds.), *Hell's Cartographers* (1975)

Amis, Kingsley, *The Golden Age of Science Fiction: An anthology* (1981)

Ballard, J.G., *Concrete Island* (1974); *The Drowned World* (1972)

Böll, Henrich, *Absent Without Leave (Entfernung von der Truppe* (1964) trs. Leila Nennewitz (1965)

Burgess, Anthony, *A Clockwork Orange* (1962; 1972)

Burroughs, William S., *The Naked Lunch* (1959; *The Wild Boys* (1971); *Exterminator!* (1973)

Carter, Angela, *Heroes and Villains* (1969); *The Magic Toyshop* (1967); *The Bloody Chamber and other stories* (1979); *The Passion of New Eve* (1977)

Cocteau, Jean, *Les Enfants Terribles* (1929), trs. Rosamond Lehmann (1955; 1961)

Diderot, D., *Jacques the Fatalist and his Master*, trs. J. Robert Loy (New York, 1962)

Franz, Marie-Louise von, *Introduction to the Interpretation of Fairy Tales: Problems of the feminine in fairy tales* (New York, 1983)

Frayn, Michael, *Sweet Dreams* (1973)

Garnett, David, *Lady into Fox* (1922)

Golding, William, *Lord of the Flies* (1958); *The Pyramid* (1966)

Huxley, Aldous, *Brave New World* (1932; 1950); *Brave New World Revisited* (1958)

Janouch, Gustav, *Conversations with Kafka*, trs. Goronwy Rees (1951; 2nd edn, revised and enlarged, 1971)

Jung, Carl G., (ed.), *Man and his Symbols* (1964; 1979)

Kafka, Franz, *The Penguin Complete Short Stories*, ed. Nahum N. Glatzer (1983); *The Penguin Complete Novels*, trs. Willa and Edwin Muir (1983)

Kermode, Frank, 'The meaning of it all', conversation with William Golding, *Books and Bookmen,* August 1959

Lukács, Georg, *Existentialisme ou Marxisme?* (Paris, 1948)

Mann, Thomas, 'Mario and the Magician' ('Mario und der Zauberer'), *Sämtliche Erzählungen* (Frankfurt, 1963)

Mottram, Eric, *William S. Burroughs: The algebra of need* (1977)

Orwell, George, *Animal Farm* (1945) ; *Nineteen Eighty-Four* (1948); *The Road to Wigan Pier* (1937); *The Collected Essays, Journalism and Letters*, eds. Sonia Orwell and Ian Angus, 4 vols, 1968–70.

Philips, Michael (ed.), *The Philosophy of Science Fiction* (New York, 1984)

Stansky, Peter and Abrahams, William, *The Unknown Orwell* (1972)
Thurber, James, *Further Fables for our Time* (1956)
Tiger, Virginia, *William Golding: The dark fields of discovery* (1974)
Vonnegut, Kurt, *Slaughterhouse 5* (1970)
Williams, Raymond, *Orwell*, Fontana Modern Masters series (1971)

5 The Medium

Beckett, Samuel, *The Lost Ones* (1966; last para. added 1970)
Bree, Germaine and Guiton, Margaret, *An Age of Fiction: The French novel from Gide to Camus* (Rutgers, 1957)
La Bruyère, Jean de, *Les Caractères* (1688; 1694)
Butler, Samuel, *Erewhon* (1872)
Caute, David, *The Illusion: An essay on politics, theatre and the novel* (1971)
Carlyle, Thomas, *Sartur Resartus* in *Works*, ed. H.D. Traill, 31 vols, (1896–1901)
Dicey, A.V., *Lectures on the relation between law and public opinion in England during the nineteenth century* (1905)
Eagleton, Terry, *Literary Theory: An introduction* (1983)
Eliade, Mircea, *Aspects du mythe* (Paris, 1962)
Fabre, J.H., *Social Life in the Insect World*, trs. Bernard Miall (1937)
Fletcher, J., *Flaubert: Trois Contes:* An Interpretation (New York, 1968)
Fletcher, John, *Samuel Beckett's Art* (1967)
Forster, E.M., *Aspects of the Novel* (1927)
Fowles, John, *The French Lieutenant's Woman* (1969)
Freeman, Kathleen, *Ancilla to the Pre-Socratic Philosophers* (1948); *The Pre-Socratic Philosophers* (1946)
Freud, Sigmund, *Totem and Taboo*, trs. A.A. Brill (1938)
Graves, Robert, *Greek Myths* (1958)
Halperin, John (ed.), *The Theory of the Novel: New essays* (New York, 1974)
Heller, Joseph, *Good as Gold* (1979)
Hytier, Jean, *André Gide* (1938), trs. Richard Howard (1963)
Jakobson, R. and Halle, M., *Fundamentals of Language* (The Hague, 1956)
Kirk, G.S., *Myth: its meaning and function in ancient and other cultures* (1970)
Lévi-Strauss, Claude, *Totemism*, trs. Rodney Needham (1964; 1973)
Lewes, G.H., 'The Inner Life of Art' (*Fortnightly Review*);

reprinted with *The Principles of Success in Literature*, Scott Library (London, n.d.)

Lewis, C.S., *The Allegory of Love* (1936)

Malthus, T.R., *An Essay on Population*, ed. W.T. Layton, 2 vols, Everyman edn (1914)

Mill, John Stuart, *On Liberty* (1859); *Utilitarianism*

Morris, William, *News from Nowhere* (1891; 1917)

Mylne, Vivienne, *The Eighteenth-Century French Novel: Techniques of Illusion* (1965)

Nordeau, Maurice, *The French Novel since the War*, trs. A.M. Sheridan Smith (1967)

Peyre, Henri, *French Novelists of Today* (1955; New York, 1967)

Queneau, Raymond, *Pierre Mon Ami* (1942), trs. J. Maclaren-Ross (1950)

Saint-Simon, Henri de, 'La parabole de Saint-Simon' in *Les précurseurs français du socialisme: de Condorcet à Proudhon*, ed. M. Leroy (Paris, 1948)

Sarraute, Nathalie, *L'ère du soupçon* (1956), trs. Maria Jolas, *Age of Suspicion* (1963)

Sharrock, Roger, 'Life and story in *The Pilgrim's Progress*', Dr Williams's Trust (1978)

Sorel, Georges, *Réflexions sur la violence*, 11th edn (Paris, 1950)

Spencer, Herbert, *The Man versus the State* (1884); ed. Donald Macrae (1969)

Tocqueville, Alexis de, *La démocratie en Amerique*, 2 parts (1835; 1840

Tolstoy, Leo, *Twenty-three Tales*, trs. L. and A. Maude (1906; 1915)

Westfall, Richard S., *Science and Religion in Seventeenth-century England* (New Haven, 1958). See also G.R. Cragg, *From Puritanism to the Age of Reason*, chapter 5 'The impact of the New Science' (1950)

Williams, Raymond, *Culture and Society, 1780–1950* (1958)

6 The Message

Bernstein, B., *Class, Code and Control*, I (1971)

Blackmur, R.P., 'Between the tiger's paws', in *A Celebration of Poets*, ed. Don Cameron Allen (Baltimore, 1959; 1967)

Bodkin, Maud, *Archetypal Patterns in Poetry* (1934; 1963)

Bridges, Robert, *The Testament of Beauty* (1929)

Capek, Karel and Josef, 'The living flame', 'The island', in *Selected Czech Tales*, trs. Marie Busch and Otto Pick (1925)

Douglas, Mary, *Natural Symbols: Explorations in cosmology* (1970; 1973)

Huxley, Aldous, *Literature and Science* (1963)

Iles, Norman, *The Resurrection of Cock Robin* (1983); *The Nursery Rhymes restored to their adult originals* (Morecambe, n.d.)

Jung, C.G., *Man and his Symbols*, ed., with Marie-Louise von Franz (1964)

de Man, Paul, *Allegories of Reading* (New Haven, 1979)

Pound, Ezra, *Selected Poems*, edited and with an Introduction by T.S. Eliot (1928; 1948)

Proust, Marcel, 'George Eliot', in *Contre Sainte-Beuve*, suivi de *Nouveaux Mélanges* (Paris, 1954)

Renwick, Roger de V., *English Folk Poetry: Structure and meaning* (1980)

Richards, I.A., 'Poetry and Beliefs', in *Critiques and Essays in Criticism 1920–1948*, representing the achievement of modern British and American critics, selected by Robert Wooster Stallman (New York, 1949)

Robey, David, *Structuralism: An introduction* (1973)

de Sade, Marquis, *Dialogue entre un prêtre et un moribund*, ed. Maurice Heine (Paris, 1926)

Santayana, George, *Three Philosophical Poets* (1935)

Snow, C.P., *The Two Cultures: A second look* (1964). An expanded version of the 1959 book on the two cultures and the scientific revolution

Sulieman, S.K. and Crosman I. (eds.) *The Reader in the Text* (Princeton, 1980)

Thompson, Stith, *Motif-Index of Folk-Literature*, 2nd edn (1955)

Tompkins, Jane P. (ed.), *Reader-response Criticism* (Baltimore, 1980)

Index

action, the: excludes inner dimension, 102; in a fable the whole of the invention, 195, 225; specific and general, 102

Addison, Joseph: inadequate conception of fables, 96–7, 99–100; 'Ancient Fables on Prayer', 256; 'On Dreams', 77; essays on Wit, 97–8; 'On Genius', 99; 'Vision of Mirza' compared with Lucian's 'Charon', 101

Aesop: the man, 5, 181; the legend, 6; the fables, *see* fable, Aesopic

Alcuin, his school and lost source of medieval collections of Aesop, 82

Aldiss, Brian, *Hell's Cartographers*, on science fiction as a genre, 166, 247–8

allegory: and ancient myths, 68–9; complications in Spenser, 71–3, 192; distinguished from allegorizing, 190; in 18th-century periodicals, 97, 99–101; a medieval habit of mind, 35, 39, 82; traditional compositions 190–92

allusive literature: Addison on, 97–8; Bacon on, 179–80

Almokaffa, Abdullah ibn, translator of the *Fables of Bidpai* into Arabic, 16

Amis, Kingsley, on structure of a short story, 248

analogy as a feature of the world, 35, 67, 71, 265

Anderson, Graham, on Lucian's comic fiction, 31–2

Andreae, J.V., *Christianapolis*, a 'Rosicrucian' document, 65–6

animal imagery, vogue of in medieval preaching, 35

animals in fables, 11, 20–21, 102, 123, 203–5, 261–2

animal stories, most are not fables, 1

Arabian Nights, 22, 94, 114, 189

Archilochus, introduces 'iambic' satirical verse, 11, 100

Aristophanes: *The Birds*, 213–14; as a model for Lucian, 179, 182; *Wasps*, 28

Aristotle: on intuitive perception of similarity, and on invention of examples, 180–81; two uses of metaphor, logical and didactic and stylistic, 210

Arnold, Matthew: contemporary French novel, 199; *Culture and Anarchy*, 218

Avianus, and transmission of Aesop, 7, 37, 38

Babrius: Aesop in Greek verse, 7, 13–14, 22; 'The Sea', 233

Bacon, Francis: *Advancement of Learning*, 68, 179–80; Aesop's fables and Baconian morality, 9; *De Sapientia Veterum*, 68–9; *New Atlantis*, 65–7; not a 'Rosicrucian', 67–9; *Novum Organum*, 67–8; 'Of Plantations', 78–9

Baldwin, Barry, on Lucian, 25, 31

Ballard, J.G., *Concrete Island*, 160–62; *The Drowned World*, 164

Barzoye, translator into literary Persian of Sanskrit fables, 16

Bate, W.J., *The Achievement of Samuel Johnson*, 109

Baudelaire, Charles, 152–3; 'L'homme et la Mer', 233

Beckett, Samuel, *The Lost Ones*, 211

Beggar's Opera, 90

Bernstein, B., restricted speech codes and frames of reference, 241

bestiaries, medieval, 34–6

Birrell, Augustine, on *Erewhon*, 127

Blackmur, R.C., on Edwin Muir's poetry, 229, 236

Blount, Margaret, *Animal Land*, 1

Bodkin, Maud, *Archetypal Patterns in Poetry*, 241

Böll, Heinrich, *Absent Without Leave*, 157–9, 248

Bompaire, J., on Lucian, 24–5, 31

Dunbar, William, 'The Merle and the Nightingale', 58–9
Dunciad, 90

Eliade, Mircea, *Aspects du mythe*, 185
Eliot, George: her ideal as novelist, 215; Proust on, 221
'Emperor's New Clothes', 248
Erasmus: 'Adages', 62–5, 186, 257; and Aesop, 5; and Lucian, 23, 24, 83
ethology, 203–5, 262
exempla in medieval literature: 39; classification of, 256
extremes, respect for truth of, 113, 168, 179

fable:
  general:
    aesthetic, 250
    compared with poetry, 225–38
    cultural conditions, 82–4, 125–6, 215–19, 222
    descriptions: a conceptual artefact, xix, 196; dictionary
      definitions, 258–9; an heuristic fantasy, 208; an intuitive conception,
      xvi, 97, 101, 178, 180–81, 224–5; a narrative device to provoke and aid
      concrete thinking, xvi–xvii; not an argument, 104, 112, 117–18, 173;
      not merely an example, xi, 175, 178, 181; not metaphysical fiction,
      199–200; 'pictures a truth', xi; a story devised to show something of
      general import and importance insufficiently recognized, 175;
      specific and general, 102; a tactical manoeuvre, xi
    distinguished from: allegory, xv, 190–92; folk and fairy-tale,
      188–9; myth, 183–6; the novel, 146, 192–202, 225; parable, xiv–xv,
      186–8
    freedom of representation: 177, 179, 242
    history, xix–xxii, 125–7, 212–14
    insight into: Bacon, 179–80; Hazlitt, xvi; Lessing, 101–3, 214;
      Lewes, G.H., 181; Lucian, 26–7, 30–31; Voltaire, 114–15
    'jester' factor, the, xviii, 178–9;
    limits, 126, 199–200, 207–8
    literary qualities, 249–53
    misconceptions of: Addison, 97, 100; Aristotle, 181; Breitinger, 102;
      Johnson, 100–01; Richardson, 87
    reasons for: 'political' and 'philosophical', xvi, xviii, 209
    samples of what fables show, 8–9, 21–2, 30–32, 248–9
    story material indifferent, xvii
    theory of, 175–9
    truth value of, 252–3
  Aesopic: ambivalence towards, 5, 6, 54; corpus, 7–8; editors of: 8, 11;
    in the Middle Ages, 39, 82–4; foundation stock, 7; kinship with proverbs,
    xix, 212–13; as poetic composition, Babrius and Phaedrus, 7, 12–15;
    Roman de Renart, the supreme invention and shaping influence, 40–48;
    use in linguistic exercises, 11, 38–9, 87, 103, 181
  Indian: 15–23; Bidpai collection, 15–17; ethos of, 21–2; *Hitopadesia*,
    17–19; *Jataka*, 19–21; widespread dissemination and popularity, 15–17,
    94; women in, 22–3